UNDER THE MICROSCOPE

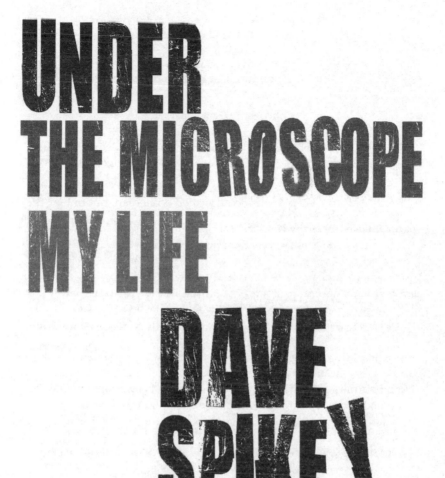

UNDER THE MICROSCOPE
MY LIFE

DAVE SPIKEY

MICHAEL O'MARA BOOKS LIMITED

First published in Great Britain in 2010 by
Michael O'Mara Books Limited
9 Lion Yard
Tremadoc Road
London SW4 7NQ

ISBN: 978-1-84317-386-1

1 3 5 7 9 10 8 6 4 2

www.mombooks.com

Designed and typeset by e-type

Plate section designed by Deep Rehal

Printed in the UK by CPI William Clowes Beccles NR34 7TL

Contents

To my wife and best friend Kay for her love, support and tolerance.

To Stephen and Jill, my wonderful children, for their
unconditional love and friendship.

To Jenny, my capricious daughter next door.

And

To my mum, for deciding that if my Aunty Dorothy was
having a baby, so was she.

Let Me Take You Back

A WISE WOMAN, a nun I believe, advised us to start at the very beginning because it's a very good place to start. And that is indeed sound advice – but define the 'very' beginning.

My *very* first vivid memory was attending nursery school for the first time when I was four. I remember the smell of the place, I remember the noise, the hustle and bustle, my first taste of crayon, Keith Wright peeing in his canvas cot during the afternoon nap and I remember clearly my first ever disappointment in life when I was allocated my peg in the cloakroom. All the pegs had pictures on them and I wanted a train or a castle or a lion or a monkey; yeah, a monkey! Monkeys are great. And I got a flower. A single flower, not even a bunch. My first ever school nickname was 'Daisy' (which was ridiculous because it wasn't a daisy, it was blue; so maybe a hyacinth or a lupin).

But I started thinking, what if that wasn't the 'very' beginning? What if there was something before that? Something important. I decided that if I was going to write a book based on and around my life it would be only right that I investigate that possibility thoroughly ... and so I did.

I visited an eccentric woman in Burnley, who was called 'Vinegar Vera' for reasons unclear, but which I suspect arose from a previous profession that involved a hot bath, a bent coat hanger and a bottle of gin. Vera put me in a trance and then took me back. That's where she took me ... back. She had me stare at a dot on a ceiling tile until my eyes got tired and then she said that it was alright to close them and have a bit of a rest. So I did and then she began to peel back the layers – and it turns out that I had been, in previous lives and in no particular order:

A dervish – not a whirly one, just your bog-standard dervish *and* listen to this! I was stoned to death for stealing a crust of bread. That's a crust! Nowhere near a full loaf, *not even a slice*! I mean, banish me to Thrace, fair enough, I'd go along with that, couldn't really argue with that, but executed, come on, be fair.

I was also Ham. Not the meat; Noah's son. While Vera had me under, I actually re-lived in vivid detail a massive argument that I'd had with my father after the rain had started coming down big time ('scattered showers' it said on the forecast!) and he was acting all smug-like because he'd built this ark (turns out he had inside information). So he's trying to get two of every animal on the earth onto the ark, which is a total nightmare. Can you imagine how stressful it is trying to separate just two sheep or two lemmings or two wildebeests from the rest of the flock/herd/whatever?

It really kicked off when I was busy trying to sex a bunch of guinea pigs (you press your thumbs into both groins and a penis either does or does not pop up) and I noticed that he was letting two gophers on! What was he thinking?! We'd already had a huge row about the termites and the woodpeckers, and now he's letting these two goofy-looking critters on, and suddenly I'm shouting, 'Dad! Check out the teeth! Remember the type of wood you used to build this thing with, yeah?' Then he's actually let them on! I can't believe it! I look around in despair and now I break into a cold sweat because I can't see the beavers anymore and the last time I looked they were definitely there, right in front of the dodos and they're still there. Surely he's not …

Staying with the animal theme, I had a rubbish life when I was a daddy-long-legs. I was born, lived for about six hours, then a five-year-old kid with buck teeth pulled my legs off – it was shit.

I was also a soldier called Yannis at the siege of Troy. We'd been there for about ten years, right, and my friends Fat Yannis, Yannis the Cheese (mad on halloumi), me and a few others got drunk on ouzo one night and somebody – it was Yannis, I think – said to a now very drunken group of soldiers …

Yannis: Do you know what I'm going to do tomorrow?

Yannis the Cheese: No, what?

Yannis: I'm going to build a horse.

All: A horse?

Yannis: A big, f**k-off horse.

Me: I'll help. Can I help? Let me help.

Yannis the Cheese: What are you going to make it from?

Yannis: Wood.

Fat Yannis: How big is it going to be?

Yannis: Massive big. Big as a house.

All: Wow! Big as a house!

Yannis: Then guess what I'm gonna do? I'm going to get inside! I'm
  gonna hide in it and then you lot pretend you've gone home and
  let's see if the Trojans will take me inside the fortress. And if they
  do, right, I'll sneak out and open the gates!

Me: I'll come with you.

All: We'll all come. It'll be brilliant.

And the rest as they say …

My final incarnation may surprise you. I was a cauliflower. That's
right: you can come back as vegetables! You know it: just have a look
around, you've met them, you've worked with them, you're related to a
couple.

Now, you might reasonably assume that this revelation must have
traumatized me, but it hasn't – in fact, quite the opposite; it's been
cathartic. You see, ever since I can remember, I've had this irrational fear
of cheese sauce. I've been in restaurants and at dinner parties and when
the waiter or hostess says, 'Cheese sauce?' I freak out and I mean proper
panic. '*No* cheese sauce! Bad, hot, *burn*, KILL!!' Of course they respond:
'It's only cheese sauce, Dave.'

So, without getting out my world gazetteer and encyclopaedia, I'm
guessing the 'very' beginning was the poor dervish – and I'm so sad that
I don't know what my name was. I'd like to think it was still Dave. 'Dave
the dervish' sort of works.

Hey, all that for twenty-five quid – which included tea, cake and an all-over body with jojoba oil. *And* that was only one session, so I can't say with any authority that that's it. I'm tempted to go back because I suspect there may be more. I'm pretty sure that at one time I must have been a dog … but more of that later.

The Best Medicine

S O ... TO MY very early memories of this *current* life. When I was very young and wanted to get out of going to school or church or getting the coal in, I would feign a vague illness.

'I don't feel so well, Mum,' I would moan feebly.

My mum would say, 'You know what you want?'

'No. What?'

'Putting in a bag and shaking up.'

'I don't, Mum. Actually, that's way down the list of things I want. That's in the bottom three, along with prunes and the Aquaphibians off *Stingray*. No, seriously, Mum! Put the bag away, Mum!'

Where did she get such a big bag from anyway?

My dad had a more philosophical approach. He would hold me gently by the shoulders and say, 'David? *Laughter*. Laughter is the best medicine' ... which is why, when I was six, I nearly died from diphtheria.

Me: *(Gasping for air.)* Dad ... I can't breathe.

Dad: Knock, knock.

Me: This isn't going to work, Dad.

Dad: Knock, knock.

Me: Who's there?

Dad: Dunnup.

Me: Dunnup who? Yes, very hilarious. Can I have some antibiotics now?

No, I couldn't. Not just yet, anyway – because if the laughter didn't work, there'd be plenty more options before a real, proper, bona fide doctor would be required. I was sort of convinced as a kid that my mum and dad, respectively a part-time wages clerk and a painter and decorator (self-employed, no job too small), must have attended a night-school class in domestic medicine at Bolton Technical College – because they did appear to be prepared for any medical emergency.

I say 'prepared' not in the sense that they would reach with confidence for the first-aid kit and medicine cabinet. Oh no, all that they needed could be found in a well-stocked kitchen pantry. Allow me to illustrate this, in the style of submitted papers to the *British Medical Journal* with some real-life case studies …

Case Study 1:
Aged six, I fell from the top of the coal bunker and landed on my head. A lump came up the size of an XL egg – you could have made an omelette. Dad triaged the injury and referred me to the emergency room (kitchen), where Mum didn't hesitate: years of training kicked in as she instinctively went straight for the butter and applied a large dollop ('a knob' I believe is the technical term).

Case Study 2:
Only one week later, I burned my hand lighting the fire. Emergency treatment? Bit of butter.

Case Study 3:
I contracted TB. Solution? Bit of butter. (Not true: but you get the picture.)

Case Study 4:
I got a bad cold. (You know, as opposed to a good one?) I had a very sore throat and the pantry nurse heaped a mountain of salt into hot water with instructions to gargle. And for that chesty cough? Mustard. Not to be taken internally – oh no, to be massaged into my chest. Dinnertime at school that day was a nightmare; all the other kids wiping their spam butties on me …

Case Study 5:
We couldn't afford talcum powder, so when my baby sister Joy was born, my mum used self-raising flour. The first time Joy got nappy rash, she broke out in scones.

Case Study 6:
I injured my ankle playing football in the back street and was carried home by a neighbour screaming in agony (me, I mean). Dr Dad took one quick look and prescribed 'knit bone' – that's *knit bone* (!) – and produced, like some ancient apothecary, a bunch of a weird-looking dried plant, which he soaked in a bowl of very hot water before plunging my swollen, throbbing ankle into it. Again, that's *very* hot water ...

Me: Arrrrrrrrrrrrrrgh!
Dad: Don't be so soft, that'll knit your bones back together.
Me: Oh, right. Is that why they call it 'knit bone'?
Dad: Yes it is, son.
Me: Have they heard about this down at the orthopaedic hospital, Dad?
Dad: Have you heard about a smack round the ear?
Me: Have you heard of Childline?
Dad: No, it's 1958.

I now know that 'knit bone' is comfrey – a medicinal herb that the marketing people of olde obviously had trouble shifting in the Middle Ages. After a brainstorming session, the 'creatives' came up with the re-branding idea: 'We'll call it knit bone – it does exactly what it says on the stalk.' Indeed, it was in medieval times that its reputation for knitting bones together flourished. That's *medieval* times, Dad!

My parents also practised preventative medicine. For example, did you know that if you go out to play with wet hair you *will* get double pneumonia, no question. Not single pneumonia: *double* pneumonia. The potentially life-threatening dangers of wet hair were well known in our family – but not, it seems, to generations of scientists since, who are still blaming it on the humble virus and/or bacteria.

If all else failed, there was vinegar. According to my mum, vinegar was 'nature's cure-all'. (Which begs the question that if that was indeed the case, why did she always use other emergency condiments first? Why not go for the 'Sarsons' straight away? She was a bit vague on that subject. I did press her on it once and she reasoned, as mums always do, 'Because I say so.')

Nevertheless, vinegar was liberally applied to my warts, acne and nettle rash. It was swallowed to combat heartburn and headaches, and used as an insect repellent in summer when I would attract midges by the thousand. Mum would rub vinegar all over me: 'That'll keep the little buggers away.' 'It'll keep everyone away, Mum!'

It was a real worry to me that in between applying or forcing vinegar down me, she also used it for descaling the kettle, cleaning the iron, getting rid of rust from the railings and dispersing stubborn soap scum in the bath.

Should vinegar, against all the odds, not come up to scratch (not likely to happen, is it?), my mum could always spit on a hankie and apply to the injured area. Apparently, mums' spit contains a powerful antibiotic which will kill 99 per cent of all known germs. (It is also the best thing for flattening your hair, cleaning round your mouth after a drink of Vimto and getting stains out of your jumper.) I think that the NHS should recruit an army of mums, issue them with hankies and send them into hospitals spitting and wiping. MRSA would be eradicated in a fortnight.

Under certain circumstances, my mum could 'kiss it better'.

Me: Mum, I fell off the shed roof and landed on my head.
Mum: Come here while I kiss it better.
Me: Look, Mum, I'm only eight, so what do I know, but there's blood coming out of my eyes and I really think I should go to casualt . . . (*Blackout.*)

Early Days

UNTIL THE AGE of twelve, I lived at 3 Grafton Street, Bolton, Lancashire: a small terraced house amongst the rows and rows of terraced houses that surrounded the many cotton mills of the town. We had a coal fire, a tin bath and an outside toilet (and other stuff, furniture and that). The outside toilet was at the bottom of the back yard and – if you hadn't burned it to keep warm – it had a door on it. It wasn't very pleasant going down the yard to the toilet at the best of times, but in the middle of a freezing winter it was horrible, even with the marginal warmth of the paraffin lamp that was burning in there to stop the cistern and pipes from freezing.

On occasions, it was just too cold and hazardous to venture down the yard holding the washing line to guide and steady you from slipping on the ice – especially if you only needed to pee and there was the temptation of an empty milk bottle on the kitchen table. Pasteurized milk bottles were best because the sterilized milk bottles had a narrow neck which was a real worry when you were aged eleven and your body was changing. Even so, in the deepest, darkest winter, it was sometimes worth the risk.

If we needed to pee in the middle of the night, we had a totty-pot (chamber pot) under our beds which you knew was getting full when your thumb went warm. Bizarrely, one of my earliest memories is sitting struggling with constipation on the totty-pot and my grannie shouting at me, 'Come on, David, thrutch!'

For many years, we didn't have the luxury of toilet paper, we had the cut-up pages of the *Bolton Evening News* or my mum's *Tit-Bits* magazine, which was sadly mostly '*Bits*' to be honest and was the *Bella* of its time.

It contained short stories, puzzles, knitting patterns, rubbish poems and of course 'Top Tips'. The winning 'Top Tip' of the week was the 'Ten-Bob Tip' and one I've always remembered was 'how to get ring stains off your coffee table' ... I was more interested in how they got on there in the first place!

So, although we didn't have the luxury of soft velvet tissue, we did at least have interesting reading material. The problem was that undisciplined toilet users would rip their sheets of newsprint off randomly instead of in strict page order, which often ruined an exciting moment in *Tit-Bits's* weekly steamy story 'Sinful Pleasures': 'Gareth took hold of Denise and drew her slowly towards him. She smelled the musk of his aftershave as his hands gently cupped her ...'

Next sheet, quick! Oh no, where is it?! This is the 'Top Tip' page! Where's Gareth? What's he cupping? I'm eleven, I need to know! I don't need to know how to clean a pack of playing cards by using a loaf! And I quote, 'Don't throw away a grubby pack of playing cards, simply rub a slice of bread over them and they will come up as good as new'; this earning the contributor ten shillings for the 'Ten-Bob Tip'. I had (and still have) a few quick questions about this:

1. How many cards can you clean with one slice?
2. How much does a loaf cost?
3. How much does a pack of playing cards cost?

I had no idea then, I have little idea now, but I imagine that there can't be much difference between the two. Just buy a new pack of cards, you idiot!

I did ask my dad about it at the time. He didn't know either although he did want to know why I wanted to know. I told him about the 'Ten-Bob Tip' – and the next thing you know, Jed's a millionaire ... well, my dad won ten bob for the top tip in *Tit-Bits*!

His top tip – unsurprisingly – concerned the art of painting and decorating. You may remember it, it went something like, 'When painting doors and window frames, make sure to paint a small piece of wood at the same time. You will never again leave fingerprints when touching the door or window frame to judge if the paint is dry; simply touch the painted piece of wood instead.' They printed that! And that only spurred him on, but he never had another one accepted. I give you, 'Do your glasses steam up when reading in the bath? Simply dip them in the water and they will clear immediately' … so, not surprising, really.

When I was four, I went to nursery. As previously reported, I remember my first day vividly: there was a big wooden slide and lots of games and we all were given a peg; a cloakroom peg onto which we would hang our outside clothes and put on some sort of tunic.

The transition from nursery to primary school was seamless, being as it was the same building. I was a mixed infant – or so it said on the entrance to Oxford Grove County Primary School – and my memories of early school are clouded. I remember my first class teacher, Miss Wilson, a 103-year-old spinster who was quite blind, which was a bonus when she administered her particular form of corporal punishment: a ruler across the knuckles. If your timing was good, you could move your hand at the last minute and yell in pain as she forcefully smacked the desk. If your misdemeanour was more serious, she would add more rulers; some would break as they smashed down on the desk.

I was in 'Hilary' house and have a photograph somewhere of me in the school football team. This is a happy reminder, of course, but I also remember my first proper game of football with acute embarrassment. As we trooped out to the pitches across the road, I noticed that all my friends and classmates sported the strips of local teams – Bolton Wanderers, Manchester City or Manchester United – while I wore a shirt that my mum had bought on Bolton market. My shirt was green with white sleeves.

'Whose strip is that?' the others asked.

I furtively glanced at the badge. 'Hibernian.'

I was a bit of a laughing stock for a while. So much so that I was forced to invent a Scottish ancestry; a family history that included an aunt and uncle who actually still lived in Hibernia!

The only other clear memory I have was of the nit-nurse who would examine our hair regularly for head lice. She always used to rummage through your hair and say, 'How often do you clean your teeth?' which freaked me out because I thought there was some way she could see through my head to inside my mouth.

Class Clown

A QUESTION I'M often asked is whether I was the class comedian at school ... and actually I wasn't; I was quite shy, quiet and studious. However, we did have a class clown called Derek Rigby, who I'm sure was just like the lad that you had in some class at school. A boy who was a complete idiot. You know the type; he was the one who would jump on the front desk as soon as the teacher had left the classroom, get his willy out and wave it about. And you'd shout, 'Do you mind, Derek, we've got our A levels next week!'

Derek was the lad you still talk about at school reunions or in conversations with old schoolmates; something along the lines of 'Remember when he did that? What a nutter! And remember when he hung Mr Nealy out of the Chemistry lab window?!'

So, as I say, Derek Rigby was our class comic – well, I suppose that 'class clown' is possibly more accurate. Derek assumed this role for the classic reason that he was bullied and thought that acting the fool might get him accepted into the gang and deflect the bullying to someone else. And please don't get me wrong, when I say he was bullied, it was nothing severe, it was a playful kind of bullying; he was simply the butt of our jokes. The worst we ever did to him was take his clinic glasses off him and burn his arm by focusing the sun through them ... Actually, when I write it down ...

The fact that Derek was selected to be bullied in the first place was surprising when you consider that we had a lad called Cliff Kidney in our class. Not only did he have a stupid name, but Cliff was the boy with the lazy eye (and I don't mean a ranch in Arizona), plus he had ringworm (and so a purple head). Imagine then how relieved he was when he was overlooked in favour of Derek Rigby.

So, why Derek? Well, where do I begin, to tell the story of how great a … Okay, well, for a start his mum and dad sent him to school wearing one of those leather helmets, do you remember them? They had a peak, ear flaps with press studs and a strap and buckle under the chin. The first time I saw him I thought he was a Japanese kamikaze pilot.

Then we discovered that Derek couldn't say his 'R's, sort of like Jonathan Ross, so he always introduced himself as Dewek Wigby, and I know you shouldn't laugh, but just say it now out loud – 'Dewek Wigby' – piss funny and kids are cruel. And you know when you start school, there's always a kid with massive ears and another kid with a huge nose and another with thick clinic glasses? Two words – Dewek Wigby: he had the full set (maybe that's why he wore the helmet). Jumbo sticky-out ears, big flat nose and thick glasses – when he stared at you, he looked like a VW Beetle with the doors open.

His eyes were all over the place, with the left one predominantly looking slightly upwards and the right one skenning to one side; our first nickname for Dewek was 'Look North-West'. He was so self-conscious about his ears that he used to go to bed at night with an elastic band round his head, in the hope that he could train them flat. Unfortunately, this only made things worse because all that happened was that he came to school the next day with a red stripe across his forehead. One night, the elastic band snapped and nearly took his eye out, so he had to wear an eye patch for a fortnight. I remember him bursting into the classroom, shouting, 'Look at me! I'm a piwate!' Don't make it worse, Dewek.

If all that was not enough – and let's face it, it is – Dewek had a nut allergy. In those days, it was a rare condition and his parents were naturally very concerned that everyone was made aware of this potentially life-threatening condition. Nevertheless, they didn't really think their plan through to see the downside of making him a big red badge that they insisted he wore throughout his schooldays, which simply read: 'No Nuts.' He didn't stand a chance, did he?

He was so desperate to be part of the gang. He would have done anything … Well, he did, actually.

We once acquired an old battered air rifle, with which we tried to shoot sparrows. I know it's wrong! But let me comfort you by saying that we never hit one ... so naturally we moved onto pigeons. Bigger, slower and easily distracted pigeons. We thought that this time we'd actually hit a couple, but although a few feathers flew, the birds didn't seem unduly troubled.

We decided the gun needed testing – and so we had this brilliant idea, and I don't use the word 'brilliant' casually. Listen to this and bear in mind that this was basic forensic science way before *Quincy* appeared on the scene, never mind *CSI*, *Waking the Dead* and *Hetty Wainthropp Investigates*. The idea was that after school, one of us would put on everyone else's jumper and then a school blazer with a duffle coat on top, and then one of the others would shoot that person and then we would examine the depth of penetration of the pellet. Pretty impressive for eight- and nine-year-olds, I'm sure you'll agree.

Suddenly, from the periphery of the crowd we heard: 'I'll do it.' And there he was, Dewek Wigby volunteering. 'Shoot me, I don't mind.'

Fair enough. After school in Queen's Park, Dewek turned up in his school uniform, very smart in his blazer, tie, little grey short pants and grey socks. We each of us gave him our jumper to put on and someone gave him a duffle coat, and then we stood him on the spot and I shot Dewek Wigby ... in the leg. Dewek howled and hopped about like mad, screaming in shock and pain. And that's bad, obviously, but it's also good because it helped us solve the problem with the air rifle. It was the sights! The sights were all to cock. We needed to aim a lot higher.

Then Dewek started to make us laugh. He started saying funny things. The problem was that you could see in his eyes that he didn't know why they were funny or indeed why we were laughing, he was just saying any old stuff that came into his stupid head. He was simply reacting to situations and questions in his normal way; he didn't mean to be funny and he really had no idea why we were pissing ourselves laughing. For the thing I haven't yet mentioned about Dewek was that he was a bit dim. No, actually, he was *very* dim; at school he was lucky if he got a tick. He was the lad who the teachers got to play the wooden blocks in the school 'orchestra' and he couldn't even do that, trapping his fingers in them all the time. As we played our recorders – 'Frère Jacques ... Frère Jacques' – you'd hear a 'Frère Jacq ... Ow! Frère Jacq ... Argh!' The only real natural talent that Dewek had was that he could make that farting noise by squeezing his hand in his armpit.

We talk about Dewek a lot at school reunions because over the years he did come out with some classic lines during lessons. We all agree that the first time he really made us ache laughing was at primary school, when we were about eight and Mrs Greenhalgh was trying to teach us basic geography. She picked Mary Hilton out and asked her to come to the front of the class and stand near the big map of the world that decorated many a classroom wall. Mrs Greenhalgh asked Mary to go to the map and point to Australia. After a moment's hesitation, Mary successfully did so.

'Very good, Mary,' Mrs Greenhalgh said. 'Please sit down.'

As Mary retook her place, Mrs Greenhalgh said to Dewek, 'Dewek Wigby. Who discovered Australia?'

He looked at her as if she were simple and replied, 'Mary did.' Then he turned to us, shrugged, and rolled his eyes as if to say, 'How dim is she?'

And we laughed and Dewek loved it and he laughed too, but you could tell that he had no idea what he had said that was so funny because Mary *did* just discover Australia, didn't she? Maybe he thought we were laughing at the disparaging look he had shot at us, which highlighted how dim Mrs Greenhalgh was.

The second time he struck was more of a sharp intake of breath, followed by giggles, followed by suppressed hysteria. One very snowy cold January, a little boy from the year below us died. He'd got a new sledge for Christmas and had been out sledging on Winter Hill and caught a chill which turned into pneumonia and he'd died. So they kept us behind after assembly and a solemn headmaster addressed us all.

He said, 'Now, as you all may know, Horace Cope [not his real name] will not be coming back to school. I'm sorry to tell you that he's gone to heaven.' Gasp from the assembled children. 'Horace went out sledging without wrapping up properly and he caught a chill, which turned into pneumonia, which turned into double pneumonia.'

We all exchanged glances and mouthed knowingly, 'Wet hair.'

The headmaster continued, 'The outlook is that this bitter winter weather will continue and so I want you all to promise me that when you go out sledging, or playing in the snow, you'll wrap up warmly. Bob hats, scarves and gloves. Will you promise me that, children?'

We all replied in unison, 'Yes, sir.'

'Good, thank you, children. And I understand that this tragic occurrence may have troubled some of you, and so if anyone has any questions, any questions at all, I'll be happy to try and answer them.'

A moment or two passed and then, almost predictably, a hand was raised. We all looked down the line and saw that it was Dewek and anticipation grew.

'Yes, Dewek?' said the headmaster. 'What's your question?'

And Dewek said, 'So ... what's happened to his sledge then?'

Of course, once he found out that he could make us laugh, he dedicated his life to this purpose. He loved the sound of laughter and tried hard, often too hard, to produce the comedy gold. Unfortunately, as I say, he didn't really have a handle on why we were laughing. He couldn't see that it was the stuff he came out with spontaneously that we loved – the stuff he actually didn't mean to be funny. Still, it didn't stop him from trying and just now and again he would deliver.

His biggest triumph was in our first secondary school Physics lesson. We were discussing 'natural phenomena' or some such, thunder and lightning, tornadoes, the sun, the moon and tides, that sort of thing, and the discussion got around to speed of light versus speed of sound, using thunder and lightning as the basis for said discussion.

Now, bear in mind when reading this that we were eleven and we'd never done physics before and, oh yes, we were a bit thick ... The teacher, Mr Bowler (with the implausible first name of Thomas), pointed to a child midway through the lesson and barked, 'You boy, Olaff Kidney!' ('Olaff' being, of course, Cliff Kidney ... until we altered the school register on the first day of term.) 'Based on our discussions of natural phenomena and in particular thunder and lightning, which is faster: the speed of sound or the speed of light?'

Olaff thought for a second or two and then replied with confidence, 'Speed of light, sir.'

'Good,' said Mr Bowler. 'Why do you say that?'

Olaff replied, 'Because as soon as you flick the switch, the light comes on. Flick switch – light comes on.'

Mr Bowler stared blankly for a moment before moving on. 'Mary Hilton? Do you agree?'

Mary said, 'No, I think the speed of sound is faster.'

'Why do you say that?'

'Because as soon as you say something, you can hear it, sir.' She suddenly shouted loudly, taking everyone by surprise, 'Say it – hear it! Say it – hear it!'

Mr Bowler knew at that moment that he had his work cut out with this class. He threw the topic open for discussion: 'Anybody else like to contribute to the debate?'

It was then that we noticed Dewek winking and nodding at us with that conspiratorial look. Surreptitiously, he gave us a thumbs-up before raising his hand. We could hardly contain our expectant excitement. Mr Bowler spotted him: 'Yes … Rigby, is it? Which do you think is the faster?'

'Neither of them,' said Dewek. I remember clearly the half-gasp, half-giggle I managed to disguise as a cough.

Mr Bowler studied Dewek before he said, 'Neither of them, Rigby?'

'No,' said Dewek, 'I don't think light or sound is the fastest phee-no-meenum [sic].'

'So what is?' enquired Mr Bowler.

Dewek paused for effect (what's the secret of comedy?). 'Diarrhoea,' says Dewek – and we all start cracking up.

Well, I say 'all', but Mr Bowler was transfixed. 'And on what evidence do you base that statement, pray tell?' he asked.

'Well,' said Dewek, his eyes smiling, 'I had diarrhoea last week and before I could put the light on or tell anybody I'd shit myself.'

Genius. A week's detention, of course.

We were once doing a project for Remembrance Day and the teacher asked us to enquire of our grandparents if they would care to contribute their reminiscences and/or maybe a memento they might have. Medals, belts, buckles, caps, helmets etc. I went with Dewek to his grandad's house to ask him. His grandad said he had a German helmet that Dewek could take, which he currently used as a plant pot holder in his shed.

Dewek pestered him for something for me to take and his grandad said he had a German pistol, a Lugar, but we couldn't take that, he'd get into trouble if they knew he had it. Dewek pestered and pestered and his grandad eventually said that the only other thing he'd kept was the old greatcoat he'd worn in the trenches, but it would be too big and heavy to get down from the loft. Dewek said we'd get it and where exactly was it. His grandad replied that it was over the tank.

You should have seen the look on Dewek's face. He was stunned, he couldn't speak for ages, then. 'You've got a tank?!' he shouted.

I said, 'Yes, course he has. A proper big tank and he keeps it in the loft, obviously.'

I asked both my grandads, but neither cared to talk about the experience. They were both lovely men who had been badly wounded on the Somme, where my mum's dad, my grandpa Alfred Ireland, lost his twin brother James in 1917.

James was a very fit young man who excelled at athletics and boxing and once in the trenches he was chosen, because of his speed and agility, to be a 'bomber'. Hand grenades as we know them didn't exist in the First World War; instead they had Mills bombs, which were similar to modern grenades, but couldn't be thrown as far. It was James's job to run at the enemy trenches, supported by two men who carried a supply of Mills bombs, and to lob the bombs into the trenches.

In September 1916, his battalion was moved to the salient at Ypres. It occupied the front line from Wieltje to Railway Wood. It was a 'reasonably quiet' sector and on 10 January 1917, the battalion decided to attack the German trenches.

I have obtained a photocopy of the report written by his commanding officer, which describes the actual attack in which he lost his life and which I often read.

```
1/5th LOYAL NORTH LANCASHIRE REGIMENT
10 January 1917
Party divided into two - left and right.
   Parties left assembled trench at 4.40 p.m. and
proceeded in file to front line, crossing front
```

ditch at 5 p.m. exactly and taking up position at
FIRST DITCH at 5.15 p.m. - zero hour - and made for
German trenches as per programme.

Right party on reaching enemy wire found it
uncut and encountered heavy machine gun fire from
KAISER BILL on their right front. It was impossible
for this party to enter the enemy trenches and it
sustained many casualties.

The left party was successful in effecting an
entry into the German trenches, meeting with very
little resistance until inside the trench, where
stubborn resistance was encountered. Many of the
enemy were killed and two dugouts and a O.P.
bombed. A bugle call 'G' was the signal for our
parties to withdraw. The enemy appeared to be in
strength and well prepared for the raid.

Our casualties were: Officers - Killed 2/Lieut
J.C. Frankland, Wounded 2/Lieut C.W.Whitaker, 2/
Lieut Alun Jones. Other Ranks - Killed 7, Wounded
48, Missing 2.

It is impossible to imagine the fear and horror experienced by those
young men on a daily basis, or the outstanding courage and valour
displayed on the battlefield. Or to picture the conditions in which they
lived and died day after day, month after month, during 'the war to end
all wars'.

My great-uncle James Ireland's body was buried on the battlefield, but
after the war, his grave could not be found; he is commemorated on the
Menin Gate Memorial at Ypres.

I sometimes wonder if he would have survived if he'd been in the left
party rather than the right on that fateful day.

Grans and Grandads ...

...aRE GREAT, AREN'T they? Well, mine were and because they lived nearby, us kids spent lots of time round at their houses at weekends, and during the week when Mum and Dad were out at work. Both sets of my grandparents lived only a few streets away from our house on Grafton Street. My dad's parents lived on Oxford Grove and my mum's parents lived on Lawn Street and I had a great many happy times at their houses, playing dominoes and cards and spin the bottle.

My maternal grandparents were quiet, but very loving. My grandad had been wounded in the First World War and had had TB so was never in the best of health, but he never complained. My gran was a typical lovely gran.

My dad's parents were a bit more outgoing. My grandad had also been wounded in the First World War and had been, in his time, a decent boxer in the army. My gran had a bit of the 'Thora Hird' in her, if you know what I mean – a forceful lady and slightly eccentric, if you like. She did that thing that grans often do for no logical reason, where they shave off their eyebrows and then draw them back in a bit higher up. My gran looked permanently startled.

When they got their first gas fire and North Sea gas started coming through, she was absolutely convinced that the flames went up and down with the tides. We'd be sitting having a chat and the flames would flare just a bit and she'd say, 'Tides coming in.'

One of the things I love about old people is the way they speak their mind. Talk straight. I took my gran shopping one day and in the town centre they had installed some new public conveniences, which cost twenty pence to use. My gran had to go, and when she came out, there was a posh-ish Hyacinth Bouquet-type woman, all fur coat and no knickers as they say round here, and she was haranguing the poor toilet attendant. Just as my gran was passing, the lady said rather loudly, 'I think it's an absolute disgrace that you have to pay twenty pence to use the toilet.' My gran, without a moment's hesitation or a break in her step, said, 'Oh, you can't put a price on a good shit' – beautiful.

Her most brilliant comment was inspired by a day of national celebration: the Queen's coronation in 1953. Like many others in our area, we didn't have a television until I was about nine, but a family in our street had got one in order to watch the spectacular event, and they invited all the neighbours round to watch it with them. My dad later told me (I was still a baby at the time) that during the lavish ceremony of pomp and circumstance, my gran actually said, 'It's all so beautiful. Isn't it a shame that the King didn't live to see this?'

My grandad had his moments as well. Whenever he was washing his face, he would rub soapy lather hard into his skin with both hands and make a weird loud noise by exhaling and reverberating his lips, a bit like blowing a big raspberry through his hands, which sounded as though a whale was about to surface. He was also a bit scary; I think that's part of the job description. His favourite trick with me was suddenly to grab my nose between his middle and index fingers and pull hard and then display it with glee: 'I've got your nose, David, I've got your nose!' And that's scary for a six-year-old. 'Aww, Grandad, give me my nose back.' But he wouldn't, he'd just dance around a bit and keep saying, 'I've got David's nose!'

Aged fifteen, when I judged myself big and strong enough, I jumped my grandad from behind and got him in a headlock and rummaged around in his mouth, then jumped back, shouting, 'I've got your teeth, Grandad, I've got your teeth!' He would say, 'Nner Dabith, nib me ma theet baa,' and I would just dance around a bit and shout, 'I've got Grandad's teeth!'

We called my dad's dad 'Spiderman' – not because he had special powers or was particularly agile, but because he couldn't get out of the bath. He lived till almost ninety and he put this down to a healthy lifestyle and a lifelong love of sports. As I mentioned earlier, he was a very good boxer, plus he also played football to a high standard, and in later years he loved playing bowls and won cups and medals for crown green bowling. I took him bowling at Mortfield Bowling Club only a couple of weeks before he died and he was a bit frail and his eyes and ears weren't so good, but we had a great time. He bowled a great wood right down the far corner of the green and because he couldn't see so well, he shouted to a bloke who was passing, 'How am I?' and the bloke shouted back, 'You're a foot in front,' and my grandad turned to me with a puzzled and stunned expression and asked, 'What did that man just call me?'

During his last years, he had a bad heart, which wasn't surprising considering his eating habits. Everything fried in dripping, plus full English breakfasts, fish and chips, pies and more pies ... I got him to go and see a cardiologist and then went round later to see how he'd got on.

As I went in the front door of the terraced house he'd lived in all his life, I heard him shouting from the kitchen, 'Arg! Ow! Jezz! Arrrggh!' When I dashed in, he was cooking a fry-up on the gas cooker – in a biscuit tin. Bacon, egg, sausage, black pudding, tomato ... all sizzling away in a metal biscuit tin! And he's burning his hands trying to shake it up, 'Arg! Ouch!'

I said, 'Grandad?! What the hell are you doing?' and he said, 'I've been seeing yon cardiologist feller and he examined me thorough like and told me that the best thing that I could do when I got home was throw my frying pan away, so it's gone.'

All my lovely grandparents have passed on now, leaving me with many happy memories. Some of my favourites centre on the rubbish they used to come out with. Well, to an eight-year-old it sounded like rubbish, but I now know that they were in fact age-old wise sayings such as 'You're barking up the wrong tree'. (Am I? I don't recall barking at all and there aren't any trees around here.) 'A stitch in time saves nine'; right, good.

The thing is that they pass this trait on to your parents and then they start. My mum was and still is very fond of saying, 'Cheap at half the price.' Maybe your mum says the same. But *of course* it is! It's *half* the price.

My paternal gran figured prominently in these sayings. My mum would often say, 'David? Don't teach your grannie how to suck eggs.' Okay, then, I won't. (Well, you wouldn't, would you? You wouldn't be so presumptuous. 'Grannie? You're sucking that egg all wrong. No, not like that, it should be more sort of sideways, about a 145-degree angle, try to just … Oh no! Now look what you've done! It's all over your chin!')

Indeed, it was my gran who starred in one of the only sayings that ever rang true to me, which was this: 'David, don't question your grannie. She knows her onions.'

And do you know what? She did. I used to go to the kitchen and get one out of the vegetable rack and then, holding it behind my back, I'd saunter into the front room and quickly produce it when she was least expecting it.

'What's that, Gran?' I'd shout.

'It's an onion,' she'd say in milliseconds, no hesitation whatsoever.

I tried to trick her with shallots and potatoes and even a pomegranate once – but no chance. She really did know her onions.

She had this party trick at Christmas where I would get a tray and fill it with all kinds of fruit and veg. Apples, turnips, swedes, carrots, parsnips – you get the picture – and then I'd mix in with this selection one small, solitary onion. I'd cover the tray with a tea towel and take it through to the assembled family and friends in the front room. With a flourish, I'd quickly remove the tea towel and demand, 'Gran, where's the onion?'

'There!' She'd point at it straight away with no hesitation; unerringly, always right; never known to miss.

I've thought often about the origins of these sayings and wondered if they maybe had, in days of old, some sort of *Sage Factor*, where wise old men and women came forward to present their latest words of wisdom to the panel of judges.

Judge 1: What's your name and from whence do you hail?

Winifreda: My name is Winifreda and I hail from Winchester.

Judge 1: Okay, Winifreda. In your own time. Pray tell us your wise words.

Winifreda: My saying is … (*Clears throat.*) Don't put all your eggs in one basket.

Judge 2: Please explain.

Winifreda: It is because, should you put all your eggs in the basket
and subsequently drop the basket, all the eggs shalt break,
whereas if you spread your eggs around in differing receptacles,
then if the basket should fall, you shalt still have some eggs
unbroken.

Judge 3: But what if I don't have any eggs?

Judge 1: Louis! Winifreda doesn't mean you to take 'eggs' literally.
She means—

Judge 2: (*Crying.*) I think it's so sad: little, fragile eggs . . . broken. We
must save the eggs!

(*Winifreda goes through to the next stage. Next hopeful please.*)

Edwina: My name is Edwina and my saying is: red sky at night,
shepherds' delight; red sky at morning, shepherds' warning.

Judge 2: Which means?

Edwina: I have noticed over many years that a red sky at night
indicates an imminent spell of fine weather, yet red sky in the
morning precedes a period of rain and wind.

Judge 1: Edwina, I didn't like it . . . I *loved* it!

Judge 2: (*Crying.*) And such beautiful imagery. I can almost see the
old, weather-beaten shepherd, tending his woolly sheep on the
hillside. And such inspired and exquisite rhyming: 'morning' –
'warning'.

Judge 3: You're through, Edwina.

(*Next contestant on* Sage Factor *please.*)

Judge 3: Hello, welcome to *Sage Factor*. Tell us your name and
where you've come from?

Edgar: My name is Mad Edgar and I came from over there.

Judge 2: And your saying is?

Edgar: (*Clears throat.*) People with glasses shouldn't throw stones.

(*Silence.*)

Judge 1: Why?

Edgar: (*Unsure, grasping at straws.*) They might break? Like the eggs?

(*Judges confer.*)

Judge 1: I'm sorry, Edgar, you haven't got the Sage factor.

But when you analyse it, Mad Edgar wasn't far off, was he? My grandparents came out with some totally mad sayings over the years. I think the best, for pure nonsensical value, included:

My gran: Stop that sulking, David, and stick your bottom lip in before a bird shits on it.
My grandad: I'm as happy as a dog with a tin dick.
My grandad: (*About a pretty girl.*) I know what she wants ... two cakes and a bun.

Over the course of my childhood, such phrases would crop up time and time again – often when I was getting told off or bossed around or otherwise instructed. Here are a few of the dumb phrases and sayings that my parents and grandparents inflicted on us children during our formative years ...

1. *You're late – you'd better get your skates on.*
   See, that's not going to help. That's going to take longer, surely? I don't know exactly where my skates are for a start and I know that my sister had them on last so I'll need to adjust them with that little spanner thing, wherever that is, *and* they've got those really big laces in them, so by the time I've tied them in a double bow and ... Ouch! Mum!

2. *You can't make a silk purse out of a sow's ear.*
   Right, because you'd probably need silk, wouldn't you? A pig's ear would be way down the bottom of the list. If Channel 4 screened the programme *100 Top Things to Make a Silk Purse Out Of*, I'm betting that a pig's ear would struggle to make it into the bottom ten, below 'a brick' and 'Keith Chegwin'. I reckon that even if you checked the

Dolce and Banana knock-off silk purses that 'Pineapple Pete' sells on Chorley market, I doubt they would have a label saying, '100% Pig's Ear – Boil Washing May Cause Crackling'.

3. *You can't make an omelette without breaking eggs.*
   See, that's where I've been going wrong.

4. *Music hath charms to soothe the savage beast.*
   It would be your last choice, though, wouldn't it? A length of 3 × 2 or some scaffolding pipe would be top of the list, surely.

5. *(In response to poor report from school) You are going to have to pull your socks up in English Literature, young fellow-me-lad.*
   That's going to help? I'll try it. (Pulls socks up.) Oh yes ... hang on!
   'Oh, for a muse of fire that would ascend the brightest heavens of invention. A kingdom for a stage, princes to act and monarchs to behold the swelling scene. Then should the war-like Harry assume the port of Mars and at his heels leashed in like hounds should famine, sword and fire crouch for employment ...'
   Bloody hell, it works! Let's just check and roll them down again. (Rolls socks down.)
   'My friend Billy had a ten-foot willy and he showed it to the girl next door. She thought it was a snake, so she hit it with a rake, and now it's only five foot four.'
   Hmm.

6. *Bob's your uncle.*
   No, he's not. Alf's my uncle. He's your brother, remember? How could you forget that? I don't know any Bobs.

Other characters who made regular appearances included 'Soft Mick', as in, 'He's had more women than Soft Mick. No wonder he's soft.' Also, there was 'Billy O', who featured in 'Run like Billy O!' How does he run then? Is he fast? Or does he run a bit weird? Does he zig-zag? I don't know anybody called 'Billy O'.

Last but not least there was 'Jenny Green Teeth', as in, 'If you don't come in before it gets dark, Jenny Green Teeth will get you. She'll come up out of the grids, catch you and suck all the marrow out of your bones.' That's scary stuff for a kid. The mad thing is, if my mum had said to me, 'David? Be in before it gets dark,' I'd have said, 'Okay, Mum.' But no! Jenny Green Teeth will get me!

NB. She actually did get my dad on the way home from the pub on a Friday night a few times and sucked all the marrow out of his bones because he could hardly stand up when he got home. He was like a rubber man.

7. *Don't rub your dad up the wrong way.*

Right then. And what would be the right way, Mum?

And then my dad would take over, especially when punishment was to be meted out re: point 5 above (the snake/rake poem) – not my fault, by the way, as I had my socks down, if you remember.

Dad: Oh, you think that smut's funny, do you?

Me: A bit. And even though she hit it with a rake, it's still five foot four! That's big, isn't it, Dad?

Dad: Stop that smirking or I'll make you smile on the other side of your face.

Me: (*Thinks: Oh no! He's taken a surgery course now!*)

Dad: Do you want a smack?

Me: (*Thinks: Trick question, surely?*) Er . . . no, I think I'll leave it, thanks, Dad.

Dad: What?! Do I look stupid?

(*It was worth it just the once, wasn't it?*)

Me: Yes, Dad.

Dad: Right. That's it! Go and fetch me something to hit you with.

(*I go. I come back.*)

Dad: This is a cushion.

Me: Yeah, I know.

One last thing. Where exactly was 'kingdom come'? My dad quite often threatened to knock me there. I imagine it's somewhere near 'the middle of next week', which was another possible destination.

My dad's favourite saying was, 'Best thing since sliced bread.' No matter what he was enjoying at that time – whether it was a meal, a book, a drink – the simple fact was that this thing, right now, was the best thing since the invention of sliced bread by Otto Frederick Rohwedder of Davenport, Iowa, USA. If you remember, a prototype Rohwedder built in 1912 was destroyed in a fire, so it was not until 1928 that Rohwedder had a fully working machine ready. Anyway, nothing in the interim period had come close to the thing my dad was enjoying at that minute: Vesta beef curry, pot noodle, JML miracle mat, etc. ...

I tried to imagine various scenes.

1. Alexander Fleming presents his discovery of penicillin to the Royal Society in late 1928.

    Fleming: 'Tis an antibiotic and will kill the majority of known bacteria. It will eradicate life-threatening infections and suffering throughout the world.

    President of Royal Society: Sorry, Alex, look at this! It's a 'Toastie' loaf!

2. Madame Marie Curie's up next.

    Marie Curie: I have discovered radium, an element that will revolutionize medicine. With X-rays, we can look inside the human body. In time, we will treat serious illness with radiography.

    President of Royal Society: Sorry, love, very impressive – but have you seen this loaf? Thick and Thin! Thick *and* thin slices in the same loaf! Can you believe it?

I have to say that of all the wise sayings and adages I was bombarded with during my childhood, I never found any of them that (a) made much sense or (b) helped me in any way. To this day, forty years later, I have still never met anybody who ...

- Poked their eye out with a stick.
- Grew an apple tree inside them because they'd eaten the core and pips.
- Broke their neck because they didn't tie their shoelaces properly. (Their neck! That's a heavy fall from a standing position for a six-year-old.)
- Could hear themselves think.
- Had to tell a donkey twice.
- Ate so many chocolate biscuits they turned into a chocolate biscuit! ('Is your David playing out? No, he's in the biscuit tin. He ate half a packet of chocolate digestives. What can you do? I've warned him often enough.')

Street Life

AFTER SCHOOL, EVERY weekend and on school holidays, we would play out in the neighbouring streets around the mills. We'd play hide-and-seek, tig, kick-outta-ball and 'What time is it, Mr Wolf?'.

Did you ever play that? Did you ever understand the rules? As I recall, you'd creep up a step at a time and ask Mr Wolf (who stood with his back turned to you), 'What time is it, Mr Wolf?' Mr Wolf would turn slowly, snarling, 'Iiiiiiit's … 3 o'clock!' And we would jump – 'Arghhhh!' – then look at each other, silently asking the question, 'Have you any idea what the f**k is going on?' Honestly, I have no idea what was supposed to happen until Mr Wolf shouted, 'Dinnertime!' and we all ran off, screaming, with Mr Wolf after us. Well, you would.

If we could get a football from someone, we'd play for hours, sometimes in the dark, in the street across the end terraces next to the mill. Chris Guffog usually had a ball, but he didn't play out much. We used to go and call for him, and when Mrs Guffog answered the door, we'd ask, 'Is Chris coming out to play?' Quite often she'd say, 'No, not tonight,' so we'd smile and ask, 'Is his ball coming out?'

Occasionally, one of us would get a ball for a birthday or Christmas, but you could bet that you'd only have played ten minutes with it before it went over Mad Mr Woodcock's back yard and there was no way he would give it back. Every street had a Mad Mr Woodcock and also a witch, or in our case two witches who lived together, dressed in black and had a black cat. Definitely witches.

We'd play cricket in summer. Stephen James had a bat and someone usually had a tennis ball. I drove past recently and our chalked cricket stumps are still visible on the mill wall. We played the alternative rules version, which meant that you could be given out if caught one-handed off the wall, and any disputed wicket was decided by a peg-leg. This involved turning the bat over, holding the blade and trying to play the next ball with the handle. Hit it or not, you had to run and there was a very fair chance you would be run out. I think it's time that these two simple variations were introduced into Test Cricket; it would make it a lot more fun, especially if there was a big wall on the offside and you could run the batsman out by hitting him with the ball: brilliant.

During Wimbledon, we'd share a tennis racquet. Because we had no tennis courts handy (and only one racquet anyway), we'd hit the ball against Mark Duncan's gable end (his house, I mean) for hours on end. The weird thing was that no matter how well and hard you hit the ball over the line drawn on the gable end, the wall always won.

Boys would play marbles (marps); the girls would do traditional skipping with a rope or the Chinese variation with elastic bands, which involved no actual skipping or reference to China whatsoever. They also played hopscotch, which I never understood, and some game that involved tucking their skirts into their knickers and bouncing a ball off the wall between their legs.

If we needed a bit more excitement, we'd play knock-a-door-run and its variant, which involved scraping dog poo into a paper bag, setting fire to it on someone's doorstep, then knocking on the door. If you were lucky (and they were unlucky), they'd see the paper bag in flames and immediately stamp on it hard – dog biz city!

Then our mums would call us in for tea. (Point of order here. Your evening meal is 'tea' – fact. Your midday meal is 'dinner'. That's why, at school, your midday meal is served by 'dinner ladies', not 'lunch ladies'.) So, okay, we'd go in to get ready for tea. Dad would soon be home from work and we'd all sit down at the table to eat. 'All' being my mum and dad, sister Joy, who is three years younger than me, and later my brother Peter, five years behind Joy. We'd have corned beef hash or hot-pot or my favourite: a meat-and-potato pie covered with Heinz vegetable soup – oh yes, you read that right. Beautiful.

Friday tea was courtesy of the chippy. My job. Off I'd go, clattering up the back street in my red plastic moulded sandals, carrying a bowl for the steak puddings, which they'd take off you and keep warm until it was your turn. Fish and chips was always cod, unless you asked loudly for an alternative as soon as you got in the queue. Dad sometimes fancied a plaice and I hated having to order it, I felt so self-conscious shouting to make myself heard: 'Can you put me a plaice in, please?'

David Dickinson continually says 'cheap as chips'. Chips round our way now are £1.80 a bag. That's not cheap! But it is a useful economic indicator of our times. If I wanted £1.80's worth of chips when I was a kid, I'd have to have taken a wheelbarrow, and once I'd got them, the chippy would have to have shut. Not enough potatoes in Bolton for that many chips.

During tea, we'd talk about our day and listen to the radio. Later, we'd read books and comics, do puzzles, play snakes and ladders or draughts, and listen to the radio some more, especially if there was a comedy programme on. Sometimes, my dad would put one of his Deutsche Gramophone LPs on the radiogram and sit in his chair conducting the Berlin Philharmonic's recording of Wagner's *Tannhäuser* (bit heavy for an eight-year-old) with one of my mum's knitting needles. We'd all look up from our comics or puzzles and watch him conducting the overture with his long hair flying, or we'd simply listen to the music and stare into the coal fire, making shapes from the flames. Happy days.

Snow and Sun

I N THE WINTER school holidays, we'd wake up to thick frost on the windows and take turns at going downstairs to get the coal fire going. Clean out yesterday's mountain of ash and, in the days before firelighters, roll up pages of last night's newspaper into tubes and then tie a knot in them. We'd pack the grate with these before adding kindling and coal.

Getting the fire going was a risky business. The technique involved standing the shovel up against the fire and covering it with a sheet of newspaper to get the flames drawing up through the kindling and coal. One lapse of concentration and the sheet of newspaper would first turn brown, then burst into flames! 'Mum? I need some butter!'

After breakfast, porridge usually, we'd be well wrapped up and out into the snow. We'd make snowmen and long icy slides and have snowball fights. Sometimes, we'd go sledging in Queen's Park if Chris Guffog's toboggan was coming out to play.

I've always thought that we should put in for the Winter Olympics in the North-West. We've started getting the weather for it, plus, if we hosted the Games, we could introduce events that the Swiss, Austrians and Scandinavians wouldn't stand a chance at. We could have 'Sliding Down a Hill on a Bin Bag'; we'd be halfway down 'Winter Hill' and the Swiss and Austrians would be still examining the bag at the top ('*Was ist das?*'). We could have 'Old Men Clearing a Path Relay' – because we lead the world in that. Our old men are limping down to the shed as soon as the first snowflake falls, nailing a flat piece of plywood to a long bit of 2×1, then they're off. We could have proper, big Olympic snowball fighting. Imagine the scene: we've drawn Germany in the quarter-finals; get a bit of coal in.

In the summer school holidays, we'd spend all day playing in the neighbourhood or we'd take a picnic to Queen's Park. We made sugar butties (mmm: nutritious. If I get asked to do *Ready Steady Cook* again, I'm going to take sugar, butter and bread as my ingredients) and we wrapped them in shiny bread wrapper. We made our own pop by getting a small packet of kali (rainbow crystals or American cream soda) from the corner shop and dissolving it in a bottle of tap water. I once tried to make a cheese toastie using my mum's iron, but that went horribly wrong and I got smacked legs.

We used to get a few sweets from the penny tray: 'fruit salad', 'blackjacks' (probably banned now) and cinder toffee. We didn't have Kinder Surprise – which, by the way, isn't ever a surprise. It's always a plastic toy that you have to assemble, always. That's not a surprise, that's cheating kids, that is. If it was a mouse's head, fair enough. That's a surprise, a proper surprise: Kinder have delivered. Or, somebody's appendix ... 'Jeez! What's that?!' If it says 'surprise', it should be a surprise.

If I'd managed to save up enough pocket money, I'd get a cider ice lolly (and of course pretend to get drunk off it!) or my absolute favourite – a frozen Jubbly. They were great: a big pyramid-shaped lump of frozen orange. Trouble with a frozen Jubbly was that sometimes you'd be so excited about getting one, you'd rip a strip of the packaging off and squeeze too hard and the Jubbly would shoot out into the air and land on the pavement about two feet away. Be alright, dust all the dirt off, oh – bit of dog poo, flick it off and try to get it back in the packet ... almost impossible, you could never get it back in properly. But it would last you all day would a frozen Jubbly, and when all the juice had been extracted and you no longer had any feeling in your mouth, you were still left with a small meteorite: the perfect projectile for skirmishes in the park.

I loved Jubblys and ice-pops. One day, during school term, the dinner ladies went on strike (at dinnertime), and our parents gave us two shillings to get our dinner from the chip shop. All my mates got pudding, chips and peas, or pie, chips and peas, or fish and chips, and then it was my turn: 'Scraps and gravy, please, with a bit of pea-wet [the juice off mushy peas].' 'One penny please.' 'There you go.'

Then off to the corner shop: 'Twenty-three ice-pops, if you please.' I stuffed them into my inside blazer pocket ... and by the time I got back to school, I was flatlining. The school nurse panicked – 'He's got no pulse!' Luckily, they discovered the ice-pops packed over my heart. Mr Freeze nearly killed me.

We spent all day playing, making our own fun. Spin round and round and round and round, get dizzy, fall over – piss funny. Picking buttercups, holding them under each others' chins and saying, 'You like butter.'

'I know!'

'Ha! Brilliant.'

Using 'sugar-stealers' (dandelion seeds) to tell the time. 'What time do you have to be in?'

'Five o'clock. What time is it now?'

None of us had a watch, so pick up a sugar-stealer and blow the seeds away, puff, puff, puff ... 'Three o'clock.'

'Plenty of time.'

We'd lie on our backs, making shapes out of the clouds for hours ... 'Polar bear'; 'Galleon'; 'Seagull. No, wait, that is actually a proper seagull.' We'd catch caterpillars, put them in a jam jar and watch them die. Simple, innocent pleasures. Well ...

Dewek Wigby also taught us lads a game where you go for a wee, but hold your foreskin tight shut, until it fills up and swells like a frog in mating season and hurts bad ... real bad ... excruciating bad. The first time, I screamed, 'What do I do with it now, Dewek?!'

He replied, 'Just let go.'

I did.

Pop – whooooshhhhhh! Talk about a golden shower! Great game.

Playground Laughs

I N BETWEEN OUR playground games of tig, hide-and-seek, 'What time is it, Mr Wolf?', football, cricket and hoperooski – a game eventually banned by the teachers because it was considered too violent[1] – we started telling jokes.

Generally, they were about nuns, elephants in a mini, shark-infested custard, frogs in a blender, and 'Mummy Mummy' jokes, e.g.

'Mummy Mummy, can I lick the bowl?' – 'No, flush it like everyone else.'

'Mummy Mummy, I don't like Grandma' – 'Well, just eat your vegetables then.'

'Mummy Mummy, I don't want to go to Australia' – 'Shut up and keep digging.'

Then there were visual jokes. My favourites included pulling the skin on either side of your neck out between your thumbs and forefingers and saying, 'Please, miss, can I have another pencil?' and hooking your forefinger into your bottom lip and pulling down hard and mumbling,

---

1 Hoperooski was a battle between two teams which could, on occasion, include every child in the playground. It was played under cover of the playground shed, and each team retreated to an opposite wall and began to hop with arms folded in front to act as a battering ram. Then the teams charged and tried to fight their way through the opposition to the opposite wall. Anyone who put a foot down during the mid-shed battle was 'out' and retreated to the periphery of the contest. The process was repeated until there were, for example, three left on one team and five on the other. Tactics came into play where a hopper from the 'three' team would be targeted by three members of the 'five' team, but the beauty of the game was that the three team hoppers might be big and strong enough to defeat the 'five' team. It should be an Olympic event. Seriously.

'Could you hang your umbrella somewhere else, please?' or squashing your face tight between both hands and saying, 'Could you open the lift doors again, please?' You had to be there, probably.

Some of the most popular jokes weren't technically jokes at all, they were riddles, e.g.

What's green and hangs off trees?
Leaves?
No. Monkey snot.

What do you call a kangaroo with no skin?
Slippy.

There was one of these riddles/jokes which I 'got', but which I didn't find funny, because it just didn't ring true. This riddle was – and I'm sure you're familiar with it – 'What's worse than finding a worm in your apple?' Of course, the answer is: 'Finding half a worm.' I never really found that funny because even at that tender age, I could think of loads of things that had happened to me that were infinitely worse than finding half a worm in my apple.

Simple things like, being sick down your nose. Your mouth's full and the sick has to come out somehow; it can't come out of your ears, can it? So whoooosh, arghh, burn, burn nose! Even worse when you've had a corned beef hash for tea and there's a chunk of carrot stuck in the top of one nostril. 'I wish I'd chewed that a little bit better.'

I'll tell you something else that is worse than half a worm: getting your willy caught in your zip is worse. I'd already done that by the age of ten, with half a dozen near misses besides. Most times, you could extract it easily, but occasionally the zip head would trap some skin – a little 'U'-shaped flap stuck tight. And the shock is exceeded only by the pain. It's an exquisite, intense pain and it demands immediate attention. But you have a dilemma – do you zip up or zip down? The pain is piercing now and then your mate runs up in a panic and thrusts a half-eaten apple at you, shouting, 'Urgh, look, half a worm!' and you scream back full in his face: 'Stick your worm! Look at my bleeding dick, you bleeding dick!'

Around the same time, something else happened to me that was worse than finding half a worm in an apple. It happened during our weekly swimming lesson, when we were marched in double file down to the municipal baths.

I hated going swimming from school. I hated it because our maths teacher took us and he was a psycho, a proper psycho who didn't have a cane for corporal punishment; he used a broken chair leg. I'm not joking, a broken chair leg! I reckon he must have thrown a chair at a kid at some time and it smashed to bits and he saw the fragments and said in his Neanderthal way, 'Chair leg – good.' Seriously, he hit misbehaving kids with a chair leg. Imagine that these days! He was as mad as a bucket of frogs. I can't tell you his name for obvious reasons, but he was married to a woman called Mrs Matthews.

I hated him, and because of that I hated maths – and so became hopeless at maths. Right from those early problems: 'If it takes two men with one bucket ten minutes to fill a bath, how long would it take one man with …' Stop it right there! Why don't they just turn the taps on? And why've they only got one bucket? Are they simple?

Alternatively, do you remember this one? 'A swimming pool is twenty-five yards by ten yards and you have two planks, one of which is five yards long and one of which is three yards long. How do you get to the other side of the pool?' *I walk round.*

I could never remember formulae in maths. I couldn't even remember the acronyms we had to learn to help us. Do you remember BODMAS? It was a way of aiding us to remember in which order an algebraic equation should be solved: **B**rackets first, then '**O**f', then **D**ivision, then **M**ultiplication, then **A**ddition and finally **S**ubtraction. But how do you ever remember the acronym BODMAS in an exam? I remember sitting in the exam room, staring blankly at my algebra equation, thinking, 'BAMSOD? BASMOD? BOMSAD? That sounds about right.'

The only one I remember was SOHCAHTOA. I don't know why, it's far more complicated than BODMAS, but it nearly rhymes with Pocahontas, the Native American princess who married John Smith. (I don't think that was his real name, do you?) Anyway, the first two syllables sort of match – 'SOCAH' and 'POCA' – so … If you recall, it is a formula for working out the other angles of a right-angled triangle. The acronym stands for **Sine** = **Opposite** over **Hypotenuse**, **Cosine** = **Adjacent** over **Hypotenuse**, and **Tangent** = **Opposite** over **Adjacent**, and I'll tell you something for nothing: that's come in bloody handy in my adult life. The number of times I have to deal with triangles each and every day. Colleagues constantly asking, 'What angle's that, Dave?' 'It's a Toblerone, just eat the pissing thing.'

There were all sorts of stupid rhymes and phrases they taught us in school, like 'Richard Of York Gave Battle In Vain' to remember the colours of the rainbow, and the other one that did my head in: the rhyme to aid you in remembering the number of days in a month. You know the one, it goes like this:

Thirty days hath September *(got it)*

April, June and November *(good)*

All the rest have thirty-one *(okay, that's simple enough)*

Apart from February *(what?!)*

Which has twenty-eight *(twenty-eight? Well, okay, then)*

Unless it's a leap year when there's twenty-nine *(no! What sort of shit rhyme is that?)*

How the hell does that rhyme make it easier to remember? More to the point, which idiot came up with that distribution? How come February did so badly out of it? Why not have: 'Thirty-five days hath December *(longer for Christmas holidays)*, all the rest have thirty.' That's it, done. Fairer all round.

Anyway … back to the swimming lesson and the thing that was worse than half a worm. The week before this traumatic incident, the teacher had told us that they'd put some special substance in the water so that if you peed in it, it would change colour and they'd know immediately who was peeing and you were out.

Well, me and my mates thought that was brilliant! We were going to do the 'Red Arrows'. We drank loads of water before the lesson, then headed for the deep end. Me, as squadron leader, gave the command:

'Right now. Peel away … and piss!' We swam and pissed; I looked behind me – nothing! It's just yellow! Yellow's no good, I can do yellow anytime!

Then it happened – this worse than half a worm thing, even worse than swimming through all your mates' piss. I was swimming breaststroke, breathing out underwater as you do, then surface for a deep breath, and this one time, as I breathed in a lungful of air, I also sucked in a plaster. There was always a plaster in the swimming pool, wasn't there? Bobbing away in that guttering thing at the side of the pool, usually. A dirty plaster with one corner folded over, usually. So, I swallowed this plaster, straight down. And it was lumpy! I thought, 'Verruca.' Urrggh, half a worm?! I'd have eaten a plateful of worms rather than swallowing that plaster!

5 November 1960

A MOMENTOUS DAY in my childhood. Bonfire Night, obviously, but also the day that my dad first took me to see Bolton Wanderers FC at Burnden Park. He'd bought me a big wooden rattle and I'd spent the last couple of days covering it with black-and-white-checked sticky tape. (Bolton played in white shirts and navy blue shorts and it was the nearest match.)

Bolton were playing Manchester City and although I was a massive Bolton fan even at that age, I was looking forward to seeing the great Denis Law. I thought that I was going to burst with excitement; and I thought my mum was simply going to burst as she was due to have a baby on 10 November and was enormous.

We walked to the match. I lived at 3 Grafton Street, just round the corner from a pub called Sally Up Steps, which was at the bottom of Chorley Old Road, so we cut through Bolton Royal Infirmary onto Chorley Street, passing two ornate elephant statues on some old gate posts (the elephant features prominently on Bolton's coat-of-arms and there are many sculptures dotted around the town still). Then we crossed the 'High Level', passing the fire station and into town. We went through the town centre to Trinity Street station, then down passed 'Edbros', crossing the railway lines on Orlando Bridge and down onto Manchester road – where we turned right and joined the huge tide of supporters heading down the road. I could see the floodlights of Burnden Park now.

I know this will mean nothing to most of you readers, but as I write it, I am reliving that happy journey in my mind, so please excuse the indulgence.

The crowds were huge in those days; I think that there were about 40,000 on Burnden Park on that day. Although my dad usually stood on the Bolton Embankment end, he took me into the Paddock to avoid the crush, which he had rightly judged would be too dangerous and scary for a nine-year-old.

When I got into my teens, I always went on the embankment, where the atmosphere was electric: the chanting, the humour, the wild celebrations and the heartbreak were mixed with the always present fear of being trapped within such a huge crowd. At the end of the game, thousands of the fans on our end had to file out through three narrow exits. Quite often, me and my mates would optimistically say, 'We'll wait here until the crush is over.'

No chance: the plain fact was that you had no say in the matter; if the mass around you started to move, you'd move with it, staring at the exit and thinking, 'We'll never get through there!' your feet sometimes hardly touching the ground. But we always did, quite often bluffing through our fear with shouts of 'Mind my eggs!' in a desperate hope that people would give you more space, but really – eggs at a football match?

Anyway, on 5 November 1960, I cheered till I was hoarse and rattled my new rattle as Bolton Wanderers took to the pitch, led by the legendary Nat Lofthouse – 'The Lion of Vienna' – who famously said, 'In my day, there were plenty of players who would kick your bollocks off – the difference was that at the end of the match they would shake your hand and help you look for them.' Also playing that day was our new golden boy Francis Lee, a local lad from Westhoughton, who was sixteen! Sixteen and playing in the first division (the Premier League of its day)!

The game was end-to-end stuff (that's how it works, usually; sometimes it's more one end than the other, admittedly, but ...) and totally mesmerizing and exciting for a nine-year-old. Bolton won 3-1 and both Nat Lofthouse and Frannie Lee scored. People say that I am mistaken when I say that I saw Nat and Frannie play in the same side; that they were of different eras and that my childhood memories have been clouded by time, but I can assure you that I remember it as if it was yesterday. Frannie Lee scored a diving header! (Not the obligatory penalty he scored almost weekly when he moved to Man City later in his career.)

After the game, we walked back down Manchester Road into town and bought a 'Buff', the football results newspaper, which was printed hastily after the game and sold from a van. On the way home, we would read the match report on the match we had just watched! How mad was that? Because of the speed at which it was produced, it often contained typo errors. I remember years later a front-page picture of Johnny Byrom, our brilliant centre forward, firing a shot at the opposing goalkeeper, who had only managed to parry the ball, such was its ferocity. It was a great picture, capturing the moment perfectly on that very cold January day, with the players' breath hanging like steam in the air. The big caption should have read, 'Byrom's Shot Warms Goalkeeper's Hands', but one little error can make so much difference and cause so much hilarity, especially when it results in, 'Byrom's Shit Warms Goalkeeper's Hands'.

So home we went, it was five o'clock and going dark and the anticipation of Bonfire Night gradually replaced the excitement of the match. Bonfire Night or 'Bommy Night' round our way used to be a massive thing, a community event which took weeks and weeks to prepare.

Each group of terraced streets had its own bonfire celebrations. In Grafton Street, we shared ours with Laburnum Street, with which we shared a back street. Our gang would start collecting wood and other combustible material for our bommys during the back end of the summer holidays and all through September and October after school and at weekends. We would take our axes (really!) and cut down dead and dying branches from trees and bushes in Queen's Park and along Chorley New Road, and drag them home through the streets. We'd raid the cotton mills for big wicker skips, which burned like mad. Some of them we'd find broken and discarded in the mill yard, but if there weren't so many, or another gang had beaten us to it, we'd actually get into the mill at night via rickety metal fire escapes and take proper good ones.

We would make our dens out of these skips on shed roofs and take it in turns to sit in them and guard our bonfires – bonfires in the plural because we had our big main bommy halfway down the back street with two 'feeder' bommys at either end. And your bommys would get raided by other gangs, so we had to repel the enemy with hand-to-hand combat or by using ingeniously constructed firework weapons.

There used to be three different types of banger, ranging from the penny 'cannon' through to the biggest, fattest and noisiest with the most potential for injury, the '3-2-1-zero', which we used to repel attack by lobbing or firing at the enemy. If you had a good arm, you could hit them with a full toss or, failing that, you could fire them from a 'gun' constructed out of a small metal tube we found in the mills fitted with a wooden handle carved from a block of wood with your penknife; the fizz from the banger fuse was strong enough to propel them from the tube over quite a distance.

The same laws of backstreet physics produced the drainpipe bazooka / rocket launcher, which obviously caused mayhem after a one-shilling 'Starburst' rocket was lit and dropped into the adapted length of drainpipe.

Of course, the days of bonfire guerrilla warfare have long since gone; health-and-safety quangos have gradually killed off another great British tradition. However, I can say, hand on heart, that I can't remember anyone being seriously injured in the skirmishes over the years. Mind you, that might be because my memory has never been the same since I got hit in the temple by a mini rocket when I was eight. There was a lad from our street who did lose an eye on Bonfire Night, but that happened when he tried to fire a 'Roman Candle' at a rival gang from the passenger seat of a moving car without having had the good sense to wind the window down first.

But on 5 November 1960, health-and-safety directives, risk assessments and standard operating procedures were just clouds on the distant horizon. I dashed in, still on a high from the match, and blurted out every memory I had of the day to my mum as I ate my cup of black peas – the first course on the traditional Bonfire Night 'menu'. Hot-pot and red cabbage would follow outside round the bonfire, with jacket potatoes and chestnuts cooked in the embers, then parkin and treacle toffee.

After the peas, I dashed to my bedroom to retrieve my metal biscuit tin, which contained the assortment of fireworks I'd accumulated over the previous weeks. I'd open the lid and do a quick inventory, then try to work out a lighting schedule. First the 'Snow Storm', then the 'Traffic Light', then 'Mount Vesuvius', then the 'Katherine Wheel', 'Roman Candle', 'Golden Fountain' etc.

Then I'd put my duffel coat on, grab my balaclava (which you needed to wear for dashing past the blazing bonfire) and run outside to where our dads were taking the back gates off their hinges to prevent the paint blistering from the heat. Now it was time to try to light the bonfire, which had been predictably (and traditionally) drenched by four days of November rain. Dads diced with death pouring petrol on it as a last resort, but then it was lit and the flames took hold and a cheer went up from the entire population of those two terraced streets as the flames began to lick the trousers of the Guy Fawkes dummy atop the pyre.

Then the fireworks started and the dads took charge of lighting them whilst at the same time announcing the next pyrotechnic as they lit the fuse at arm's length. Roman Candles shot their coloured balls to 'oohs' and 'aahs', sky rockets burst above the roofs and families cheered, bangers exploded accompanied by shouts and screams, and Katherine Wheels spun a dazzling pattern … then got stuck … then got prodded by a dad with a stick and resumed the spin … then stuck again. The biggest screams and shouts of the night were caused by the 'jumping jacks' – small concertina-shaped firecrackers that exploded a segment at a time, each explosion causing the firework to jump in an unpredictable pattern, but always, always following you as if they contained some sort of homing device!

On this night, 5 November 1960, a jumping jack went down my heavily pregnant mother's wellie (obligatory wear for Bonfire Night). Such was the shock that she straight away went into labour with my brother Peter, who was due on the 10th. People always say that it must have been terribly traumatic for her, but I say, 'Yes, but look on the bright side – if her waters hadn't broken when they did … she'd have suffered third-degree burns to her foot.'

Bonfire Night was a real family and community event. We've lost it forever and that's a great sadness. I spend a lot of time in Spain now, where the values of community and family are cherished and celebrated at every opportunity. Throughout the year, there are fiestas small and grand celebrating saints' days, historical and national events. The stunning 'Moors and Christians' festival celebrated over three nights is amazing; the Fallas – where massive, beautifully crafted effigies are paraded through the streets before being burned as the fire brigade hose down the surrounding buildings to protect them from the heat – is unbelievable. Communities line the streets of villages, towns and cities to watch these stunning processions, thrilled by the awesome costumes and stirred by the magnificent music of the marching bands.

Once the main event has ended, the street parties begin. In small avenues and squares, friends and families assemble around tables and chairs and eat and drink, laugh and talk, sing and dance as their marching bands play again and again and again ... until the early hours of the morning.

BWFC

ON THAT UNFORGETTABLE day, 5 November 1960, I became a loyal Bolton Wanderers FC fan. I was born in Bolton and that's how it works, you don't get a choice; I was just lucky that I was born where I was because I loved the club then and I do now. BWFC is a great club with a great history, and above all it is a great family club with a warm welcome for everybody.

Over the next few years, me and my mates never missed a home game and also got to the nearer away games. There was nothing like cheering your team on to a well-earned 2-1 win on a cold, wet and grey January afternoon, before trudging off home for tea, a welcoming fire, pudding, chips and peas, bread and butter and a mug of tea. Once we got a TV, it would be *Doctor Who*, *Emergency Ward 10* and *The Black and White Minstrel Show* and then later, if you were lucky, coming down in your pyjamas to watch *Match of the Day*. Not changed much, has it?

In the school holidays, we'd go down to watch the Wanderers train. We'd make BWFC albums out of old exercise books using photos cut from the *Bolton Evening News* and tried to get the players to sign their photo when they arrived for training. Most were very generous with their signings; some were more difficult: for example, Gordon 'Chunky' Taylor, now chairman of the PFA and a lovely man, wouldn't sign if he saw that he'd previously signed a photo.

In stark contrast was Barry Fry. We'd signed him one close season and I'd cut out loads of pictures of him from the papers for my book. I dashed over to him one afternoon as I recognized him getting out of his car. He took my album and signed every single photo 'Best Wishes, Barry Fry' – every one! I wanted to get away because Wyn Davies had arrived and I desperately wanted his autograph, but Barry wouldn't let go of my book!

Once they'd all arrived and got changed, we'd follow them over to the training ground on Bromwich Street and watch the full training session. We had some great players in those years. In addition to the players I've mentioned, we had two great fullbacks – Syd Farrimond (Syd – that's a proper name, that is) and Roy 'Chopper' Hartle. You wouldn't want to be a winger playing against a fullback whose nickname was 'Chopper', would you? Roy was built like a tank and was hard but fair. Syd was also a class act.

One of my greatest thrills now I've achieved a degree of success and become a 'known' Boltonian is that I have got to meet some of these sporting heroes of mine. Roy Hartle is a charming, well-spoken man and Syd is an absolute gent. When I see them at the Reebok and they shout, 'Alright, Dave?' it is still the biggest thrill.

We had a great goalkeeper, Eddie Hopkinson, who got a well-deserved England cap or two. He was a great shot-stopper and when I was ten or eleven I cut out a magnificent photo of him flying through the air, arms flung high, back arched and legs extended behind him majestically – and he signed it. A couple of years ago, just before he died, bless him, I brought my album down to the Reebok and showed it to him. I said what a fantastic picture it was and he looked at it, smiled and said, 'Aye, but I missed it!'

Another legend I've had the pleasure of meeting is Freddie Hill. Freddie was one of the most cultured, skilful midfield players I ever saw; how he didn't get more England caps is baffling. I once saw him, away at Gigg Lane, take the ball wide of the box and shape up as if to cross. All the defence, including the goalkeeper, took a step out ready, as did most of the crowd to get a better view, and then Freddie dummied the cross and passed the ball into the empty net from about twenty-five yards. Brilliant, he was.

One of my best memories from the Bromwich Street training ground was that during the 1966 World Cup, Brazil trained there for a time.

There were no restrictions on us watching them and on one occasion I bet there were about 10,000 fans down there. Watching Pelé, Da Silva, Gerson ... in Bolton!

Blow Me, It's Christmas

CHRISTMAS AS A kid, of course, was brilliant – and the countdown started after Bonfire Night. In the weeks building up to the big event, we'd be making our hugely ambitious Christmas present lists and rehearsing carols with the school choir and 'orchestra'. I was on triangle and vocals, with Dewek Wigby still on wooden blocks. I had a fair soprano voice and once sang the opening verse to 'Once in Royal David's City' as the choir entered the church for the Christmas Carol Service.

From December the 1st, we took turns opening the doors on the advent calendar. A couple of weeks before, we'd put up the Christmas decorations and make new ones. Yes, that's 'make' new ones, usually the coloured banners made by gluing a packet of paper strips together into interlocking hoops.

On Christmas Eve, we'd be ready for bed early and Dad would get in late after having had a few celebratory drinks after work. He'd always dash in in a fake panic and tell us that he'd just seen Father Christmas on a roof on Vernon Street and we'd freak out and hurriedly put out a mince pie and a glass of sherry for the big man and a carrot for Rudolph. One year, I wanted to leave carrots for all the other reindeers, but we had a count-up and we only had three.

Of course, we couldn't sleep for the excitement – and then started to panic when he didn't show up within the hour because Vernon Street was only about ten streets away so maybe he'd missed us! Eventually, we'd sleep and then wake up at three o'clock in the morning and almost burst with happiness when we saw our pillowcases full of Christmas presents. Mum and Dad would wake up and insist that we could only open one present and then had to go back to sleep.

In the morning, we opened our gifts. There were various techniques, ranging from opening the smallest first, slowly and deliberately, to make the whole joyous process last longer – or tearing into them in a mad frenzy starting with the biggest!

We got selection boxes, comic annuals, games compendiums, footballs, Dinky and Corgi cars, train sets or accessories, *I Spy* books … These last were pocket-sized books in which you earned points for the objects you 'spied', so for instance you might have *I Spy Cars*, where an Austin A40 or Morris Minor would earn you 5 points and an E-type Jaguar 25 points. For one Christmas, I got *I Spy Birds*, which was for the most part a waste of time where we lived, among the mills in Bolton. I got Sparrow (5 pts), Starling (5 pts) and Pigeon (5 pts), but the chances of spotting an Osprey (25 pts) were as remote as seeing a Bentley (35 pts) pull into Grafton Street garage. At the bottom of the pillowcase were tangerines and nuts … and when, in the history of man (well, let's say after the Neanderthal period), have children *ever* liked fruit and nuts in any setting, on any occasion, least of all as a present?

Possibly the worst presents you can get as a kid for Christmas are items of clothing. When you're eight, clothing is definitely not on your Christmas list; toys are on the list, where does it say 'balaclava'? I once got a pair of red plastic moulded sandals for Christmas! Fair enough, this was in the days before Nike, Adidas and Puma and when the only other alternative leisure footwear was a pair of pumps – but red plastic sandals! They didn't only look a bit shit, but they would often smell of it, as inevitably you would run through a dog turd and it would get squashed into the moulding on the base of the sandal and you'd spend hours sitting on the kerb trying to flick it out with a lolly stick.

Mentioning 'Puma' actually stirred a distant memory about a great pair of shoes I once received: a pair of shoes that not only had animal prints embedded on the sole, but also a compass in the heel. I think they were called 'Pathfinders' and they were of course invaluable if you grew up in Lancashire and stumbled across a wild animal print when you came out of Bridgeman Street baths. No need to panic: all you had to do was take your shoe off (and pray that the animal wasn't waiting nearby, ready to pounce as soon as you'd incapacitated yourself by doing so) and compare the animal prints on the sole ... It's an Arctic wolf! Or possibly a biggish dog. Anyway, best not chance it, head for home – but now it's going dark and you're a bit disorientated with fear and trepidation! What to do? Try not to freak out, just check the compass in the shoe heel because you know your house is north-north-east from here. It's either head in that direction or catch this bus that's coming.

Just as Nike, Adidas and Puma were brands of future footwear, beachwear by Billabong, Ripcurl and O'Neill were waves on a distant ocean. When I was thirteen, I got a pair of knitted swimming trunks for Christmas. Yes, I said 'knitted'. These had to be held up with a striped 'snake' belt. Not only did they look rubbish, but also, when you were paddling in the sea at Blackpool, your swimming trunks were two feet behind you, full of shrimp.

When you're on holiday at thirteen and developing an interest in girls, the knitted swimming trunk is not a good look. Dewek Rigby told me that I should put a carrot down my trunks and that would help and so I tried it – but the reaction was exactly the opposite I was hoping for; girls would pull their faces in disgust and point at me in a bad way. I found out later from Dewek that I should have put the carrot down the front of my trunks!

If you were very lucky, you might get that extra special game that you dreamed of unwrapping on Christmas morning. The game that all great footballers were privileged enough to receive from good old Saint Nick at one time or another. The game that bred in them not only skill, dexterity and concentration, but also honesty, fairness, truth and a love of the beautiful game. I'm talking two magic words (not 'Open Sesame') – Blow Football.

Two opponents armed only with a straw would try skilfully to manoeuvre the ball and power it past the opposing goalkeeper. No outfield players required.

Tucked away in the three corners of the world, from a council flat in Salford via the beaches of Rio de Janeiro to the industrial landscape of the Ruhr valley, future stars of the beautiful game would blow till they could barely breathe ... then they'd blow some more. Fortified by a simple glass of pineapple juice, dandelion and burdock or Umbongo,[2] they'd blow the extra mile.

This great game slowly disappeared over the years, replaced by miniature players to flick! Flicking – where's the skill in that? Other players pierced by long silver poles were destined to spin forever. Is it any wonder that greed and cynicism crept into the game?

Presents opened, half a selection box eaten and at least one toy broken, we'd sit down for the traditional Christmas meal. Sometimes our grandparents would come over, but most Christmas Days we'd go round and visit them before the Christmas dinner.

We mostly had chicken instead of turkey, but with all the trimmings. We pulled Christmas crackers, laughed at the plastic toy gifts, wore the paper hats and told each other the jokes. I collected my favourites over the years and I present them here for your delight:

How does Santa Claus like his pizza?
Deep *pan*, crisp and even.

Two snowmen in a field and one says to the other, 'Can you smell carrots?'

Man: Doctor, doctor, I've got a cricket ball stuck up my bum.
Doctor: How's that?
Man: Don't you start.

---

2 So 'Umbongo Umbongo, they drink it in the Congo'. I bet you any money that they don't. They struggle trying to find a decent supply of water half the time; my guess is that there are far more important things on the shopping list than a tropical fruit drink. I think the 'creatives' in some ad agency came up with an idea that people would love this refreshing drink in a hot climate and settled on Africa. So then they had to come up with a name that (a) sounded ethnically African and (b) rhymed with an African country! An idea that is (a) offensive and borderline racist and (b) ridiculous. How many hours did they spend working on presentations, proposing, 'Umberia Umberia, they drink it in Nigeria'; 'Imbwana Imbwana, they drink it in Botswana'? Bollocks.

How do you make a door laugh?
Tickle its knob.

Two cannibals eating a clown and one says to the other, 'Is it me or does this taste funny?'

Patient: Doctor, I've got some lettuce sticking out of my bum.
Doctor: I don't like the look of that. That could just be the tip of the Iceberg.

What happened to the hyena that swallowed an Oxo cube?
He made a laughing stock of himself.

Holidays

TRADITIONALLY, EACH MILL town had its own 'wakes' week, when the mills closed down and the workers had a well-earned – although unpaid – break, and the local population migrated to the seaside. The 'wakes' evolved from village festivals, which were quite often staged to celebrate the anniversary of a church or chapel, into mass industrial holidays. When Bolton Holidays came round, we would go to the Fylde coast most years – so Thornton Cleveleys, Lytham St Anne's or, of course, Blackpool.

We always went on the train, because we didn't have a car until I was about nine or ten. This was always a great thrill for me because I loved steam trains; still do. If I hear a steam train's whistle or the characteristic sound of the steam chugging from the funnel, I have to try to locate the source and find a vantage point from which to see the engine power past.

I know steam-engine enthusiasts are considered anoraks – but this is a very unfair tag. Steam engines in any shape or form are awesome creations and a tribute to man's skill and invention. From the massive single-cylinder fixed steam engines that drove the hundreds of spinning, weaving and carding machines in the cotton mills of Lancashire to the steam locomotives that hurtled from one end of the country to the other, pulling freight or passenger coaches at speeds of up to a hundred miles an hour, they are all impressive feats of engineering. Consider that they achieved all of this using steam. Just steam power. Plenty of coal to get the fire burning hot to heat the water, which in turn created vast amounts of steam, which was then channelled in the right way to produce this awesome power.

I spent many, many days at weekends and in the long summer holidays train-spotting with my mates. We'd walk down through Queen's Park and across Spa Road to the main Bolton–Blackpool line, or down to the vantage point of the big iron bridge at Trinity Street Station so we could also take in the Bolton–Blackburn line. The problem with these locations was that neither line was what you'd call a 'main' line, and so the engines we spotted were mainly the 'workhorses' of the steam train world. These included 'Jubs' (Jubilee Class), Pats (Patriot Class), Standards (Standard Class) and any number of the ubiquitous 'Tank' engine (Thomas Class). We'd only very occasionally see one of the big, pedigree express engines capable of hauling a huge number of coaches at high speed, which would include 'Brits' (Britannia Class), Scots (Royal Scots Class) and Semis (Coronation Class). We usually had to travel further afield in our region to see these – unless odd trains were rerouted due to engineering works, or they were pulling the main 4.30 p.m. Blackpool Express, which we dashed down after school to see most days.

I vividly remember the excitement of standing on Trinity Street bridge and watching the appropriate signal go up. 'Pegs up!' was the shout and we'd squat down low to try to see the front of the engine, which was largely hidden at the platform. The excitement built if someone shouted that it had shields (those massive metal plates fitted on the front sides of some engines) because on the whole, in our region and 'Pats' apart, only the big powerhouses had shields.

Then we'd hear the whistle and the engine would start loudly, very loudly – chug chug chug – building and building … then occasionally: chgchugchugchg! Wheel spin! The power would cause the big wheels to spin on the track, frantically trying to gain friction, which often meant it was a big engine (sadly not always the case).

Then the train itself would start to emerge from the station under the road bridge and the excitement was amazing – 'It's a Brit!' 'No, a Scot!' – and now it's clearer and yes, it has got shields, but it's still shrouded in steam and we can't make it out … until it suddenly clears and we see the shape and beautiful green livery … it's a Brit! What's its name and number? Could it be the holy grail '70000' – 'Britannia' itself? Please, God. No, it's 70008 'Black Prince'! Ohmigod! Black Prince: and the bridge packed with 30–40 schoolboys is cheering and shouting and jumping for joy. It's just like that feeling you get when your team scores the winner against Man Utd in the last minute.

But hang on! There's another engine behind it! A double-header, hardly ever heard of in Bolton, two engines hauling a train in tandem – but what's the second engine? Groans all round; it's a Black 5 … but hang on! It's got a name plate and there are only a handful of named ones; it's 45156 'Ayrshire Yeomanry'. Oh no, that rings a bell. Get my Ian Allen LNWR book out, which lists all the engines working in our region, look it up, here we are: 45156 'Ayrshire Yeomanry' – and it's underlined. That means I've got it. I've seen it before; what a bummer. Why couldn't it be 45154 'Lanarkshire Yeomanry' or 45158 'Glasgow Yeomanry'; I've not got those. But there are still wild double celebrations going on for those who haven't seen it before.

A big treat was scrounging the fare from our mums and dads to get a return ticket to Wigan. Oh yes – because Wigan had two lines, the local line from Bolton to Southport through Wigan Wallgate station, plus the main west coast line from London and the south to Glasgow and Edinburgh via Wigan North Western station. We'd make a couple of big doorstop cheese sandwiches, put them in our duffel bags and off we'd go, early on a Saturday morning in summer when all the special holiday trains had been added to the timetable.

We'd get off at Wallgate and walk down a small, cobbled, dead-end street at the side of the station, which gave a good view of the embankment north of North Western and, believe me, when you saw those express engines hammering past on that raised embankment it was awe-inspiring. One of the highlights of my youth was seeing 70000 'Britannia' *twice* in the same day at Wigan.

Another highlight occurred at Manchester Exchange station (it's gone now – Victoria station which it adjoined is still there). It was a bitter, biting cold February late morning and all but two of our gang had called it a day and caught the train back to Bolton. We were going to have our cheese butties and make our way home when we saw, half hidden up against the far buffers, a 'Brit'. Suddenly, the world was a brighter place, no warmer but brighter as we hurried over to get the name and number.

We approached from the buffers and saw its number first, 70033, didn't recognize that, excitement building as we looked on the shield for the name, 'Charles Dickens', stunned for a second, then ecstasy, unbridled joy, two ten-year-olds hugging each other, punching the air and dancing around in circles. 'Charles Dickens' was a rare sight round here: none of our friends had seen it and it was celebration time.

As our mad victory dance subsided, we stood with big stupid grins on our faces breathing heavily, our short breaths exhaled as 'steam', quite appropriately. The driver had observed all this and then did something I will always remember; he invited us into the cab to warm ourselves and eat our sandwiches in front of the open roaring furnace. How great was that? Very great – double great. The only other time that I stood on the footplate as a child was when the driver of 'Glasgow Yeomanry', observing the delirium prompted by my having spotted it at last, invited me up into the cab and drove the train the length of platform number 1 at Bolton station.

As an adult, I was lucky enough to be invited up into the cab of the restored 'Sir Nigel Gresley', flagship (!) of the Nigel Gresley A4 Pacific Class, possibly the most beautifully designed class of engine in the world. It had a stunning blue livery and was the first class of real streamlined steam engines. We train-spotters called this class of engine the 'Streaks', due to their shape and speed, but sadly they belonged to the LNER (London and North Eastern Railway), so we never ever saw them in Lancashire.

The only exception was probably the most famous 'Streak' ever, which was 'Mallard': the fastest steam engine the world has ever seen, reaching a top speed of almost 126 mph. 126mph! Driven by steam. Can you imagine that? Please take a moment to try. 'Mallard' came through Preston station on its farewell tour before the steam era sadly ended, and soulless, homogenous diesels and electric trains replaced them. All our gang made a pilgrimage to see it. Unfortunately, our train from Bolton was delayed and as we approached Preston station, the great Mallard was pulling out, towards us. We clamoured for room at the windows to get a last view of the legend, and I decided I was going to touch it. I don't know what the combined speed of the two trains was as we passed and

I don't know the outside temperature of 'Mallard' generated by the furnace – but I do still bear the scar.

So where was I? Wakes week, right. Yes, we'd arrive in Blackpool on one of the specially organized Wakes Excursion trains (usually pulled by Black 5s or Tanks) and make our way to the boarding house. I remember several lovely home-from-home boarding houses in Blackpool – and one horrible one that was run by a sour-faced old cow.

She greeted us with a stern, 'Are you half board?' and my dad couldn't resist the golden opportunity and came out with the classic (if misplaced), 'Well, we're not very interested to be honest.' He thought she'd see the funny side. Do you recall the witch on *The Wizard of Oz*? Enough said because her stony face never cracked and just got stonier as she followed it up with the equally tempting, 'Have you got reservations?' Dad wisely resisted the urge and said, 'Yes, under the name of Bramwell,' even though I know that he was dying to say, 'Yes, we wish we'd booked somewhere else.'

It was a dismal, humourless place and so boring that I had to send down for another Bible (He dies in the end). I remember that there was a confusing sign in the hallway that read: 'Please be in bed before I am.' The landlady caught me ridiculing the sign to my sister Joy and snapped at me, 'It's "Please be in bed before one am."'

Blackpool was great. We'd go on the beach most days with our brand new buckets and spades, make sand pies and have a ride on the donkeys. (Q: What do donkeys get for their dinner at Blackpool? A: Half an hour.) A tip about choosing your donkey – always take one from the middle because they do tend to lean against each other in a line, and so if you take an end one, sometimes they will all fall over. We'd walk down the promenade and the piers to see 'Uncle Peter's' junior talent show and maybe visit Blackpool Tower and the Pleasure Beach. My grandad always called Blackpool Tower the 'Fairy Shite' because when we used to get to the resort, I'd shout, 'Look, Blackpool Tower!' and my grandad would say in his broad Lancashire accent, 'Aye, it's a fairish height,' and then laugh at his own perennial joke.

One of my favourite days in Blackpool was at the boating pool on north shore, where you could drive a proper motorboat, have a ride on the small funfair, or catch crabs by tying a mussel to a piece of string and dropping it to the bottom of the pool. We used to catch dozens of them; I say 'catch', when in fact what happened was that they climbed onto the mussel for a snack and we just pulled them up. Some of them were huge and would climb out of our buckets to terrorize all the small children, mums and grans. We'd empty them back in the pool at the end of the day.

Sometimes, we'd take a tram up the front (have you ever taken a tram up the front, Mrs? Oh, a Ken Dodd moment there). We'd go to Bispham (hilarious place name for a kid – Biz-Bum) or Fleetwood for a day out. My gran was terrified of the tram lines and she once asked a tram driver, if she stood on the tram line, would she get electrocuted, and he replied, 'Only if you cock your other leg over that wire up there.'

On the Friday night before we came home on the Saturday, Dad would take us all to the 'Café Royal' and we'd have chicken and chips. I loved that.

We got a car when I was about ten, I think. My dad and Uncle Brian (not a real uncle, just a good family friend; we had dozens of pretend uncles and aunties when I was growing up and all as good as the real thing – they'd do anything to help), who was also a painter and decorator, had decided to set themselves up as an independent self-employed business ('no job too small'). Of course they needed transport, and so purchased a Skoda Estate car, which was that strange sort of dirty-underpants colour with a contrasting blue passenger door (as they do). My dad was learning to drive and my Uncle Brian was teaching him. I can't remember if Dad had actually passed his test when he decided we should drive to North Wales for our holiday week. We were so excited – we were going abroad!

It was to be the first (and most eventful) of many wonderful holidays in North Wales. I'll always remember that inaugural journey for all sorts of reasons: the stunning beauty first of all; I'd never seen hills and valleys and so much green on that scale as we drove the long way round, through Ruthin, round Lake Bala, passed 'Swallow Falls' and down the winding road through the mountains by Betwsy-coed ... And what else happened on the journey? Oh yes, the brakes failed as we hurtled down a particularly treacherous stretch towards Ffestiniog! Instinctively, Dad pulled on the handbrake and somehow steered us into an inviting pub car park, where we rolled to a halt. Unbelievable. We waited for the AA and they came and fixed the problem (I think! The memory is a bit blurred). It was a rubbish car and when we came to a big hill, which happened quite a lot as we made progress to the coast, us kids had to get out and walk up because the car wouldn't make it to the top fully loaded.

We eventually got to Ffestiniog and the slate mines and dropped down into Porthmadog, before approaching our destination of Criccieth. In my mind's eye, I can see it now as I saw it then, and recall the amazement of travelling along that coast road and then following the road around the bend created by a headland and there it was, Criccieth. The sun was shining and the small waves on the sea in the near-perfect bay glittered its reflection – and there on the headland was a castle! A real-life castle. I was dumbstruck. I'd somehow found my way into a 'Famous Five' book. We returned to Criccieth and surrounding villages for many years after that, and every time that first sighting of the bay always lifted my spirits.

The beaches and coves were so different than Blackpool (well, obviously). 'Blackrock Sands' beach was immense and there was beautiful 'Whistling Sands' beach, where, if you walked barefoot, the sands would actually whistle underfoot. Around Criccieth there were rocky coves to explore and Cadwalader's ice-cream parlour. We nearly always visited Ty Newydd, Llanystumdwy where David Lloyd George lived and died, and we'd walk up the river and sit on the rocks and dangle our feet in the water.

Another day out would be to Caernarfon, which has a stunning castle right by the harbour there, but some days I'd just go off with my dad and try to catch trout in the small stream behind the house we'd rented in Chwilog. My dad said he could tickle trout – a traditional skilled way in which to catch them, which involves submerging your hand in the river and slowly moving your fingers in a tickling motion; for some reason known only to trout, they swim over your hand because they are attracted to this particular action and then you very, very quickly flip them up and out of the water. Sounds simple. Isn't. After two hours, I persuaded Dad to take his strangely blue hand out of the stream and try a fishing rod instead. I suggested that Welsh trout probably weren't as ticklish as the English ones anyway.

When I got married for the first time, aged twenty, there was only one place I wanted to go to for my honeymoon: Criccieth. Problem was that I couldn't drive, so my mum and dad said that they'd take us to the B&B we'd booked for the week. And so it was that, the morning after the wedding, we got into my mum and dad's sky-blue Vauxhall Viva EUT 613C and took that same journey that I'd taken as a ten year old.

The B&B was fabulous and the landlady persuaded my parents to stay for an evening meal before they drove back. They stayed and I am not joking when I say that that meal was stunning. So stunning, in fact, that my mum and dad decided to stay for a couple of days. And the landlady gave them the bedroom under ours! Happy honeymoon.

Sex Education

Gran: We didn't have time for sex in my day; we were too busy having babies.

DEWEK WIGBY TAUGHT me some swear words and rude jokes. The first one he told me went like this:

Dewek: What's the difference between light and hard?
Me: Dunno, what's the difference between light and hard?
Dewek: You can go to sleep with a light on.

(*I laugh loud and hard. Too loud and hard: Dewek knows I don't 'get' it.*)

Dewek: You don't get it, do you?
Me: Yeah, course I do.

(*So straight away he told me his second joke.*)

Dewek: What's the difference between an egg and a wank?
Me: Dunno.
Dewek: You can beat an egg.

(*I have no idea what this means, but laugh manically.*)

Dewek: You don't get it, do you?
Me: Yeah, course I do, because you can beat an egg, can't you? Beat the egg, yeah.
Dewek: But you can't beat a wank.

(*I laugh again, now a little hysterical.*)

Me: I know! You can't . . . so that's funny as well. So that's really two jokes, isn't it? It's brilliant.

You had to say that you 'got' stuff, didn't you? You didn't want to be seen to be a wimp, immature and inadequate, so you lied. Do you remember that a lot of jokes at school involved nuns? Like the one where the Mother Superior goes into the convent bedroom at night and shouts, 'Right, girls, candles out' and you hear 'pop, pop, pop' (that noise you make by inflating a cheek and 'popping' it with your finger). I didn't 'get' that joke for years – I said I did, obviously, but I didn't. There was loads of stuff I said I knew about at school that I didn't. You know in Biology when you got given pond water and had to look for amoebas and spirogyras? I always said I saw them, did you? I even drew them in my science book, but I never did see them though, not ever. Not one.

Anyway, back to Dewek Wigby, who wouldn't let me off the hook with the egg-versus-wank question …

Dewek: Go on, then, what does it mean?

Me: You can beat an egg. Because you can, can't you? Beat it up, like.

Dewek: It means, you can beat an egg, but you can't beat a wank.

Me: I know! And that's funny as well, 'cause you can't beat a wank so … that's like two jokes in one.

Dewek: You've never had a wank, have you?

Me: Yeah, I have … I've had nearly four.

So then it's straight home and get the dictionary out. Turn to the 'W's … 'Wank'? 'Wank'? Where's 'wank'? Ah, here it is: 'A stick that when waved about causes magic.' What? Oh no, that's 'wand'.

'Wank' wasn't in. Most of the words Dewek taught me weren't in, although I did find one, which was 'shag' – but the elation of finding it was tempered by the confusing definition offered: 'Shag, a seabird of the cormorant family.' Some time later, Mary Hilton asked me if I wanted a shag and I said, thanks, but I'd nowhere to keep it, and really she should find somebody with a big pond as it was one of the deepest divers of the cormorant family. And then there's feeding it. Think of all the fish – and I only got five bob pocket money and two and sixpence for my paper round.

As it turns out, the 'S' section has quite a few rude words in it: 'screw', 'scrotum' and 'spunk', which means 'spirit', apparently! There's also 'sperm' and 'semen' – names for the special seed.

'Spunk' is a great word, isn't it? I once got into trouble in English when we were learning about onomatopoeia; the example always given is 'ping pong' because it really does sound like the sport in action. The class were asked for other examples and I offered up 'spunk' because I think it's tremendously onomatopoeic, as I demonstrated to a stunned-looking Mrs Woodcock. 'SssssspppppppppppppUNK!' Say it and really emphasize the 'p'. It did not warrant one full week's detention in my opinion.

Anyway, having been told these jokes and learned all these dirty words, naturally the first thing I did was to repeat them to my little sister Joy – and my parents overheard. I received a good hiding and had my mouth washed out with soap and water, but it was also decided that, based on the words I was using, it was time that I was taught the facts of life.

(Actually, it wasn't time; I was only nine, I didn't know what the words actually meant and anyway, at that age I had more important things to worry about. For example, if I stood on a nick, I'd marry a stick! And a beetle would come to my wedding and I'm pretty sure that didn't mean Paul McCartney.)

And so it was that it fell to my dad to explain where babies came from. He was rubbish.

Dad: Do you know about the birds and bees?
Me: Er, yes.
Dad: Good. (*Exits.*)

I remember thinking, 'What the hell was that all about? Birds fly about, make nests, tweet, and bees buzz around and make honey. What can he mean? What is his point?' I asked my mum and she made him have another go.

This time he mumbled a lot and basically told me this: 'A man passes his special seed to a woman.' Right, so I had this vision of a man holding out his hand to a woman and going, 'Here you are,' and she says thanks and puts the special seed in her cardigan pocket. So this special seed then – maybe it's bird seed – maybe that's where the birds come into it? Just need the bees now. So far, not so good.

Then I thought he said, 'The seed swims to her room.' That's what it sounded like. So now we have a special seed that can swim upstairs to her room – and let's be honest, that *is* special.

Lastly, he said that once there, the seed swims into her egg. So let's get this right: it's got to be Easter, a special seed has swum into her room and got into her egg; don't know which egg; does it have to be a specific egg, maybe a Creme Egg?

Confused? You bet.

The sex subject was rarely raised again – until two years later when I started secondary school and my dad took me to one side and gravely told me that I should always wear a condom or I would catch some terrible disease. In retrospect, I now know that I took him too literally, but he did say, '*Always* wear a condom,' and as I didn't want to catch a terrible disease (who would?), I started wearing condoms. Admittedly, it did make me a subject of ridicule in the showers after PE, but I always just smiled to myself and thought, 'You'll not be laughing when I'm the only one here without smallpox.'

It was around age ten that my body chemistry started to change and I began to notice things that had previously gone unnoticed. I remember being enthralled by the sight of two dogs doing it in our front street and asking my mum what they were doing, thus presenting her with an ideal opportunity to explain to me the basics of sex and procreation. She passed on the chance and instead told me that they were dancing. Dancing! Inevitably, the first school disco I went to I nearly got expelled. I asked Christine Hargreaves to dance and she said yes, so I said, 'Turn around, then.' She was surprised – but even more surprised at what happened next!

Then my body began to change: well, a small part of it did. The first time was very, very embarrassing, happening as it did at the school sports day with our proud parents watching. My first hard-on wouldn't have been so bad if, say, it had happened during the egg-and-spoon race. It would have been equally okay if it had popped up during the sack race – but no, it happened as I had hold of Christine Hargreaves's ankles at the start of the wheelbarrow race.

Erections regularly popped up first thing in the morning on the bus going to school. The throbbing of the engine as it turned over at every stop worked its way up through my feet and legs to my groin. There is a recognized term for this, which is 'Diesel Dick'. And I'd sit there praying that it would go down before my stop, but it never did, so there was always the risk that if I stood up suddenly, I could overbalance and pole-vault off the back platform of the bus.

So there I was, just turned twelve. I realized I would have to do my own sex 'research' to get to the bottom of the special seed versus egg thing – and exactly where did my five-times-a-day stiffy fit into the equation?

I'd started looking more closely at naked women in books and magazines. Not in the 'dirty' mags, which were always displayed on the top shelf at the newsagents (which was confusing in itself, because my mum had warned me that if I played with myself, it would stunt my growth; so how did people ever reach them?). The nudey women I looked at appeared in publications which were included in my paper round.

I especially looked forward to Thursdays, because a bloke on Greenmount Lane got *Amateur Photographer*, and about one week in four there would be a naked lady in there in an 'artistic' pose, illustrating the use of light to create a soft and sensual image. I also delivered *National Geographic*, which often had the bushmen of the Kalahari on the cover – and the bushwomen inside! Oh yes, completely starkers with nipples you could hang a coat on. Next week: the first pictures of a lost tribe from Peru who haven't heard about clothes. Brilliant. I also learned an obscure fact from *National Geographic*, which was that your female giraffe sometimes gets so bored during sex that she wanders off. I had a girlfriend like that once.

I progressed onto soft porn; well, my mum's Gratten catalogue: lingerie section. Big women in corsets, middle-aged women in industrial bras, and my favourite – the knicker page. This page was split up into a grid of 5 × 5 photos of girls wearing knickers. The photos just showed the knicker area and a bit of midriff and upper thigh – how sexy is that?

I did wonder how they got those shots. I thought that they might have one of those passport photo booths, and the girls jumped in quickly one after the other, having just the knicker area photographed, then jump out, change knickers, back in line and pop, in again.

As well as being very arousing for a twelve-year-old, it was also a bit of a puzzle trying to guess from the brief snaps (sorry) which model was wearing which knickers – sort of a 'Match the Snatch'. I was always disappearing into the bathroom with my mum's catalogue.

'What are you doing with that, David?'

'Just looking at the Scalectrix, Mum.'

It was round about that time that I noticed that my 'girlfriend' Mary Hilton had changed. Changed a lot! Her nickname was 'Bubbles'. You know how little girls with short blonde curly hair are usually called Bubbles? Well, that wasn't the case with Mary; we called her 'Bubbles' because she would not blow her nose. Anyway, it suddenly struck me that Bubbles had grown up. We were sat in my front room, I was doing my Meccano and she was holding my nuts and I thought, 'Wow! Hang on! She's a woman! She's got winnebangos and everything!'

My mum obviously noticed what was going on and thought that it was time I learned a bit more about sex and relationships. Her way of doing this was to lend me one of her Mills and Boon-type books. It was called *Cruel Desire* and it was very confusing.

The man in it was called Guy, the woman was called Deirdre, and quite early on she was stirred by the sight of his 'manhood'. 'Manhood': I made a note, thinking, 'Well, I've got a duffel coat, so that sounds as though it might do.'

Next paragraph, and he's found her mound of Venus. Now I'm struggling, because where am I going to get a star chart or telescope from?

Then he's caressing her love-bud; and we've not got a garden, just a back yard, so boy am I in trouble.

Then I noticed that my mum had underlined a sentence, which was, 'Every fireball from Guy's rigid cannon exploded like molten lava inside

Deirdre's fluttering love purse.' My mum popped her head in my room: 'Everything clearer now, David?'

'Oh yeah, got it, thanks Mum.'

'Good boy.'

But of course I hadn't and was still getting confused reading the Cathy and Clare page in *Jackie* with the girls at break time. What the hell was 'heavy petting'?

So, to the first time I had sex. I was terrified; well, being on my own and that. I was in the bath as usual with an old catalogue on the corset and suspender page, and it took ages and when it happened, I thought I was dying and that the back of my head had fallen off! Brilliant!

I told Dewek Wigby immediately that he was right, you can beat an egg but ... and he told me that the best way of doing it was to lie on your hand until it goes to sleep and then you 'do it' with that hand and it feels like somebody else is doing it to you! Great in theory – but have you ever tried to do anything with a hand that's 'gone to sleep'? Anything at all? Turn the alarm off? Pick up an object? No – useless.

Much later in life, when I worked in the NHS, a man was admitted with a ring-spanner stuck on his penis. He became an instant star in the Accident and Emergency department, with everyone in the hospital turning up to examine him using some ridiculous pretence or other. Double funny.

The patient explained that he'd been out drinking with mates and got very drunk. Afterwards, they all went back to his for a takeaway and a few more cans, and they were watching European Championship highlights and he must have fallen asleep. And for a laugh (brilliant), for a laugh, one of his mates must have got his willy out and put a ring spanner on it. He explained that he must have had a reaction to the cadmium-nickel alloy and his knob had swollen up and he couldn't get it off!

And we thought, 'Great story, my friend, but no way!' He'd been masturbating with a ring spanner, hadn't he?!

All Change

I N THE LAST year at Oxford Grove County Primary School, I had to take my 11-plus exam. If I remember rightly, there were two parts to this. The first paper was called a 'Space' test and had nothing to do with *Space – The Final Frontier*; it was, I think, more or less an IQ test. The second was a general paper that tested you on the three 'R's – Reading, Writing and Arithmetic (so only one 'R'). Thanks to my teachers at Oxford Grove, and my wonderful parents, who had encouraged me to read and write from an early age, I found the paper relatively easy and thankfully passed.

I was rewarded with my first choice of secondary school, which was Smithills Grammar, a relatively new school set in a lovely part of Bolton. Smithills Grammar was one of three schools on the same 'base'. The other two were Smithills Technical College and Smithills Secondary Modern. I believe that this base system was an experiment and Bolton had been chosen to pilot two of these; the other being the Hayward Schools complex. I don't understand why the system wasn't implemented nationwide, as it was fundamentally a great idea. Children who showed real aptitude for academic studies in the 11-plus exam went to the grammar school, those who showed more technical ability went to the technical college and those who did poorly in the exam for any number of reasons went to the secondary modern.

One of the positives of the system was that there were eight 'houses' on base, which were named after local areas. Irrespective of which school you went to, you were allocated a 'house', which encouraged pupils to integrate at lunchtimes and in sporting activities. The real benefit of the system was that if a child was a late developer and began to show aptitude at a later stage, they could be moved up to the grammar or technical. Similarly, if pupils failed to live up to early promise, they could be relegated – although this very rarely happened because, as each school was also 'streamed', they usually just ended up in the bottom stream. I was in 'Ainsworth' house and had my lunch on second sitting in the technical college.

On my first day at secondary school, my mum waved me off in my new uniform (I know I should have been the one wearing it). Grey short trousers, grey socks, white shirt, black tie with red and thin yellow stripes, black blazer with the school crest (which was essentially a large red rose and a motto in Latin that translated as 'Pride and Respect'), and a black cap with the badge on the front and a red stripe on the rim.

The cap was the first to go. Some older kids spotted the new boy (I'd foolishly gone upstairs on the double-decker bus) and within minutes my cap was winging its way, Frisbee-like, through one of the small sliding windows. I got off the bus on the way home near the spot, but never found it. My mum and dad were displeased and I got my first stern telling-off by my housemaster for turning up on my first day without cap.

My first class was 1G. We weren't streamed until the second year and so classes were named after the form teacher and ours was Mr Green. All the teachers wore gown and mortar board around school and were quite scary to an eleven-year-old, but Mr Green was a lovely man and put us new kids at ease with his warmth and good humour. He used to transpose the first letters of Christian name and surname to produce comedy names, so I became Bravid Damwell, Paul Crook became Caul Prook and Sally Hart became Hally Sart, etc. That's funny to an eleven-year-old. He stopped doing it when we got a new boy in the class called Sam Whitehead and he did Wam Shitehead. That was double funny.

Mr Green taught us Latin and I don't remember too much, apart from *amo, amas, amat, amamus, amatus, amant*, and that most of our translation concentrated on Hannibal coming over the Alps on his elephants. I also vaguely recall an embarrassing yet hilarious conjugation of the past tense of a verb which was something like *uraco*; the translation for 'they were *whatever*' ended up as *urac**t*. Or that might have been a dream.

Most of our teachers in first year were pretty good and I enjoyed my introduction to grammar school. I joined the chess club, did well at swimming – the school had its own twenty-five-metre pool – and I played football for the house.

After exams at the end of first year, I was put in 2B. I was disappointed because I wanted to be in the top stream 2A, but I was rubbish at maths. I can't remember much about that year from a school point of view (see elsewhere for the appearance of hormones and changes to my blood chemistry), except that I got beaten up by a hard, wiry-looking lad from the secondary modern, who as it turns out was 'cock' of the third year; a title that was amazing considering his shortness of stature.

I was climbing the steps to the bus terminus at Halliwell when he dropped a cigarette end on my head. I was bigger than him and although I'd never had a proper fight before, I thought, 'I can't let him get away with that,' so I said something like, 'Don't you ever try anything like that again,' and he said, 'Or what'll you do?' and I, like an idiot, said, 'You.'

That's when he headbutted me and broke my nose. Every credit to me, though, because I fought back and momentarily held the upper hand as I pinned him against the low stone wall at the top of the steps. Then I did, almost instinctively, a very grammar school thing. I thought, 'This isn't fair,' so I stepped back and let him off the wall. That's when he kicked me in the balls.

I was a mess when I eventually made it home. Bloody nose, black eyes and a huge busted lip. My dad demanded to know what I happened and I did what every schoolboy with an ounce of backbone would do; I lied. I said that I'd tried to jump onto the back platform of the moving bus, missed, slipped and fallen; that I was, in fact, lucky to be alive.

In the third year, we were streamed by subjects and I was in 3L, which meant that I was to continue to study Latin and other languages; German and French were added. Mr Holden taught Latin and he was really old school but fair, and Mr Jasper taught us German. And what a great name for a teacher, Mr Jasper; that would strike fear into the heart of any thirteen-year-old – Mr Jasper! And he looked the part: big, dark, bushy hair and a beard. Although very strict, I remember he was a good teacher.

Thinking back now, I can't remember who we had for French, or most of the other subjects. I know all us boys wanted Miss Hanley for Biology because she was fit, but we got Mr Farr. Joe Farr when you got to know him was a laugh and a great teacher, but to be fair he didn't have the same appeal as Miss Hanley in her miniskirt.

Lyrically Speaking

PERHAPS UNDERSTANDABLY, MISS Hanley in her miniskirt raised (sometimes quite literally) the sex issue again. By now, I'm a dab hand at the masturbation thing, so I need to know more about this whole sex lark. After all, I'm fourteen and I want a girlfriend (well, I want Miss Hanley, but that's not likely to happen). I need a steady girlfriend to experiment with, you know? My hormones were rampant; you could smell the testosterone through the Clearasil.

So learning how to flirt and chat up girls was now top of my list. The trouble is that when you're fourteen, you really think it's cool (and girls will like you) if you act stupid and do amusing things like pull their hair, or tap them on the wrong shoulder, or trip them up by kicking their back foot ... Is it any wonder they fancied lads in the sixth form?

One day, I was in the dinner queue behind Christine Hargreaves with our trays piled up with cottage pie and veg and bakewell tart and custard and drinks etc., and I did that thing where you knee the person in front of you in the back of their knee and their leg folds and crumples. I thought it would be cool if I did both Christine's knees and it worked well; too well, actually, and she went down like a ton of bricks, throwing the tray up in the air. Milliseconds later, she was anointed by gravy and custard while I stood there like a goon and said, 'I like you.'

We have a saying in Lancashire, which applied to me at the time. It is: 'If I sewed castanets in my underpants, I still wouldn't click.'

Like a fool, I asked Dewek Wigby's advice. Yes, I asked advice from a lad who still thought at fourteen that steam train drivers actually steered trains – and that's why they were leaning out of the window all the time; so they could keep the train on the tracks! God knows how he thought they coped in tunnels.

He told me that you could use song lyrics as chat-up lines. He explained that that was what they were written for anyway. He said he'd had some success with 'If I said you had a beautiful body, would you hold it against me?' and was contemplating, 'When your body's had enough of me and you're lying right down on the floor; when you think I've loved you all I can, I'm gonna love you a little bit more.' Which is a bollocks lyric and a bollocks promise. It is a well-known fact that the only time a bloke feels like doing it twice is just before he's done it once. In his head, he's thinking, 'Right, we'll just crack a quick one off, then we'll have a session' … snore …

I resolved to try this lyrics approach. At the next school disco, I bumped into Christine Hargreaves. My seduction didn't go according to plan, even though I'd memorized all the words to my favourite song …

Me: Hiya.

Christine: Hiya.

Me: I've been across the desert on a horse with no name.

Christine: What? When?

Me: It felt good to be out of the rain, I can tell you.

Christine: Did it?

Me: Yeah. There were rocks and birds and plants and things.

Christine: Things?

Me: Things, stuff, yeah.

Christine: What sort of things?

Me: Oh, you know, sand, cacti and that.

Christine: Have you been drinking?

Me: No, I was just saying that . . . In the desert, you can remember your name. 'Cause there ain't no one for to give you no pain.

Christine: I liked it better when you tripped me up.

I reported back to Dewek and he reluctantly agreed to sell me his best, solid gold, proven, infallible chat-up line. It cost me: one frozen Jubbly, half-a-crown (2s. 6d. … oh alright, about twelve and a half pence), and I had to do his maths homework. His chat-up line went like this: you say to a girl, 'Can you tell me what Brazil is famous for?' and she says, 'Coffee,' and you say, 'Your place or mine?' And you appear mature and sophisticated and witty and they love that.

I tried it with Christine Hargreaves.

Me: Hiya.
Christine: Oh, it's you again.
Me: Yeah. I was wondering if I could ask you a question?
Christine: If it's a quick question.
Me: It is. What's Brazil famous for?
Christine: Nuts.
Me: (*A beat.*) Thanks.
(*Wanders off.*)

I didn't try any more of Dewek's chat-up specials, which included:

- 'Are those real?'
- 'Do you sleep on your stomach? Can I?'
- 'Do you know that there are 206 bones in your body? Do you want another?'

I did point out to him that there actually wasn't a bone in his penis and he just smiled as though I was joking and said, 'Yeah, right.'

It is amazing that at school we received little or no information about STDs and contraception and that the playground was the only place this information (misinformation) was available. According to playground gospel, methods of effective contraception included using a crisp packet as a condom, strapping a watch with a luminous dial around your testicles (because the luminous material had a radioactively lethal effect on sperm; it would be mobile phones today, probably) and of course wrapping your cock in clingfilm.

Proper sex finally happened and I'm guessing in a similar way to many of us – at a house party after too much Woodpecker, in the spare bedroom on the coats. I tried to look macho and ripped open the condom packet with my teeth, but the foil hit a filling and I jumped and shouted out in shock. The whole act was very unsatisfactory, really – and really difficult. I remembered reading that the hymen is very elastic and hard to break the first time, but I thought that at this rate, if I continued to push this hard and it didn't give, I could get catapulted through the window and into the off-licence across the street. Anyway, I broke through and it was over very quickly. As I lay there, I thought that I'd better say something caring and sensitive and tried to remember something from *Cruel Desire*, so I said, 'If I'd known you were a virgin, I would have taken more time.'

She responded, 'If I'd have known that we had more time, I'd have taken my tights off.'

Memories of the next couple of years at school are sketchy. I know I got back into the 'A' stream in the fourth or fifth year after we got a new maths teacher who was quite fit with big breasts and whose name I sadly forget, but I think began with a 'W'. As well as being nice to look at, she was a brilliant teacher who made me understand the subject better.

I also remember getting into the school football team second eleven, which was quite an achievement for somebody from the fifth year. I have an embarrassing recollection of getting injured on a muddy pitch on a bitter winter's day: the teacher in charge, who might have been Mr Oxenby, rubbed my thigh and I got a hard-on. Look! I was fifteen, alright! Chemistry raging through my veins.

I started going out with Helen, who lived in a big bungalow on Longridge Crescent (a 'crescent', how posh is that?). I say we were going out, but I only remember going to Heaton Cricket Club Disco, Bolton Fair and seeing Cat Stevens at Bolton Odeon – performing, I mean; he wasn't watching *From Russia with Love*. Helen and I never even kissed as far as I recall, but I was devastated when somebody told me during a cricket match at school that she was going out with one of the Keltie brothers.

The only proper 'serious' girlfriend I had at school was Joan, and she was lovely. As it turned out, my dad knew her dad and older brother through the painting trade. She came away on holiday with us once and we must have gone out for around two years, but it finished when I started work and she stayed on at school.

Joy to the World

M Y SISTER JOY was three years younger than me, but we were always very close and I protected her when necessary ... usually ending up in the Infirmary down the road.

The first time it happened we were playing in the old churchyard on Park Street when a lad called Carl, who was a couple of years older than me, started teasing and bullying her. Of course I intervened. He was a lot bigger than me and so when I confronted him and told him to stop, he simply pushed me hard and I fell backwards onto the church railings – and one speared my thigh! (Arghhh! It makes me cringe just thinking about it.) I limped home from the Infirmary with Joy following behind me, telling me that 'all your flesh is sticking out'. Thanks for that, Joy. Chris Buckley ran ahead to warn my mum by saying, 'Your David's got his intestines hanging out!' Mum went to get the butter.

Though I acted as self-appointed bouncer, Joy actually had a secret weapon, which was her unexpected skill at boxing. Boxing was a passion of my dad's; we three kids all had a pair of boxing gloves at some stage in our childhoods. I remember Joy getting some when she was about five or six, and while Dad was adjusting her guard and telling her to keep her head down, she hit him with a sweet left hook that nearly put him hospital – because she ruptured his uvula and there was blood everywhere.

When she was older, Joy started going out with a lad called Andy, who was a couple of years behind me at Smithills Grammar. I wasn't impressed with her choice because he was always in trouble at school and at the end of assembly when they read out the names of the pupils in detention, his name was invariably there. Anyway, paying absolutely no attention to my advice, she married him! And they are still together all these years later.

Andy came good and turned out to be a top bloke. He entered the RAF as an apprentice armourer, I think, and over the years rose up through the ranks to become a Squadron Leader or something equally impressive.

The downside of having family in the forces is that you hardly ever see them. Joy and Andy were constantly on the move as his career progressed and in addition to various postings all over the UK, they spent huge chunks of time on bases abroad. I would guess that since she married in the seventies, I've only seen her a couple of dozen times, tops. She has lived in Cumbria and Anglesey in recent years, but we still don't see much of each other. She comes to some family celebrations, most recently Mum's eightieth birthday party, and when we get together, it's immediately like old times, like she's never been away.

Never Lie at Interviews

I'D JUST STARTED the sixth form at school. I was studying Maths, Physics, Biology and Chemistry and I had a vague idea that I'd like to go to university to study medicine. A vague idea was as far as it got – because my dad had an accident at work and as a result I had to leave school and get a job.

As you know, my dad was a painter and decorator (self-employed, no job too small), and he was painting the hands on the Town Hall clock in Bolton when he slipped and fell off. Well, it was half past six so he had nothing to hold on to – quarter past, he'd have stood a chance – and the doctors said he was lucky to walk away with two broken ankles. This meant that he was going to be off work for at least six months. We'd just moved house and my parents had taken on a big mortgage, but now there was no money coming in, so it was obvious that I'd have to get a job.

My dad had noticed, while he was at the hospital, a sign in the Department of Pathology advertising a job vacancy for a Junior Medical Laboratory Technician – six O levels required, including Maths, Physics, Biology and Chemistry. He suggested that it might be an idea to apply because, once he was fully recovered, I could return to my studies and the medical laboratory experience might prove valuable if I pursued the medical career.

And so it was that I presented myself for interview at Bolton Royal Infirmary in September 1968. The interviewing panel was daunting and comprised Mr Parker the Chief Scientist, some bloke from Personnel and Consultant Pathologist Dr Manning.

Dr Manning was a very grand, old-school-type consultant pathologist. Immaculately turned out, right down to the flower in his buttonhole. Think

James Robertson Justice in the *Carry On* films. He was also very shrewd and a great judge of character, which is why, when I told the lie in the interview, he knew immediately. Rather than challenging me on it directly, he played me like a fisherman plays a salmon, allowing me just enough line to keep running, but he was in fact slowly, inexorably and painfully reeling me in.

The interview had actually gone pretty well and we were up to the easy bit at the end where they try to find out what makes you tick. Hobbies, interests, sports, that sort of thing. I made the mistake of lying to impress when Dr Manning asked me about my hobbies. It went something like this ...

Dr Manning: So, David, what do you do in your spare time? Do you have any hobbies?

Me: Stamp collecting.

Dr Manning: Philately?

Me: Probably.

Dr Manning: I'm a great philatelist myself.

Me: (*Smiling on the outside, but on the inside thinking, 'Oh shit.'*) Really?

Dr Manning: Yes. I specialize in United Kingdom and the Commonwealth. Which country do you specialize in?

Me: China.

Dr Manning: China! That's unusual.

Me: (*Ohmigod.*) Is it?

Dr Manning: Why China?

Me: (*He knows I'm lying.*) Because my uncle lives there and he sends me them.

Dr Manning: Whereabouts in China?

Me: (*Eyes pleading: 'Please let me off.'*) Er . . . (*Why didn't I do Geography?*)

(*Mr Parker and the bloke from Personnel are now exchanging knowing smiles, then Mr Parker leans slightly back in his chair out of Dr Manning's eyeline and mouths something to me. I think I know what he's saying.*)

Me: Saigon.

Dr Manning: That's in Vietnam.

Me: (*Sweating now.*) Is it? Shanghai, then? Yes, that's it definitely, Shanghai. I'm always getting them confused.

Dr Manning: What does he do in Shanghai, your uncle?

Me: (*Oh, please be merciful.*) He's an engineer.

Dr Manning: What sort of engineer?

Me: A marine engineer.

Dr Manning: A marine engineer in Shanghai?!

Me: Alright! I don't collect stamps!

I got the job!

Howzat?

I MET MY friend Sean, who would become a mate for life, at the interview; he was in after me. When I came out, he nervously asked me how the interview had gone, and I said, 'Brilliant.' Then, because I thought there was only one job going, I helpfully suggested that if he wanted to impress the panel, he should say that he was a stamp collector.

Despite falling for this, he got a job as well. It turned out that they needed seven junior laboratory technicians at the time, so it wasn't such a big deal getting the post as I'd thought.

The following Monday, four of the seven started in the Department of Pathology at Bolton General Hospital and the other three – Sean, myself and a bonny girl called Yvonne – started at Bolton Royal Infirmary. We were allocated departments and my first rotation (we would eventually work in all the departments) was in Bacteriology, which sounded pretty exciting, but turned out to be a nightmare.

I don't mean a proper nightmare; not a crazy man in a black hooded cloak chasing you with two machetes and your legs can't run and it feels like you're wading through treacle, and now you've no pants or underwear on and you're trying to pull your shirt down to cover your balls, and then suddenly, for no reason, all your teeth fall out! And now you're hitting him, but he's laughing because you aren't hardly touching him because your arms seem to be made out of jelly!

Not that sort of nightmare – but almost as bad because I found that one of my main duties was as assistant in the animal house, with responsibility for all the laboratory mice and guinea pigs. This was an aspect of the job that I had never considered; I'd never dreamed that even in 1968 hospitals still used animal testing. I love animals, always have, and so, as it turned out, this was possibly one of the worst jobs in the world for me.

After being allocated my four white lab coats, pens, pencils and a chinagraph marker (common name: 'grease pencil') required for writing on glass laboratory apparatus and microscope slides, I was given the usual fools' errand handed out to naive, gullible and wet-behind-the-ears kids fresh out of school. And so it was that I waited patiently in a queue outside the pharmacy department for eighteen inches of fallopian tubing. When I looked down the queue, I saw both Sean and Yvonne on similar missions; Sean asked the pharmacist if he could have a 'long stand' and she left him waiting there for an hour and a half, while Yvonne politely asked for a bucket of steam. Oh, how we laughed.

Sean was on the receiving end of one of the best impromptu practical jokes ever when he needed to sharpen his chinagraph pencil. He asked where he might find a suitable pencil sharpener and was told to go through a set of double doors. He barged through – to discover himself in the mortuary, where Dr Manning was straddling a dead body, wielding a Black and Decker saw in the process of sawing off a cadaver's skull to examine the brain.[3] Dr M knocked off the electric saw and glowered at Sean, who stammered, 'Have you got a pencil sharpener, please?'

So, on that first morning, after my fruitless and humiliating mission to obtain fallopian tubing, I was given a guided tour of Bacteriology. First stop: the animal house. I was incredibly apprehensive as we made our way across to the unit from the main lab block.

Unfortunately, my darkest fears proved well founded because as we entered the main door and turned onto the corridor, some object whizzed passed me at head height and I ducked instinctively and then heard a weird sort of 'splat' noise. I turned slowly to see the current incumbent of my post wielding a cricket bat, upon which was a large patch of white and red. As I stared in disbelief and some horror, a splatted mouse slowly slid off the bat.

---

3 They take the brain out, then put the 'lid' back on and tie the skin into a big bun at the back. It's no wonder friends and relatives often say, 'At least she died happy. Look at the smile on her face!' To which I sometimes reply, 'No, she got struck by lightning and thought she was having her photograph taken.'

'Watch out!' the batsman shouted, and I turned just in time to see another technician drop a white mouse into the nozzle of a CO_2 fire extinguisher and then aim it towards his colleague before pulling the trigger. The mouse flew past at something approaching Mach1, before the batsman played a haymaker of a stroke and missed the poor thing (there might have been a slight edge) and the mouse hit the suspiciously stained brickwork behind him.

"Owzat!' the bowler screamed at me, obviously confusing me for an umpire. I just stared, open mouthed, shocked beyond belief.

John, who was showing me round, explained that every week we received mice that were surplus to requirements. We never knew exactly how many tests would be requested and so how many mice we might need. We had a standing order for a certain number – and any surplus mice had to be disposed of. For the last six months, these two technicians had implemented different ways to expedite this ... but now I was in charge.

Mice were used in testing for Gonadotrophins.[4] Mr Parker and/or Dr Greenwood, a big genial forensic pathologist, injected the mice every morning, Monday to Thursday, in the scruff of the neck with differing concentrates prepared from the patient's urine. It was my job to catch and identify each mouse from a batch of four (not easy, as most white mice look pretty much alike) and present it to the injector in a 'spread-eagled' manner by pinching it by the neck while simultaneously pulling down on the base of its tail.

On Friday, the mice were killed and dissected and the uterus and ovaries removed and weighed. I had to kill the mice and I had to do it effectively and quickly, which wasn't a perfect science. I had to drop one patient's batch of four mice into a jam jar and then gas them, via a tube fitted into the cap and connected to the bench gas supply. It was disgusting watching them trying to escape the deadly fumes by attempting to climb the inside of the glass jars, before they quickly succumbed to the gas. Mr Parker and Dr Greenwood worked at incredible speed and

4 Recommended Reading: 'Pregnancy Gonadotrophins on the basis of Induced Ovulation in Mice', H.O. Burdick, H.O. Watson, Vincent Ciampa and Thomas Ciampa – Department of Biology, Alfred University, New York, 15 May 1943.

keeping them supplied with dead mice in the correct patient order was a very stressful job for a seventeen-year-old who hated every second of the process.

Sometimes, in the rush, I failed to administer the right amount of gas, and the mice would start to come round during dissection. When they did this, two things would happen: Dr Greenwood, who as it turns out was terrified of mice, would go berserk and run off to his office; and Mr Parker would go ape-shit because he now had to finish off all the dissections by himself, and so I would get it in the neck (be on the receiving end of his wrath, I mean, not the concentrated piss).

Early on in my animal genocide career, I asked the Chief Medical Laboratory Technician (CMLT) if I could be excused these duties on moral and ethical grounds. He got hold of me by the throat on the main corridor, in front of staff and patients, and explained to me that this would not be possible and if I ever mentioned it again or refused to do it, I would be sacked on the spot, and I couldn't let that happen; we needed the money.

So, I used my initiative. Within about four weeks, I had a hidden colony of mice that had been deemed surplus to requirements. I told my bosses and my fellow technicians – who were in the early stages of planning a laboratory-mouse-based Wimbledon tournament – that I was gassing them humanely every week, when actually I was putting them in a large cardboard box hidden in the guinea pig room.

One day, I looked in the box and realized a major flaw in an already heavily flawed plan – and that was that, mice being mice and doing what mice do, I now had twice as many mice than I started out with. Inevitably, something would have to be done.

After much soul-searching, I realized there was nothing else for it but to dispose of them. The logistics of this posed an enormous problem. If I tried to gas them four at a time as per Friday's process, it would take me hours because I reckoned that I had about 150 mice in the box by now. I formulated a plan. The plan was this: I'd get a Winchester bottle (2.5 litres) of chloroform and a roll of thick cotton wool, which I would soak with the chloroform and deposit in the cardboard box. Next, I'd close the air holes up. The mice would simply fall asleep and never wake up.

Simple and humane, I thought, and so it turned out, as within fifteen minutes all the little things were well and truly dead.

Next problem = disposal, and here I had another plan. Part of my duties was to take certain items of laboratory waste (let's leave it there!) to the hospital incinerator – and so I thought cremation of the poor mice was the obvious solution. I carefully carried the box, the cardboard coffin, down through the hospital grounds to the incinerator and pulled aside the heavy door to reveal the furnace inside. I said my goodbyes, which took about ten minutes (I had given them names), and then slid the box into the blazing inferno. As the flames engulfed the box, I bent my head in silent prayer.

It was then that the box exploded. Idiot that I am, I hadn't figured out that chloroform and its fumes – being highly inflammable, especially when concentrated in a confined space – might react in this fashion. The incinerator spewed forth a huge flame of exploding gas and I just had time to put my hands up to protect my face before it hit. I staggered, dazed and confused, back to the lab with my hands badly burned, my eyebrows missing and my 'Paul McCartney' fringe smouldering.

I spent the next two hours in Casualty, and the hour after that with Dr Manning, trying to explain exactly what had happened. I lied again, of course. He didn't believe me again, of course, although I might say that my 'chloroform and chlorine disinfectant bottles being easily confused' was a fair excuse in such a short space of time. I said that I had mistakenly cleaned the sluice and sinks down with chloroform and put the rags and paper towels used in the process in the bag for incineration. Alright, so the nurse in Casualty freaked when she found half a mouse in my hair … but I feigned ignorance about that.

And just when you think that it can't get any worse … you have to kill half a dozen guinea pigs. We used guinea pigs in a test for TB. Dr Greenwood would inject a tissue biopsy concentrate into a guinea pig's groin and then, after a period of a few weeks, the animal would be killed and dissected to examine for signs of TB growth at the site of injection. I only had to do it the one time (thankfully), but I had to kill a batch of the little fellas.

The thing about guinea pigs is that they've got more about them than mice. They're bigger, obviously, and cleverer and prettier in my opinion, with their own character traits … and so you sort of get more attached.

At the time, the prescribed 'humane' method of execution of a guinea pig was by breaking its neck. This could be facilitated either by hitting it with a metal pole or by our laboratory's preferred method: hitting the poor creature really hard on the edge of the bench. Just writing it again and picturing it after all these years brings home how absolutely barbaric this is.

On the day, it took me three hours to kill six guinea pigs. I say 'three hours to kill', but if I can break that down: it took me five minutes to kill them, and the remaining time to psyche myself up into actually doing it.

It was obviously very important not to get the guinea pigs mixed up, which would result in misdiagnosing patients. We had a Home Office book to fill in with all patient and guinea pig details. The guinea pigs would be accurately described, for example, 'Abyssinian, predominantly white with black patch on right eye and rear right leg,' or 'Golden with white patch on head,' and I labelled large pieces of paper headed with the patients' names in the same manner, ready to accept the body.

I must have picked up that first guinea pig ten times, ready to do the deed – only to panic and return it to its cage. You have to understand that in order to break the poor thing's neck, you had to cradle it on its back within your two hands and press its two little paws down with your thumbs, so that just the head and neck protruded above your hands; so it's lying there looking up at you, staring into your eyes with a quizzical look that seems to say, 'What?'

After two hours and five threatening phone calls from my boss, I knew I had to get it over and done with. The deed passed in a blur as I picked up each beautiful guinea pig and quickly smashed its head and neck against the bench edge. Once I'd done all six and placed them on their allotted paper, I turned away, shaking in disgust, totally traumatized.

After a couple of minutes, I composed myself and turned to look at the pieces of paper – and discovered that four of the guinea pigs had gone! I searched frantically for them and found each one in turn, wandering dazedly around the benches, shaking their little heads and going, 'What the f**k was that all about?'

I realized immediately what had happened. In my panicky state, I simply hadn't hit them hard enough; it's understandable, I suppose, when you do something half-heartedly. I grabbed them and hit them again, poor things, and finished the job. All dead.

I'll probably go to hell for that. I probably deserve to.

Blood, Spit and Tears

THE ANIMAL HOUSE management formed only part of my duties in Bacteriology ('Bugs' as it is known in the trade – and why, by the way, would anyone want to work in a place called 'Bugs'?). I also did a lot of work in the main lab, where we would receive all sort of human biological matter (and, believe me, I was really not attracted to a job in which much of the day's work involved taking the lid off yet another pot to discover yet another lump of poo). The lab would then try to identify firstly which, if any, bacteria were present in said sample, and secondly which antibiotics worked best to prevent that particular bacteria's growth. I saw a car sticker once, which said, 'Microbiologists Do It With Culture and Sensitivity', and I laughed out loud because culture to a microbiologist is a Wallace and Gromit T-shirt.

Although that's what a microbiology lab does, as a junior, of course, I didn't get to do any of this very interesting detective work. Instead, I had to make up solutions and reagents and liquid stains. I had to boil, clean and polish the microscope slides, clean the benches and fume cupboards, autoclave the used glassware … and so on.

The only actual laboratory testing juniors got to do involved preliminary testing for TB. I don't know why we got that job because it was quite important, but I suspect that it was because it was a horrible nasty job. We would receive from 'Wilkinson's' – our outlying TB unit – metal tins which contained samples of patients' sputum (that's phlegm to you). We would sample a globule of sputum and spread it on a special nutrient agar called a Jenner slope and a glass slide, and then stain the smears on the slides with ZN stain. The way we did this was by placing them on a glass stand and 'flaming them' by lighting a wad of alcohol-soaked gauze, which was attached to the end of a metal probe. We flooded the slide with the stain and then heated the slide from underneath with the burning gauze until the stain bubbled. I set my hair on fire again doing this, tragically destroying what was left of my 'Paul McCartney' fringe.

A couple of years later, we had a junior called Janet, who knocked a Winchester of methanol over whilst flaming ZNs and set the bench and one wall of the lab on fire. She famously wandered into the main Bacteriology lab staffed with six technicians and said matter-of-factly, 'Hey, kid, come and look at this.'

It was great fun in the TB lab in those days. Sean was rotated in and there was a girl called Elaine, a couple of years older than us, who was great fun. We used to tape a transistor radio to the fume cabinet in which we did all the TB culturing and we would sing along to the sounds of the sixties. I remember the great yet scary Dr Manning appearing at the door in the middle of a Beatles medley and giving us a death stare, which made us freeze with fear, and then saying in a totally deadpan manner, 'Keep it down, will you, my patients are joining in.'

He was a great man, Dr Manning; he didn't suffer fools gladly, but he acknowledged good work and rewarded you with a few well-chosen words of praise. Sean got on with him particularly well considering our lowly status. Whenever Dr Manning ventured into our lab, resplendent in three-piece suit, dicky bow and buttonhole flower, Sean would always indicate the flower and make up some preposterous botanical name, 'Is that a *roboticum siphillicum*, Dr Manning?' Dr Manning always permitted himself a little smile before putting Sean right.

Before I move on from Bacteriology, I must mention another job that came under my responsibilities and that was the collection of outpatient urine samples, faeces samples and seminal fluid samples – for which an appointment was required. This was all very embarrassing for a young man straight out of school, but I soon found it to be routine.

Instructions for a mid-stream urine? For a woman, issue a disposable bedpan, instruct them to wee a bit down the toilet, then a bit in the pan, then the rest down the toilet. Same for a man, except substitute a small glass bottle for the bedpan. Simple enough – although you could and did run into difficult patients.

I particularly remember one old man, who looked at the neck of the bottle and said, 'I'll never be able to get it in there.'

'Not a problem,' I said, producing a large plastic filter funnel, which I placed in the neck of the bottle. He grabbed my arm tight and it was only then that I noticed that he looked a bit strange. Time may have blurred my memory, but whenever I remember the incident now or recount it to friends, I seem to think he talked like a pirate.

'That's no good, either,' he said.

'Really?'

'No, and do you know why?'

I shook my head and he came a little closer and said, 'Because I'm a woman.'

Right, don't panic; even though you're in a toilet cubicle with a demented pirate, just smile and think of something appropriate to say. But now it's too late because he's saying, 'I might be able to manage if you can hold it for me.'

'*What*?!'

'The bottle, I mean,' he said, 'because I am a woman.'

I'll be honest; he didn't look like a woman. He looked like a pirate. I just said, 'Of course you are. I'll just go and get some help ...'

He gave me a twisted smile and said, 'No, look!' and dropped his pants – and I saw immediately what he meant when he said that he was a woman because he had no penis. Well, none to speak of. He had the testicles, but just a tiny stump where there used to be a penis.

'I got it shot off in the war,' he explained, and immediately I felt both ashamed and compassionate. 'These little things are sent to try us,' he said, and I apologized sincerely for my abruptness in dealing with him. I asked him about the circumstances surrounding the event and we chatted for about ten minutes before he had to go and he was such a kind, gentle old man.

Arranging the appointments or collecting samples for seminal analysis was also embarrassing, but it was the source of much hilarity too. Quite a few men, most but not all non-English speakers, couldn't quite grasp (pardon the pun) exactly what I was telling them to do – and so I had to resort to mime, which would occasionally cause offence and heated argument. While booking in appointments, meanwhile, you might tell them to attend on Friday. They quite often said, 'I can't come on Friday,' to which you might reply (childishly), 'Well, that could be your problem. Don't do it on Fridays.' Others would bring in samples of urine and occasionally faeces, and you'd think, 'No wonder you aren't having any children!'

I rotated from Bacteriology into Biochemistry, where blood, urine, stomach washouts and other bodily fluids are analysed for their biochemical constituents. It was here that I first learned how to take blood from patients (phlebotomize). Small samples were obtained with a lancet from a thumb prick, and larger samples by venepuncture, using a needle and syringe to take blood from a vein in the arm. This was quite a traumatic and scary learning curve. We first practised on rubber tubes of various internal diameters, getting the angle of insertion right and making sure we didn't go in too deep and go right through the other side of the vein. Then we practised on volunteer lab staff – or Junior Technicians as they were called; practically, each other! I had been volunteered many times and now it was my turn to tighten the tourniquet.

Eventually, of course, you were let loose on real patients, who had all sorts of dodgy-looking veins, flabby arms and needle phobias. I actually became very good at phlebotomy. I liked the patient contact, enjoyed the chat and the teasing – when we had to go on wards to collect samples, the gynaecology wards were the worst, with the shouts of, 'Here he is with his little prick!' 'Don't hurt me when you put it in,' etc. – and it was very satisfying when you managed to get a decent sample from patients who were classed as difficult to bleed because their veins were hidden or stringy, or their arms were so flabby that it was difficult to get the vein stable.

I once had a bit of a trauma bleeding a patient in our outpatient department. I had almost finished and asked her to bend her arm up, but she reacted too quickly for me and knocked the blood-filled syringe and needle up in the air. Time went into slow motion as the syringe described a perfect parabola in the air before plunging back down towards the desk. Instinctively (madly!), I tried to catch it. I completely miscalculated its flight and made my grab as it landed upright on one end, with the needle pointing upwards on the desk. I didn't have time to halt my interception and my hand pushed down hard on the needle (what were the chances of it landing vertically?). The needle pierced my hand through the skin at the base of my middle and fore fingers. The patient looked horrified and asked, 'Are you alright?'

I smiled, grabbed the syringe and pulled the needle back out through my skin as if it was an everyday occurrence. I said, 'What am I like? I'm always doing this.'

I'll not dwell too much on the preparation of faeces for faecal fat analysis, or the pitfalls in the mouth pipetting of stomach contents prior to testing for salicilates, but suffice it to say I'm pretty bloody sure that half of those laboratory procedures wouldn't be permitted under the most lenient of health-and-safety procedures these days.

I was, after a suitable period of training, given responsibility for glucose tolerance tests (GTTs), which were and still are, I think, the definitive test for diabetes. Patients fasted overnight and a urine sample and blood test from a thumb prick were taken at 9 a.m. in the Outpatients' Department. The results of the glucose level in these samples was taken as the base measurement and then the patient was given a glass of glucose solution to drink. I had to make this up by measuring out the glucose and diluting it with an appropriate amount of water. It was very sickly sweet and quite unpleasant, and we had to cajole some patients into finishing it off as we needed to see how the patient tolerated this massive increase in blood sugar. Five further blood samples and two more urine samples were taken over the next two and a half hours.

For my first session in charge of the GTTs, I had three elderly patients and the responsibility had made me very nervous. Anyway, it all seemed to go well and at twelve o'clock I returned to the Biochemistry lab with my eighteen blood samples (six per patient) and nine urine samples (three per patient), all carefully labelled up with times and names. One of the biochemists, Pete, took the samples from me and asked me how it had gone.

'Good,' I said. 'Very good.'

He took out his pen and enquired as to what time exactly had I given them their glucose solution drink. Do you know when you get those icy fingers running down your spine that make you shudder involuntarily? And your shoulders sort of contract and your throat constricts and that awful feeling of dread and panic starts to rise up like a heavy cloud from the very core of your being, and yet your face just sort of goes a bit blank? That's what happened to me then – because I'd forgotten to give them their glucose. I'd done the first ever glucose tolerance test without glucose!

Pete's enquiring smile was now slowly fading as he started to detect the fear and panic in my eyes. He went ballistic. Fair play, he didn't get me up against the wall like the mad bloke from Bugs, but he gave me a right royal bollocking, which only ended when he thrust the patients' request cards at me and told me to rearrange the tests for as soon as possible.

And so it was that the three old ladies returned the following Tuesday and I found myself apologizing profusely for the 'technical failure' which had caused this to happen. 'All this modern technology, eh? What can you do?' So we started again. Because our outpatient rooms were rammed that morning, I had to conduct the tests in the packed waiting room. After the first blood and urine tests, I produced the glucose drink. One lady said in a very high voice, 'Oh look! At least he's giving us a drink this time!' Another said, 'No thanks, love,' and the third said, 'I'll have a cup of tea, please, two sugars.'

I told them that they had to drink it and number one took a sip and pulled a face, 'No! I can't drink that! It's much too sweet!' The others concurred: 'Too sickly.'

'Look,' I said firmly, 'you have to drink it for the test.' The rest of the patients in the waiting room stared at me in disgust.

'We didn't last time,' one of my GTTs pointed out.

'Well, you do this time,' I insisted. I made them drink it, but they complained for the next two and a half hours, as only old ladies can. I didn't care; I got it done.

I enjoyed Biochemistry on the whole, but it didn't grab me. A lot of the senior staff were very stuffy and full of their own importance – mainly the biochemists. Clinical biochemists, in my experience, were pedantic, grey, humourless characters. Let's put it this way: it's no surprise that it was a biochemist who invented the laboratory dipstick.

They are notoriously obsessive about protocol, standard operating procedures and quality control. I performed at a clinical biochemists' conference once and found that I had to tell one joke that was not very funny, one that was quite funny and one that was very, very funny; just so they'd have a low and a high control.

There were 300 biochemists at this conference; I'll always remember that overwhelming smell of Old Spice and all that corduroy! I'd never seen so much corduroy in one room. And beards! I thought at first that they were all wearing balaclavas, but no; big bushy beards. I recall thinking, 'Three hundred clinical biochemists at this gala dinner. Just think if they all got food poisoning and were off sick for a week; hospitals the length and breadth of the country probably … wouldn't notice.'

There is a popular story that highlights the role of clinical biochemists, which goes like this:

Two hot-air balloonists, having been blown off-course, decide to land in a field and ask for help. Just as their basket has safely touched down, a man rides down the adjoining lane on a bicycle. One of the balloonists shouts to him, 'Excuse me, but could you tell us where we are?' The man on the bike stops and looks at them before shouting back, 'You're in a little basket.' The balloonist turns to his companion and says, 'He has to be a biochemist.' His companion replies, 'How can you possibly know that?' and the first one responds, 'One hundred per cent accurate, completely bloody useless.'

Next stop for me was Histology, a quiet backwater of the lab, where the highlights of the day were watching wax set and an afternoon game of shove-ha'penny. There were only three other staff in Histology: David was the Chief, Phil (who became a good friend) was the basic grade, and Joan did mainly cytology – cervical smears.

We received assorted bits of people from either the operating theatre or mortuary. The pathologist dissected the bits and the trained staff embedded these bits in wax, and then sliced them micrometres thin on microtone; a sort of ultra-sharp bacon slicer. These one-cell-thick sections were then placed on microscope slides, fixed and stained, so that the pathologist could examine them under the microscope and then provide a detailed report.

Again, as a junior, I didn't get to do any of this! Much of my time was taken up preparing solutions, stains and reagents, and my main job was in the 'cutting up' room, i.e. the room in which we received and dissected the samples, which arrived in small jars, big jars, bowls, buckets and the odd bin (limbs, mainly). We used to play a game called 'What's in the bucket?' which would make an interesting Saturday night TV quiz programme for Ant and Dec, I reckon.

My job was to receive the samples and arrange them in dissecting order – big organs first – and to prepare glass jars and small tickets, on which I wrote the patient's reference number. You might need several per sample and experience guided you in this. An appendix, for instance, would usually only require one jar and one ticket, on which you would write 'TOT in 4', meaning it was the total biopsy dissected in four sections. A cancerous bowel, by comparison, might need four jars, with sub-reference numbers and descriptions for the suspect tumour and associated lymph nodes.

At the same time as I was frantically labelling my tickets, I was taking dictation from the pathologist on his findings during the dissection. This would include the description of the sample, the tissue changes and tumour presentation and much more. It was a frantic hour or two which put you under a lot of pressure. You simply could not afford to make a mistake.

I enjoyed Histology a lot. Apart from the cutting-up pressure in the mornings, it was a laidback sort of place. I was a little sad to leave, especially when I discovered that my next rotation would be in Haematology at Bolton General Hospital. This was two bus rides away and a lot less convenient than Bolton Royal Infirmary, but it had to be done.

Bloody Hell (Not)

I VIVIDLY REMEMBER walking into the Haematology lab on that Monday morning – and thinking that I'd found my spiritual home!

The Pathology Department at the General was a scaled-down version of that at the Infirmary, and seemed a warmer, friendlier and happier place. That said, I found the girls in Haematology and Blood Transfusion to be very intimidating; they could unnerve you with the most withering of remarks. I once came to work in a new tank top (it was 1970, alright?) and walked straight into it. 'That's a nice tank top, Dave, is it new? It suits you … it's plain, isn't it?'

Another time, a new friend of mine, Glenn, who'd started a short time after me, was floored with, 'I like your tie, Glenn. Isn't it an unusual pattern? It looks like that wallpaper in Indian restaurants.'

They could cut you like a knife, but, in time, once you gave as good as you got, they became good friends and the banter was brilliant.

Haematology is the study of the disorders of the blood – so anaemias of every type, leukaemia, lymphoma, polycythaemis and thrombocytopaenia, as well as blood-clotting disorders such as haemophilia, Von Willebrand's disease and so on. Most of the work was routine screening of samples from patients prior to operation, in pregnancy or referred from medical wards or GPs with a multitude of symptoms that might suggest anaemia, infection, inflammation and so on, or patients on anticoagulation who needed their clotting factors monitoring.

I was immediately gripped by it. I think part of the reason was that I could actually look down a microscope and see these cells, compare normal cell appearance and number with abnormal cell appearance, detect the presence of immature cells or changes in platelet numbers …

I loved this hidden, fascinating world of haematology, which was only visible under the microscope.

Whereas in Biochemistry, by contrast, I could never see anything, so much so that I began to call it Alchemy. Okay, I'll give you glucose, sodium, potassium, cholesterol … but gamma-glutamyl transferase? Pull the other one. They've made half of them up to expand the science and make themselves look important.

As a junior in Haematology, I still had to do all the basic jobs I'd done before, plus I had to spend most of the mornings on the wards and units taking blood from thumb pricks and prepping the samples at the bedside for the various tests required. Once we got back to the lab, all the tests could be run straight away as we'd done the prep as we went along.

This part of the job could be quite stressful, dependent on which wards you were allocated. Routine medical and surgical wards were relatively easy, the patients on the whole being helpful and amenable; the gynac and obstetric wards were okay (apart from the heckling and sexual innuendo); but some of the geriatric wards were difficult; and the worst of all were the paediatric wards. I tell you, the kicking, screaming kids on these paediatric units had to be seen to be believed; you just had to walk away from some of them or there could be serious injury.

Due to the range of tests we had to run, we required a fair amount of blood from a single thumb prick – so you had to make sure you stabbed the kids good and hard the very first time (that sounds all wrong – but you know what I mean) In theory, this should be relatively manageable, but is of course a massive problem when you're simultaneously wrestling with a hysterical six-year-old and engaging in hand-to-hand combat with them, you with a lancet in one fist and therefore at a serious competitive disadvantage. Even if you did manage to surprise them with your first attempt, most of the blood ended up smeared all over your hands and lab coat as the shrieking child tried to hide his pricked thumb under his arm while fending you off with the other, so it was often a traumatic yet complete waste of time.

I loathed and detested taking blood on the kids' wards; the only upside was that you could sometimes get an attractive nurse to help by holding the little monster!

However, although the paediatric wards presented a challenge, overall I absolutely *loved* the job. Best of all was the fun we had as a department. For this daily round of dedicated work that we conscientiously undertook was complemented by some truly mad antics and comedy moments. It was fun, fun, fun.

Every day, we tried to get all the lab work done by four o'clock so that we could have a game of bench-top cricket with a homemade mini cricket set, or a game of football with a mini 'ball' made out of layers of surgical tape wrapped into a ball shape, or a mini Grand Prix, where we'd hurtle round the labs and corridors on our wheelie lab chairs, while wearing stainless steel specimen bowls on our heads as 'crash helmets'. We brewed our own beer and wine in the lab; we also had a tap-dancing competition, which comprised a grand opening through the lab's double doors, a two-minute routine to the soundtrack from *42nd Street*, and then a big finish.

Phil G from Immunology was up first: as the music started, he burst in through the double doors, sliding on one knee, carrying a pipette as a cane and wearing a steel sample bowl as a hat. We cheered as he started tap-dancing – but then confusion reigned; we couldn't hear a thing. Then we realized he was wearing Hush Puppies. How can you enter a tap-dancing competition wearing Hush Puppies? Disqualified.

Sean was next up and I expected big things as he has always been quite the extrovert. The music started, the doors flew open and Sean entered in a similar fashion to Phil, but then he tap-danced … well, he made a lot of noise with his feet. He tap-danced all over the lab, then jumped on a bench and danced among the apparatus to wild cheering. How could he top this with his big finish? Easy, he jumped out of the window.

Now, okay, the laboratory was on the ground floor, but (and this escaped Sean's memory at the time) the building was built on a kind of raised embankment, so that effectively we were on the second floor, with quite a drop to the (thankfully) grass lawn outside. I vividly remember to this day the cheer that accompanied his dancing changing suddenly to a collective gasp and a stifled scream as he exited the large open window. Then it was like watching a scene from a Loony Tunes cartoon as Sean seemed to stop in mid-air as Wily Coyote does after going through a door marked 'Diversion', which Roadrunner has placed on the edge of a cliff.

It seemed that time stood still for that fraction of a second as Sean looked first at us and then down, and then in quick succession his legs, his body and then his elongated neck and head disappeared out of view. How he escaped unhurt I'll never know.

We had a spell of playing practical jokes on one another. In addition to the usual laxative spearmint, the soap that turned your hands black and that plastic dog poo, we got together to organize some more elaborate japes. Someone enrolled me on a Charles Atlas course because, believe it or not, I was quite thin at that age. Sean and I enrolled Glenn as a member of a sailing club and invented a set of initials after his name – S.K.I.P. – and for years he received brochures about the latest dinghy or lifesaving equipment, and he even had a rep from a yachting company turn up to see him one day.

The worst practical joke was played on me. I had just had a medical and my full blood count was being analysed while I took my morning break. My haemoglobin was okay, but my white cell count was top normal, so I decided to spread a blood smear and look at it under the microscope. I left it staining while I went for my coffee.

As soon as I left the lab, my colleague Kay spread a similar-looking smear (she later said my technique was so rubbish it took her ages to make a replica) on a slide and swapped it with my own sample. However, she used the blood sample of one of our patients who had acute leukaemia. So my question to you: is this funny? No, it isn't – and yet she still laughs when she remembers the look on my face immediately after I slipped it under my microscope, scanned it briefly and experienced that terrible aching panicky fear.

I looked up at Kay, who sat on the opposite side of the bench, and her expression gave nothing away. I looked back down the microscope – surely there's some awful mistake, those cells are just big lymphocytes, aren't they, and not immature, primitive 'blast' cells? I looked back up and said to Kay, 'I've got leukaemia,' and still she never gave anything away, but there was something odd about this – and then it suddenly hit me. The blood smear was identical to one I'd looked at earlier from a patient with acute myeloid leukaemia. I removed the stained smear and studied the name on it – and although it did say 'Dave', I was pretty sure that wasn't my writing. Then Kay laughed, as did the others who were in on the plot. I have to say, I didn't laugh, and I still don't. Kay does; she's laughing now reading this over my shoulder.

It was also around this time that Glenn took a blood sample from a dead patient and I encountered a seriously unbalanced old lady on one of our psychiatric wards.

Glenn first. He'd gone to one of our long-stay geriatric wards to take a blood sugar thumb prick sample from a Mr J. This patient had a very unstable reading and had to be tested every day. Glenn made his way onto the busy ward and, knowing where to find Mr J (and only slightly surprised that the screens were round the bed), he tried to take a sample of blood from the patient's thumb – but it wouldn't flow. He tried the other thumb: nothing. A finger or two and as a last resort the ear, which yielded just about enough blood after a deal of squeezing. 'Well done, Mr J.,' Glenn said, as he finally took the sample.

Back in the lab, he tested the blood and rang the ward with the result. It went something like this.

Glenn: I've got a blood sugar result for Mr J.
Sister: Which Mr J?
Glenn: Mr Arthur J.
Sister: I'm sorry, but Arthur passed away.
Glenn: Oh? When?
Sister: A couple of hours ago.
Glenn: I thought he was quiet.
Sister: When did you take the sample?
Glenn: Thanks, bye.

I'd drawn another short straw and had to take a blood sugar sample from a Mrs Alice D on Russell 1, which was a female psychiatric ward. When I got there, she wasn't in her bed and so I asked the nurse where she was and she indicated the entrance hall. I wandered through and discovered her sitting on a chair near the large double-door entrance, gazing with some agitation down the driveway. She was dressed entirely in black: black coat, black shoes, black hat – you get the picture.

I told her that I needed a sample and she took a glove (black) off and asked me to hurry as she was going out for a drive. I knew this was unlikely, but she was dressed up and I thought that maybe she'd been allowed a couple of hours on the outside. As I prepared the lancet and alcohol swab to sterilize her thumb, I asked her where she was going and she said ...

Alice: Three bishops are coming for me in a big black Rolls-Royce.
Me: Bishops?
Alice: They come every Tuesday, all dressed up in black they are, and they take me for a drive up round Rivington.
Me: It's nice round Rivington.
Alice: Mmm, it is. We park near Anglezarke Reservoir.
Me: Lovely.
Alice: Then they all f**k me! Hard! All of 'em. Big cocks.
Me: Right, well, have a good time!

Dirty Old Town

DURING MY LABORATORY rotation, I had day-release to study for my ONC in Medical Laboratory Sciences at Salford Technical College. All seven juniors enrolled and we had to go on different days to minimize disruption to the laboratory. I went on my own, on the bus every Tuesday, and studied Maths, Physics, Chemistry (organic, inorganic and physical), Biology and Medical Laboratory Science.

It was a long day at college, starting at 9 a.m. and finishing at 8 p.m. in order to cram in the heavy mix of theoretical and practical sessions. I met and studied with other junior staff from a variety of local hospitals, and we were lectured by a motley crew of ex-lab staff and academics. I remember Dr Maddox, who was a big, slightly scary, imposing bloke, and some mad old physics lecturer who looked like Wilfrid Hyde-Wight, whose name escapes me. I do remember, however, his early explanation of atomic theory, in which the electrons were butterflies fluttering around a flame, which represented the nucleus. He demonstrated this with his hands becoming two butterflies (!), showing that every time the butterfly dropped out of its orbit and came closer to the flame, it felt the intense heat and started to burn and shouted, 'Ow, ow, ow, ow!' and with new-found energy fluttered quickly back to its orbit. That's atomic theory in a nutshell.

I didn't make any great friends during that time. We did all come together, however, in our baiting of a weak and frankly rubbish teacher of Chemistry. The pack instinct kicked in and he was so ineffectual that he never stood a chance. Once, during a particularly rowdy Chemistry practical session, he pleaded again and again for silence and concentration, but to no avail. He sort of lost it a bit and shouted, 'Right! That's it!

You've pushed me too far and now you will have to suffer the consequences!'

We stared open-mouthed; he'd never reacted like this before. What was he going to do? We soon found out when he said, 'I'm going to go out into the corridor and I'm going to stay there until I hear complete silence in here' – and with that he stormed out.

We exchanged puzzled glances. 'He's not quite got this right, has he? He's not quite grasped the theory behind this type of punishment.' We gave a collective shrug and resumed our noisy, high-spirited behaviour. Every now and then, we'd see his worried, sad little face peep through the glass window in the door ... then, with a shake of the head, he'd be gone. Later, he actually popped his head into the class and shouted above the din, 'I'm still here!' We acknowledged him with a thumbs-up. 'Well done, sir, only another fifteen minutes to go.'

After two years, we had to sit the ONC exam. There were theory and practical exams, which both contributed to the overall score. In order to progress to study for the HNC at Manchester Polytechnic, we had to pass four out of the five subjects. Most of the exams were very hard as I recall, although one was a complete farce and predictably it was the Chemistry teacher's Medical Lab Science practical exam.

I forget exactly what we had to do, but it involved some blood coagulation testing and some preparation of agar, and I think blood sugar testing. Anyway, most of the techniques required incubating in a water bath at body temperature or in an incubator – and the hopeless teacher had forgotten to switch them on. As we only had ninety minutes or so for the exam, there was no way we would get any meaningful results. He told us to do the tests and make up the reagents anyway and we'd be assessed on those techniques. I thought that without the pressure of obtaining results in some of the tests, it would be a bit of a breeze.

We received our results a month or so later and I found that I'd passed everything – except Medical Laboratory Science! Not one of the other six juniors had attained the necessary number of passes, all failing at least two subjects. We were hauled before the bosses and asked to explain our poor showing. They banged on angrily and told us how disappointed they were with us and how much it reflected badly on the department that every one of us would have to re-enrol and take the year again.

While we were on the receiving end of this bollocking, I suddenly had a thought, which was this ... As far as I was aware, we needed to pass four out of five subjects in order to progress – and I had! When I outlined this to the assembled senior staff, scorn was poured upon my suggestion that I should progress to the HNC. 'What? Are you an idiot? Progress to Manchester Polytechnic without a pass in Medical Laboratory Science – you know, the very science you are studying?'

When I got a free minute, I telephoned Manchester Polytechnic's admissions officer and explained my situation. He looked at the rules, made a few phone calls, then called me back ... to say that, although it was highly irregular, my results did actually fall within the rules of admission to the HNC, as I had effectively passed an ONC in Sciences.

Much to the surprise and dismay of some of the senior staff – and a few of my contemporaries – I was on my way! I'd shed my 'Junior' tag at last! Now, with my ONC under my belt, my job title changed to Medical Laboratory Technician. My main feeling wasn't elation – rather relief that I wouldn't have to take the year again.

Medicine Man

IN THE MONTHS leading up to the ONC exam – and with my dad back at work – I was encouraged by my parents to resume my academic career and apply to study Medicine. Dr Manning very kindly wrote a glowing reference for me, which I sent with my CV to several universities. I was offered places at three, provided I passed my ONC and secured a grade A or B in A level Biology. I applied to the A level board to take the Biology exam and was given a date a couple of weeks after my ONC exams.

Slight problem was that I'd not done any studying for my A Level Biology. I know that sounds mad, but I convinced myself, rather stupidly – no, incredibly stupidly – that the Biology I was studying at ONC would see me through. After all, I passed the Biology module easily at ONC, so I should walk the A Level. I was so confident that I didn't even use the two weeks before to swot up. Idiot.

I walked confidently into the laboratory at Bolton Tech on the day of the practical exam – and within five minutes I realized, as a cold shiver ran down my spine, that the grade I was destined for was Grade A Prat.

How did I know that so quickly? Because the lecturer gave me a dogfish to draw, label and dissect. I drew the dogfish and labelled up as much as I could – 'fin', 'another fin', 'fin', 'tail', 'tail fin', 'mouth', 'eye', 'nose' (not sure about that one, probably has a different name, 'snout' maybe). The dissection went better; I recognized most of the internal organs from my time in Histology and from the Human Biology I'd taken on ONC.

Yes, that's 'Human' Biology – but oh no, what's this approaching? Looks like some sort of plant to draw and label – 'stalk', 'bud', 'flower', 'fin', 'leaf'.

What's next? Something human hopefully or … a worm. Not much to label on a worm, I think you'll find. There's that lumpy girdle thing on it, don't know what that's called (tempted to call it a 'fin'). You know, I've always meant to look that up, but I never have, so I'll do it now … google 'worm anatomy' … there! It's called a 'saddle'. I could have guessed that!

What next? Oh shit, he's bringing a jar with a twig in it now! In despair, I take the top off and the 'stick' jumps out! Who in their right mind would give unsuspecting students a real live locust to study?

'Look! I wouldn't have taken the stupid lid off if you'd told me it was alive. No, I don't know where it went. What if we release the gecko? He'll find it and eat it. It's what? A newt? And how exactly is that different to a gecko? Oh, right.'

I didn't pass A level Biology. I didn't care, really; I was having such a great time in the labs, I was earning a decent wage – £3. 11s. 6d. a week – had some great friends, *and* the icing on the cake was that I was surrounded by fit nurses … and you know what they say about nurses. They say, 'She's a nurse.'

D-I-S-C-O

DURING THESE YEARS, I was transformed from a quiet and shy lad straight out of school into a slightly more confident eighteen-year-old. I loved 'belonging' and being part of the teams in each laboratory.

I also discovered and immersed myself enthusiastically in a vastly different social life than I was previously used to. While at school, I'd attended the occasional discos at Heaton Cricket Club and St Thomas à Canterbury's youth club … but now there was a new world of pubs, clubs, doctors-and-nurses parties and hospital dances!

There was a period while working at the General Hospital when most of the staff went to the Wednesday night disco at Bradford Ward Labour Club just around the corner. This was where I started to have the occasional drink. My first drink I remember was half a pint of mild, which cost 11*d*. – so about five and a half pence in new money.

None of us juniors had a car, which was obviously limiting, but we could always get around by bus. Saturday nights were spent in Bolton town centre drinking in The Lower Nags Head, The Three Crowns, The Trotters, The Old Man and Scythe (one of the oldest pubs in the country), The Swan, The Brass Cat (Golden Lion) and then onwards and upwards to the Cromwellian Club (The Crom). I say upwards because it had dance floors on three floors, playing Tamla Motown, Stax and Atlantic Soul Music. They never played Northern Soul at The Crom; you had to go to Wigan Casino for that.

Then Bernard, one of my colleagues, got a car, a Triumph – the car, I mean – and we would go to Placemate or Rowntrees Spring Gardens, which were Manchester clubs that were in a different league to The Crom; or sometimes we'd go to the Elizabethan Ballroom at Belle Vue, a huge place where thousands packed the dance floor. Me and Bernard got thrown out one night for having a drunken gunfight to 'Ride Your Pony' by Lee Dorsey. There's a bit in it when Lee sings 'Ride your pony and shoot! shoot! shoot!' accompanied by gunshots, and me and Bernard drew our imaginary guns and shot each other. We got thrown out for that!

Then a terrible thing happened. The monthly discos held for hospital staff suddenly stopped. The DJ wanted more money; mobile discos were few and far between in 1970 and he was in demand. The hospital couldn't afford his new fee and so these brilliant nights – when doctors, nurses, lab staff, cardiology techs, physios, radiographers, cleaners, porters and Uncle Tom Cobley let their hair down on pay day – were to come to an end. Outrageous.

But Sean and I had a plan. I had a load of singles I'd collected – mainly Tamla Motown, Stax, Atlantic and Brit Soul; like the Foundations and Johnny Johnson and the Bandwagon, but with a fair number of Beatles, Kinks and Stones thrown in too – and Sean was quite a whizz with audio and electrical stuff (he was also into the Moody Blues, which was to pose a problem later …). We decided to start a mobile disco!

Where to begin? A pair of record decks would be an idea, then an amp and a pair of speakers might also be useful. I'd got an old dansette record player, we could use the deck out of that, but what to put it into? My mum's bedding box was just the right size; and with her being on holiday, it seemed like fate was playing a part. Get the tools out, install a base plate, cut a hole for the deck, drop it through – perfecto. Now down to HW Audio to buy another cheap deck and see if they've any second-hand amps and speakers. They have – an old Carlsbro guitar amp (!) and a pair of Peavey speakers. Sean fitted them all together with suitable connections and now the moment of truth as I bang on 'Bringing Down the Walls of Heartache' … It works! It all works!

We go to see the administrator in charge of social functions and convince her that the show can go on. We advertise the new Friday night sessions as 'THE PAY DAY RAVE – WITH SEAN AND DAVE!' Genius.

We sort of get away with the first one, even though the vibrations from people dancing make our flimsy bedding box bounce about like mad, causing the record to jump all over the place and occasionally one of the decks to fall through the hole we've cut out not quite precisely enough. And we are certain we have enough records, but you get through quite a lot in four hours, and some were recycled more than once. But we are DJs: the crowd are too pissed to care and are so happy that the party is back on that they'll tolerate Stevie Wonder being 'Up up up up up up tigh tigh tight' three times in one night.

We realize one major flaw to add to the smaller flaws and that is that we are without disco flashing lights. The next week we go back to HW Audio, but discover that the light boxes (plus control units that enable them to flash in sequence, or randomly, or more impressively 'sound to light', when the music bass and treble govern the flashing) are way out of our price range.

Hmm. What to do? I know! We'll make one. We buy three lamp holders plus lamps, some cabling – 'What rating do you need, lads?' (*Who knows?*) 'Give us some of that thick white stuff' – and three button touch switches and Sean works his magic. He completely reconstructs the speaker cabinets, so that the speaker is at the top and a bright coloured lamp surrounded by Bacofoil is housed in the bottom, and he wires the lamps through the button switches to a plug. Simple to operate: while one of us plays the records, the other will sit and push the button switches sequentially or randomly or to the beat – our own sound-to-light unit at a fraction of the price! We should have got more substantial switches really, but everyone's wiser in hindsight.

At the next 'Pay Day Rave with Sean and Dave', I was IC Lighting FX. I noticed quite quickly that the small buttons on the wooden box, sorry 'unit', seemed to be getting hot. It's fair to say that the crowd were loving the light show right up until the moment of the explosion.

We got a booking for a wedding at the Brooklyn Hotel near the hospital, so Sean went down to the electrical suppliers again and bought more substantial switches and new connectors to replace the old ones, which had melted a bit in the explosion. We hastily drafted Sean's cousin Martin and his Triumph Herald into the set-up, having realized, perhaps a little late in the day, that an intrinsic part of operating a mobile disco was actually being mobile, and neither Sean nor I had a car or could actually drive.

I still remember the excitement I felt as we unloaded our gear from Martin's car, carted it up the three flights of stairs and set it up on the dance floor. In our haste to set up, we didn't notice that the new connector for the lights (with power going through them) was exactly the same as the connector for the speakers (which had sound going through them). We connected them the wrong way round – and it was all going well until the explosion. One of the wedding guests, who by coincidence had seen our most recent performance at the 'Pay Day Rave', was awestruck. 'Brilliant, wow! What a light show! You guys rock!' We had to slowly pack up and walk out. They still paid us! Must've been a cracking light show.

We did eventually get our act together and, after a few successful paid gigs and more in the diary, we decided to invest in better equipment. We bought the now legendary 'Hawaii Citronic' twin decks, a new Vox amp and bigger and better speakers. We bought better lights and a sound-to-light unit and called ourselves 'Atlantic Mobile Discos'. 'Discos' plural because we wanted to suggest that we were a large professional outfit who managed multiple roadshows nationwide (!), and 'Atlantic' to indicate that we played the best in music from both sides of the pond – American soul and UK pop.

It was a source of endless arguments between Sean and myself about which records to buy. I would want the new Chairman of the Board or George McCrae single, while Sean insisted that The Moody Blues and Bread were the way to go. Over the months, we built up a decent collection and I picked up a load of cheap ex-jukebox bargain hits from a shop I passed near Victoria station on my way to Manchester Polytechnic.

It's fair to say that in our excitement and enthusiasm at being DJs, we didn't always think through our selection of records. During the buffet at wedding receptions, our LP of choice was usually The Carpenters' *Greatest Hits*. Someone pointed out that it was somewhat insensitive to play Karen Carpenter's plaintive rendition of 'Yesterday Once More' while everyone was stuffing their faces with mini quiches, given she'd only recently died after a long battle with anorexia.

It also took us ages to realize that Freda Payne's 'Band of Gold' was perhaps not the record to play as the opening dance track at weddings. We'd simply thought, '"Band of Gold"? That's a wedding ring; this is a wedding: perfecto.' We were mystified as to why couples were reluctant to dance to this guaranteed floor-filler … until we actually listened to Freda. 'Since you've been gone, all that is left is this band of gold, all that's left of this dream I hold, is a band of gold.' Singing as she sits 'waiting in the silence of my lonely room, filled with sadness, filled with gloom'. Hmm.

Then, the big time beckoned. We got a regular gig at Farnworth Old Vets club. On our first night, we supported an old-time famous woman singer – like Vera Lynn, but not. Alma Cogan! That's who it was, remember her?

The second gig there was an amateur football club end-of-season awards night, which finished prematurely when rival teams, fuelled by Tetley's bitter, decided to start a war. We hid under the decks as the bottles and glasses flew and blood ran in rivers. We packed up our gear and negotiated the walking wounded (and there were some serious injuries) as we carried it to the car. A couple of weeks later, the place burned down … so we lost our regular gig.

Atlantic Mobile Discos wouldn't be defeated that easily though, and in time we picked up a monthly gig at Harwood Golf Club. This residency lasted for years and they were always great nights.

After one such gig, we were invited to Kay's (she who gave me leukaemia) twenty-first birthday party at her parents' posh house on Harpers Lane. She'd banished her mum and dad for the night and organized a big fancy-dress bash. It was late when Sean and I got there; me dressed as the 'Cisco Kid' in full cowboy outfit, complete with sombrero and six-guns. (I can't remember what Sean went as, but it was probably a sack-based costume.)

The party was in full swing and the place was bouncing. I was dancing in the packed lounge when I saw Ron, the boyfriend of one of the girls from work, enter the room dressed as a white hunter. I went for my guns in jest and he raised his rifle. I drew quickly and he fired – and I mean proper fired! I felt the .22 bullet whizz past my head and we both stood staring at one another in shock. He'd obviously had no idea that the rifle was loaded.

The noise of the gun had been masked by Stevie Wonder on the stereo and everyone was still dancing, unconcerned. I turned slowly to look behind me and saw a bullet hole in the French windows. Ron gulped and exited slowly and I carried on dancing. Shame it wasn't Lee Dorsey's 'Ride Your Pony' playing at the time.

The bullet hole wasn't discovered until the next morning. Kay, naturally, got in deep shit with her parents. When she came into work on the Monday, she interrogated everyone who'd been at the bash to find out if anyone knew anything. I don't know why she suspected me – maybe I looked guilty, I don't know – but within minutes of talking to me, she was absolutely convinced that I was the culprit. I pleaded my innocence, but by now everyone had judged and condemned me. Kay wanted money to pay for the damage and I wouldn't pay up because it wasn't me! I was in the bad books for months and months, it might even have run into years: branded a coward because I wouldn't admit I'd done it or tell her who had. (Didn't they know that I could have died that night?! Rhetorical question, obviously.)

It became apparent that I had to do something. I'd confided in Sean about what had really happened and we decided to gather evidence to clear my name. As these things always are, it was going to be difficult because Ron had by now stopped going out with the girl from work. However, he still played football with us occasionally (more on that later), and so Sean and I devised a plan. I would phone Ron under the pretext of asking about his availability for a game, and somehow steer the conversation around to the night of the shooting, while Sean would listen in on the extension and record the chat on a cassette recorder, MI5-style.

Once in position, our mission began ...

Me: Hiya Ron, it's Dave.

Ron: Hi mate, long time no speak.

Me: Yeah, well look, we've got a hospital football match coming up and I wondered if you fancied a game?

Ron: Love to, mate. Where do you want me to play?

Me: Up front, I thought. Well, you've always had a good shot on you, haven't you? Oh, and talking about good 'shots' ...

With that seamless link, I said that I'd been chatting to Sean about the party, particularly the moment Ron had nearly killed me – and he laughed and recounted the whole incident from his point of view. Result! We presented the evidence to Kay in dramatic style and she thankfully forgave me.

Later, Sean and I started doing a monthly disco in the doctors' mess at Bolton General. We put on quite a show, with new and improved sound equipment, a bigger and better light show – even, would you believe it, the occasional bubble machine and pyrotechnics! We had a great idea to obtain a super-8 cine projector and show old black-and-white films on the back wall over the heads of the dancers, and this was a winner as the crowd danced and enjoyed the adventures of 'The incredible shrinking man'. The added bonus – which we'd hoped for, but which worked much better than we'd expected – was that the projected film created a strobe-like effect, which added to the disco experience!

The doctors' parties were the stuff of legend and tickets were highly sought after. The drink flowed, the hospital staff let their hair down, the music played and it was totally magic. They sometimes had themes – like the cocktail party that got out of control because they made the four cocktails up in bulk beforehand. People initially asked for a pina colada or a mojito, but then, soon affected by the excessive strength of the drinks, started shouting for 'A blue one!' Or 'A red one!' Or 'A blue-and-red one!'

One party was fancy dress. I went as a flasher with a rubber chicken strapped around my privates – 'Wanna see my cock?' – and Sean went as Eccles the Goon. A good friend, Dr John P (who went on to become Professor of Surgery), turned up as a fairy, complete with wings, tutu, magic wand etc. About an hour into the party, his fast-bleep went to signal cardiac arrest and he sprinted off to Medical Emergency. He was successful in reviving the poor chap, who slowly opened his eyes to see Dr P stood there, resplendent in fairy attire, and said, without hesitation, 'I'm dead, aren't I?'

Sean and I made good friends with many of the house officers through these parties, and were often invited as guests to formal dinners in the mess. The price of us getting in was that we had to get up after the meal and tell a few jokes, which we regularly did, trying to get the biggest laughs. These were in effect – although I didn't know it at the time – my very first stand-up gigs.

Much later, we did a gig in a church hall and, because we wanted a drink, we decided to leave the gear there overnight. We stacked it neatly in a corner, but it must have been in the way because when the cleaners came in the morning after, they had to move it. Someone put our box of music on a storage heater, which came on an hour later and melted all the records.

We were naturally devastated: this was likely the end of the road for the 'Atlantic' lads because we couldn't think of any way we could (a) afford to replace the, by now, hundreds of singles or (b) find replacements for many of the classic 45s we had collected.

Then I had an idea! If we pitched this tale of woe to the local paper, it would make a good hard-luck story for them and generate a good deal of free publicity for us (and there's no such thing as bad publicity, is there? Yes, there is). I thought if we could get the *Bolton Evening News* to tell of our sad tale, it would be a free advert for our disco and potential clients would be secured! Clever thinking, eh?

Well, no! Who in their right mind would book a disco which has no f***ing records, eh?

The Discovery of DNA

MY MOBILE-DISCO career aside, I was simultaneously getting on with the other job in my life. Having winged my way to studying my HNC, I was now faced with a big decision: much like on *Mastermind*, I had to select a specialist subject. This choice would affect the rest of my working life as I would be committed to working in and studying that subject exclusively.

It didn't take me long to choose Haematology and Blood Transfusion. The inarguable positives were:

1. It was a fun place to work, with the radio always on (low) and great staff, who were always up for a laugh and who were, without doubt, far more attractive than those in any other department = Sex, Blood and Rock and Roll.
2. There were a great variety of tests to keep you busy and interested.
3. At the time, Haematology was one of the fastest expanding branches of medical science, providing the chance to be involved in the exciting developments of the department.
4. They brewed their own beer and wine and went to the pub almost every dinnertime.

An added bonus was that, if and when you qualified, you could apply to go on the out-of-hours on-call emergency work rota – dashing into the lab at any hour to cross-match blood for transfusion, test a patient's clotting factors, perform white blood cell counts and then differentiate the different types of cells present, and much, much more – making a difference, contributing in some small way to helping patients and occasionally saving lives. In my eyes, Haematology and Blood Transfusion staff were the SAS of Pathology.

I started my HNC in Haematology and Blood Group Serology in the John Dalton Building of Manchester Polytechnic in September 1970. We still studied Physics, Chemistry and Biology, but there were more sessions on Haematology and Transfusion, usually scheduled in the evenings, with guest lecturers from the big labs in and around Manchester. This was good, but it was also bad because during the break for tea prior to the lectures, we would go to the pub across the road, The Salisbury, and down a liquid tea.

I was soon joined by Glenn, who had been fast-tracked onto the HNC course after a year on ONC due to his good A Level grades. To be fair, we had a great time on the whole. We had a bit of a close call in one of the practical projects that counted towards our final grade – because we decided we couldn't be bothered doing it.

We had to extract DNA from, I think, rat liver (the process of which is too complicated and boring to detail here). Although we got all the equipment out and mixed the reagents and set up burettes for titrations, we actually gave up twenty minutes into a project that was to take four weeks. We decided that we'd just follow everyone else around and do what they did and carry what they carried. So if they went to the biohazard store and got some acetone for part of the extraction process, we went too; if they set up a bunsen burner, tripod and gauze and boiled blue stuff in a beaker, we did too; and once when they all put their samples in the big centrifuge on high spin for fifteen minutes, we pretended that we had too.

This was where our plan almost crashed and burned – because the scary and imposing Dr Maddox appeared at the centrifuge just as it was slowing down to enquire of our progress. We said it was going really great, all according to plan, etc. Then the centrifuge stopped, someone opened the lid and everyone dived in for their samples. There was an awful pause as Glenn, Dr Maddox and I peered into a now empty centrifuge and slowly exchanged a look. Glenn's face was a cross between panic and terror, but I decided to go on the attack: 'Somebody's taken our bloody sample!'

I stormed off and into the lab, shouting, 'Somebody's got my sample, please check your test tubes!' I stole about ten yards on Glenn and Dr Maddox and approached Darryl, with whom we'd sort of mated up, and said under my breath, 'Lend us your sample for a minute, Darryl, or we're in the shit.' Darryl sussed out what had happened and gave us his sample as Dr Maddox entered. I held it up, 'It's here! Panic over.' Thankfully Dr Maddox walked away and Glenn started to get his colour back.

We were in the organic chemistry lab later and by sheer chance I found a small vial of the DNA we needed for the exam, which I 'borrowed'.

When the month was over and everyone had presented Dr Maddox with their extract and he'd run each one through the Gas Chromatography system, he appeared back in the lab, looking stern and troubled. He said, 'No one, *no one* has managed to extract a significant amount of DNA. One month's work wasted. You're hopeless, the lot of you!'

Then he continued, 'Well, I say "the lot of you", but there is one exception.'

'Oh shit!' I thought, as he went on, 'Bramwell and Richardson have somehow produced an almost 100 per cent extract. How do you explain your success, gentlemen, when you followed the exact same protocol as everyone else?'

I just shrugged. 'Skill and dedication?'

Like Dr Manning, he didn't believe me – but he couldn't prove otherwise.

The Haematology element in the evenings was, on the whole, excellent. Keith Hyde from Manchester Royal Infirmary, who is some sort of professor now, bless him, organized it and was aided by Len Seal ('Ron' to us – he does exactly what it says on the sample) and they lectured us, aided by guest consultants and specialists from local hospitals. Because we worked in a pretty basic general hospital lab in Bolton, much of what Glenn and I heard was news to us. We'd read about it in textbooks, but never practised anything at all of a specialist nature.

It became clear quite quickly through attending these lectures and discussions afterwards that we in Bolton were way behind most labs in terms of the services and diagnostic testing we offered. We didn't offer any cytochemical staining for use in leukaemia diagnosis, we didn't offer testing for genetic defects in haemoglobin or enzymes; we did nothing other than the most rudimentary tests for blood clotting. We were embarrassingly out of touch.

Much of the problem was that we didn't have a consultant haematologist. Our consultant was a forensic pathologist with an interest in haematology (not much of an interest, as it turned out). The senior staff in the department – although a great team – were not highly qualified. Through our studies, Glenn and I, although basic grade staff, in fact became far more knowledgeable than the senior staff, who had qualified under an earlier system, when the pathology sciences were nowhere near as advanced as they were under the ONC–HNC system.

I decided to push for cytochemistry staining and abnormal haemoglobin testing at the lab and ordered all the necessary reagents and equipment we needed. Glenn decided to concentrate on blood coagulation (which was good because I couldn't stand it, or understand it, to be frank).

I must say that everyone was very sceptical about the new tests I was introducing, but I followed the methodology – and, stuff me, it worked! I got the techniques to succeed and I cannot tell you the sense of pride and achievement. I'd set them up on my own. Ordered the apparatus, equipment, reagents, applied the science and made it work; brought some credibility to the department.

Glenn did the same for blood coagulation, introducing assays for blood-clotting factors; and later Sean did the same in the new science of Immunology. The class of '68 made a massive difference to the service offered by the department – and I believe to the lives of many patients.

Cadet Nurses

BEFORE THE IDEA of graduate nurses ever saw the light of day, the hospital employed a grade of nursing staff straight from school at sixteen as cadet nurses. This was a great idea and, like many great ideas, it has long since been abandoned.

Cadet nurses rotated for two years around all the hospital wards and departments in a sort of apprenticeship. During that time, they learnt rudimentary nursing skills, became familiar with the workings of most hospital departments and did a lot of mugging about. As I say, it was a sound idea because by the time they started their nurse training, they had gained an amazing amount of basic knowledge from that work experience, which meant, for instance, that if they had to take a blood sample to Haematology urgently, they would know exactly where the laboratory was, who best to deliver that sample to and a little bit about the significance of the results.

We had cadet nurses in the Pathology department. I only really remember three. One was Val and she was the niece of the great Nat Lofthouse, Lion of Vienna and Bolton sporting legend. One had red hair and was a laugh and lived on Church Road. The other was Julie and I remember her very well because I married her. Julie was tall and slim and pretty and looked great in the yellow cadet uniform. She was also very bright and had a sarcastic sense of humour, which was why, even though Ken, the senior in Haematology, called her 'pigeon legs', I still fancied her.

I honestly don't remember much about our courtship, except that it was great most of the time. I was very happy with Julie. We went clubbing a lot because she loved dancing and I remember us going to see a midnight premiere of *Butch Cassidy and the Sundance Kid* at the Odeon. We went to Southport on a day trip with (I think) Bernard and his girlfriend, and I tried to impress Julie by taking her to a cocktail bar. I'd read somewhere about Pimms and I thought that I'd be Mister Sophisticated and order one for her.

'I'll have a pint of bitter and a Pimms, please.'

'Which Pimms?'

'What?'

'There are different types of Pimms; we've got number one or a number two?'

'Two, please.'

'What do you want that with?'

'With it? Forget it, have you got Babycham?'

Julie lived with her mum, dad and brother Bernard on Oldhams estate. Her mum was – still is – a lovely lady; her dad was a sound bloke; and I vaguely remember some uncle or neighbour, who may have had narcolepsy or something, who would pass out on the rug in front of the fire, which led to a slightly surreal hour where the rest of the family ignored him and watched TV over his lifeless form.

We were married at Holy Infants RC Church on Friday 29 September 1972, a week before my twenty-first birthday. Sean was my best man. Because I wasn't a Catholic, I had to have 'lessons' with the priest to learn all about Adam and Eve and God's plan for us and Jesus and all that. I forget the priest's name (Fr Barr?), but I was struck by the way that he took the Bible absolutely literally; as an actual written history of Jesus's life.

I remember that he wasn't impressed by me enquiring about Jesus's carpentry skills: if, as he suggested, the Bible was a factual account of our Lord's life, then Jesus was actually a real bona-fide carpenter – in which case, where was the written evidence in the Bible to support this? No mention of him making so much as a pencil case or even knocking his mum up a bookshelf. I wondered if He employed the same methods as demonstrated in His many miracles. 'Water – wine. Wine – water.' (I have him presenting it in a Tommy Cooper-style.) 'Wood – coffee table. Coffee table – wood.' Surprising that he still married us.

On the night of the wedding, we stayed in our new house on

Cloverdale Square (a nice semi-detached for £3,300 in 1972!), after a reception at Smithills Coaching House just up the road from where I went to school. We honeymooned in Criccieth on the beautiful Lleyn Peninsula, one of my favourite holiday destinations as a kid.

Our son Stephen was born on 11 March 1973. That afternoon, I was due to play in an important game for the Bolton Hospital's football team and Julie was admitted to the maternity ward to be induced into labour. This was timed to occur at five o'clock by the obstetrician on call, who couldn't do it any earlier because he was playing centre half. Just before kick-off, his bleep sounded and he answered the phone to discover that he may have mistimed the drip because Julie had gone into labour.

I sprinted across to the maternity ward, still in football kit. This was an amazing coincidence because my dad was playing football when I came into the world on 6 October 1951; no bleeps in those days. Julie had a difficult labour and had to have an episiotomy, which required many stitches. Only the obstetrician could perform this procedure – and by my reckoning the second half had only just started. She had to lie there, poor thing, until the game finished.

We were expecting a girl; I don't know why. Maybe my gran had held a spinning needle over Julie's bump or something, but we were so convinced that we decorated the baby's bedroom pink, with lots of girlie stuff in there … and here was Stephen – all nine pounds, twelve ounces of him. That's stretching it a bit, as they say.

Truth is that we didn't have a name for our new baby straight away, so surprised were we at having a boy, so we called him David temporarily. It was Alison, a good friend of Julie, ex-girlfriend of mine and nurse on the obstetrics ward, who suggested Stephen, and we both liked that immediately.

Stephen was a beautiful baby, but he wouldn't sleep at night. We took it in turns to get up in the night for hours with him; well, Julie probably did more than me. We tried everything and still he wouldn't sleep. He wasn't crying a lot, he was just, well, awake and noisy and wanted attention. We tried all the usual medications, Calpol and various recommended cures, to no avail. It was absolutely wearing us out. I was going to work dead on my feet.

One day, as a last resort, I went to see the sister in charge of maternity and asked her advice. She told me to put a bit of brandy in his late-night milk and that would send him off. I tried it, expecting a miracle – but all I got was a pissed-up baby kicking off.

Finally, a miracle did happen; a friend told us that Stephen might need a 'comforter', something to suck or hold at night. She said a piece of ribbon or satin often worked and we remembered that the pink blankets we'd bought for the expected baby girl had a satin edging, so we put one in Stephen's cot and stood back and then … Hallelujah! He started crying, but then reached for the satin and started rubbing it on his nose, sighed and started to snooze again. He had the comforter for years. Even when it fell apart, we kept strips of the satin for him to use.

Stephen was a model child. He was everything you'd want from a boy growing up. Good-natured, kind and bright, and I have so many happy memories of that time. There was one awful incident that I remember vividly, which happened just as I was getting out of my car after work, not longer after we'd moved house to New Hall Lane, to a beautiful big semi-detached in a really nice area of Bolton. I heard a scream, an awful pained scream, and I knew it was Stephen. I dashed round the back of the house and there he was, with a finger mangled in between the chain and cogs on his bike. I wound the chain back to free his finger, the top of which was hanging off; Julie wrapped a tea towel around it; and we drove down to Bolton Royal Infirmary.

They looked at him immediately and the consultant reckoned that as it was still connected via a small flap of skin, he could re-attach the fingertip – but there was a problem. Stephen had just eaten his tea and so could not have an anaesthetic for some hours, so we had to sit and wait. I can't imagine the pain he was in or what was going through his young mind; I do remember how brave he was, how he never moaned or cried or complained and how proud I was of him, especially when he looked up at me after a couple of hours and said, 'I think it's fallen off.' The surgeon did re-attach it successfully, although Stephen did have some loss of feeling down one side. They say that every cloud has a silver lining – and the silver lining for Steve was that he could stop his school violin lessons, which he hated.

My beautiful daughter Jill was born five years after Stephen. We couldn't believe our luck in being blessed with another lovely child. Jill slept through the night more than Stephen had done as a baby, but it was difficult getting her to sleep and I remember lying on the bed next to her singing 'Nellie the Elephant' over and over again, just like I'd done with Stephen. She did have the odd tantrum, which involved her throwing herself on the floor and screaming a lot, but I just picked her up and took her up to her bedroom, threw her on the bed and slammed the door and she stopped doing it.

I experienced another awful moment when Jill ran into the kitchen just as I was pouring the boiling water off some spaghetti. She was only a toddler and ran up to me and grabbed my leg. I jolted the pan and one big drop of boiling water was thrown out. I can see it now, watching it rise then begin to fall, and me unable to do anything as I held the pan of boiling water. The drop hit Jill on her bare shoulder and she screamed. Although I was devastated, I just thank the Lord that it missed her pretty face, because it has scarred her for life. It's not a big scar, thank God – but it's there.

Regrets – More Than a Few

JULIE AND I divorced when Stephen was ten and Jill was five. I don't want to go into it too much. Mainly because I'm ashamed of myself and I don't believe that sharing it will benefit anyone. Suffice it to say that after the first couple of years of our marriage, I became a terrible husband and I treated Julie badly. I was selfish, uncaring and immature and I behaved in a way that must have really hurt her and that I will always regret. I was never violent or abusive, but my behaviour at times was unforgivable. I'm very sorry.

I suppose you could say that it was a classical case of getting married too soon and then growing apart. After all, I was only twenty and Julie nineteen when we wed and we really didn't have any life experience, but when things started to go wrong and we ended up arguing and fighting, I didn't make any effort to try to make things right. I was very immature as I say, and this new vibrant world of hospital work, with all my new friends and colleagues, together with all the associated social aspects, really opened my eyes and made me want more of everything … and I neglected my responsibilities. Unfeeling, uncaring selfish idiot that I was.

I moved into a terraced house around the corner. From that moment, I'd,see the kids at every opportunity – although I'm ashamed to say that, on occasions, I still put myself first. Julie had now qualified as a nurse and was working shifts, which meant that I got to see Stephen and Jill very regularly as I covered for her. I think that some weeks I saw my children more than when I was married and living at home.

Stephen and Jill took the divorce badly, I think. It would break my heart, putting them to bed at night and Jill saying, 'Don't go home,

Daddy, stay here.' I used to go home and lock myself in the bathroom and break my heart, cry and cry, distraught for hours, especially at Christmas and birthdays. But this was my punishment and it was well deserved. I just wish with all my heart that I hadn't hurt my wonderful children so much, but I did.

I still did a lot of the dad things. I think I got better at putting them first as time progressed and I took them both to swimming lessons, Jill to ballet and tap, and Stephen to Cubs.

We got Stephen a Commodore 64 computer as a present one year. It was second-hand but immaculate and came in its own carrying case. I will never ever forget the look of sheer joy that appeared on his face when he opened that present. We used that computer a lot together.

Both of them did exceptionally well at swimming and took all the lifesaving badges. Jill did very well at dancing and then she grew about two foot (taller, that is) in a week and her ambitions to be a ballerina faded a touch. Steve got a remote-control car kit one year and we built it (a Mitsubishi Shogun) – and then found out that there were events where you could race them. We would go to Leverhulme Park on a Sunday and he would race his car in the novice class and I remember that he won an event and a small cup one day. That was a brilliant moment.

My children have grown up to be fine people. Julie takes much of the credit for that, as do the kids themselves. My father was always my hero – being kind, caring and compassionate – and when he died in 2001, my children took his place.

My son because he's such a good man. He has many admirable character traits that I've not. He gives everyone the benefit of the doubt, tries to find the good in everybody and is far more generous and giving than I ever was. Stephen has also always been very artistic, a trait I think he inherited from his grandfather, to whom he was very close. In fact, right up to taking his GCSEs, he was half decided on a career in design, but then he announced that he wanted to go to music college. This surprised his mum and me because he'd not taken music at GCSE level, but we'd bought him a guitar soon after our divorce and I think that he lost himself in learning to play as an aid to dealing with the break-up, although I've never asked him if that is the case. This is another failing of mine: I'm a bit useless at communicating with people, friends, colleagues and family alike, especially if it's concerning a particularly delicate topic. I've fudged so many important conversations which leads to misunderstandings and backtracking and confusion.

Anyway, regarding the music issue, Julie wasn't thrilled with the idea, but we decided after much discussion that if that was what he wanted, he should do it. He auditioned for and won a place at Leigh College and studied Performing Arts and took his GCSE Music. He did really well at college and became an accomplished guitarist. He's played in a variety of bands all around the world, Irish, Mexican, you name it, and once famously got lost in a scary suburb of Moscow after winning a vodka-drinking competition held after he'd played at a St Patrick's Day concert there! How he won the contest is beyond me (and him), as he doesn't normally drink so much. He's recently made the leap into playing for touring musical theatre shows and won a place at the Academy of Contemporary Music, making us all very proud of him again.

My fab daughter Jill is joint hero because she is loving, caring, dedicated, kind and funny. She had always wanted to be a teacher and after leaving school she won a place at Lancaster University to study for her BA. Since she qualified, she has worked so hard to become one of the most respected and accomplished teachers you will ever find. She applied for an Assistant Head post a couple of years ago and asked me to check her CV. When I read through the document, I was amazed at how much she'd crammed into her career so far. Extra classes in teaching special needs, organizing the school choir and so many other achievements, too numerous to list. I was both stunned and so proud to discover this 'hidden' portfolio and the dedication it must have taken to achieve.

She got the job and is as enthusiastic as ever in her new role. Jill also has a fantastic sense of humour and could have been a comedian; she has everyone in stitches with her animated stories about school life and life in general. Stephen is also very inventive and very funny. I'm absolutely serious when I say that both of them could have made a career out of comedy, had they wanted.

Nurse Bramwell

I'VE SPOKEN ABOUT my father earlier and how much of an influence he was. I want to take a moment now to outline to you just why. He was a remarkable man for many reasons, but mainly, in my eyes, because although he had no academic qualifications, he appreciated, understood and was knowledgeable about all aspects of the arts.

He had books and books covering the works of his favourite artists, notably the Impressionists with Renoir and Van Gogh amongst his favourites. He had a small but impressive collection of classical music and loved opera, singing along enthusiastically to 'La Donna è Mobile' from *Rigoletto*, 'Il Mio Tesoro' from *Don Giovanni* and 'Nessun Dorma', long before it was sadly used (and devalued) as a World Cup anthem. I think he made half the words up – but languages were never his strong suit.

He also loved literature and was a fan of Tolstoy, Camus, Dostoevsky and contemporary American writers. I have many of his books and I have to admit I struggle to finish many of them. His favourite book, however, *The Ragged-Trousered Philanthropist*, became one of my favourites too, dealing as it does with working-class painters and decorators 'subsidizing' their rich employers and the efforts of a handful of men to try to organize others into a union to gain their rightful rewards.

My dad wrote short stories and took a creative writing correspondence course for years, and had a couple of poems published. I take his handwritten stories out from time to time and trace the words of his perfect handwriting, trying to feel his presence, his inspiration in the ink.

He was always interested in religion, psychology and philosophy, and flirted with Buddhism, Quakerism and Methodism. In one famous incident, he spoke at length on the subject of Zen Buddhism to the family and friends of my Chinese accountant during a party at his offices. I emerged from a meeting with the accountant to find my dad holding forth to a large group of Chinese people, a can of beer in one hand, peanuts in the other. I could tell he was a bit drunk because he had the habit of speaking out of the side of his mouth like Robert Mitchum when he'd had a few and he was doing this now, allowing the occasional peanut fragment to escape. The crowd listened to him enthralled, hanging on his every word, and it was only later during a chat with my accountant that I learned the reason for their rapt attention. It turned out that they were all Christian, but found my dad's depth of knowledge of Buddhism fascinating.

My dad was a communist and we were possibly one of the only houses in Bolton that had the *Morning Star* delivered every morning. He was a champion of the working classes and even stood for election to Bolton council as a communist and gained 212 votes, bless him.

It should have come as no surprise to me that shortly after I started working at the hospital, he became acutely interested in psychiatric nursing. He was a caring person, he was intrigued by philosophy and psychology; the surprise was that it had taken him so long to find this direction. There was one massive stumbling block, and that was that, as I previously mentioned, he had no academic qualifications. There was, however, an entrance exam, which he was allowed to take. He passed impressively and began training to become an SRN (State Registered Nurse).

It was sort of weird going onto wards to take blood or assist in bone marrow aspirations with my dad attending as senior nurse, giving me the odd smile and wink! He was a painter and decorator by trade, this was completely mad – what was going on? It was brilliant.

Over the years that followed, my dad passed all his exams, qualified as an SRN, then an RMN (Registered Mental Nurse), then became a deputy charge nurse (staff nurse), and then finally a charge nurse (sister). There were hiccups along the way; one of his patients once ate all the tropical fish because the dinners were late. Dad found him sitting by the fish tank, buttering slices of bread then diving in for another couple of guppies. Later, he prevented a murder when a patient, irritated by the bloke in the next bed's snoring, went to the kitchens across the road and returned with a meat cleaver with which to decapitate said snorer. Luckily, Dad popped into the side ward to check up on things in time to see the patient raise the cleaver ready to strike.

And what else? Oh yes, my dad bathed a visitor. Yes, he did. He was working nights on Vickers 1 ward with another male nurse called Brian, a big bruising bloke who liked a drink and a laugh, when they received a phone call to say that, although it was approaching midnight, they should expect a new patient called Mr Richards for admission. Mr Richards was schizophrenic. As it was late and he was more than a little agitated, they were advised to bathe him, as he smelled rather badly, and put him to bed.

Half an hour later, a man with a suitcase wandered onto the ward. Seeing my dad, he explained that he was a little disorientated and asked if he could please be shown the way out.

My dad said, 'Of course. Mr Richards, is it?'

'Yes,' the little man replied. 'Which is the way to the car park?'

My dad shouted for Brian and introduced him. Brian asked him where he was off to and the man said, 'I'm going home,' and Dad and Brian got hold of him gently and said, 'You can go home after you've had a bath.'

'I don't want a bath!' said the little man.

'Yes, you do,' said big scary Brian, and he and my dad took the man into the bathroom, stripped him, threatened him when he started shouting, and then bathed him, put him in pyjamas and sat him in bed.

About an hour later, the senior nurse on his rounds popped in to see if everything was under control. He apologized to my dad for not letting him know earlier that Mr Richards had been admitted to Vickers 2, where he'd been a patient before. My dad and Brian looked at one another before my dad said, 'No, he's here. We admitted him an hour ago.'

'You can't have,' said the Senior Nurse, 'I've just seen him on Vickers 2.'

'So who's that, then?' said my dad, throwing his head back to indicate the bed in the corner. They approached the little man, who was sat up in bed, face grim and arms tightly folded.

'Hello, Mr Richards,' said the Senior Nurse. The little man sat stony-faced as the Senior Nurse turned back to Dad and Brian. 'That's his brother. He accompanied him into the hospital and he was taking his clothes home in the suitcase.'

D'oh!

My dad loved working there, but, by and by, his interest in sociology increased. He applied for and won a scholarship to Leeds University to read sociology, in preparation for another change of career into social work.

And that decision led to a happy meeting with him later in my own career. Despite our scam with the rat DNA test, I passed my HNC in Haematology and Serology in 1972 – at the first attempt – and immediately embarked on what was called at the time the 'Special Exam', which is now equivalent to a Masters degree. No one at Bolton had ever taken this two-year advanced course, but I was so gripped by the ever-expanding science that I had to progress. As well as completing a tough, three-paper written exam, I also had to endure an oral exam with an interviewing panel, comprising two consultant haematologists and a senior biomedical scientist.

Mine happened to take place at Leeds University. And so it was that on the day I passed my Haematology Special Oral Exam, I met my dad, who was studying at the adjacent university, for a couple of celebratory pints. How great is that?

Senior Service

NOW I WAS fully qualified, three big things happened. The first was a promotion to Senior Biomedical Scientist. The second was that I was asked to become an occasional lecturer on the 'Special' Haematology course, which was a great honour and achievement. I started off doing a couple of lectures a term, but after a few years I was giving around ten in total upon a variety of topics (although no blood coagulation, obviously).

In a foreshadowing of my later career, I tried to introduce an element of comedy into the lectures, hopefully to make them more memorable and less tedious. I remember tackling the subject of haemoglobin breakdown and using a series of slides to illustrate the molecular progression from haemoglobin to biliverdin to bilirubin, and then I slipped in a slide of Leeds United legend and captain Billy Bremner as being the final breakdown product. It got a laugh, trust me! In later years, I stopped lecturing when I became too busy with stand-up and when the students got more and more anal – and actually started drawing Billy Bremner in their lab books, believing he was a haemoglobin breakdown product. Honestly.

The third big event was that I was deemed qualified to undertake emergency out-of-hours on-call work, which was a massive boost, not only in professional achievement, but also financial terms. I saw myself as that SAS operative I'd aspired to be when I chose Haematology as my specialist subject; a one-man SWAT team called in to work alone, under pressure, with lives at stake.

On my first night, a Sunday, I waited anxiously by the phone, which rang as early as 7 p.m. – it was promising to be a baptism of fire! The hospital sent transport to pick me up (as I didn't have a car at the time) and we hurtled in to do a full blood count on a lady who'd had a PPH – a post-partum haemorrhage. If the haemoglobin was low, I might have to cross-match blood for an emergency transfusion!

As it turned out, it wasn't low, so I came home – and the phone didn't ring again that night. No matter, I'm £2.50 up and I'm officially an experienced on-call technician.

Ah, but the glamour soon wears off ... Within a couple of years, you absolutely dread that phone ringing – and now, of course, it's always ringing. We're on ten calls a night, maybe two sessions a week, not getting any sleep and still having to turn up for work at 8.45 in the morning.

And driving in from home is such a bloody pain, especially at three o'clock in the morning when you've only been in bed for ten minutes after returning from the last call. It's February, it's pitch black, and you're battling through the snow and sleet; your windscreen wipers aren't working properly and the heater's on the blink and you're dashing in to do a six-pint cross-match for a ninety-three-year-old with an aortic aneurysm and you know that that's only the start of it. If they attempt a repair of the aorta, which they will, he's going to need far more than six pints of blood cross-matching and you can say goodbye to any more sleep tonight because he'll also need his blood counts and platelet count checking regularly and his blood coagulation monitoring and chances are that that woman who was bleeding on maternity and the bloke with oesophageal varices on C2 are going to want more blood and God knows who else will be admitted; and the only thing that keeps you going on that cold drive in, the one thing that gives you hope as you batter through the wind and snow and hail, is the thought that by the time you get to the hospital, he could be dead. Oh yes – sorry, but it's true, and he was ninety-three so he'd had a good innings and I NEED TO GET SOME SLEEP!

And you get in and he has died and you say a prayer of thanks and head for bed, but then the phone rings and a woman on the gynae ward has had a bleed and can you check her haemoglobin level please? That's not a problem, that's a two-minute job – but then the doctor hits me with a gem. He tells me that if the haemoglobin level is less than 10 g/dl, I'll need to cross-match two units of blood.

'Right,' I say, thinking, 'Less than 10 g/dl at three o'clock in the morning? What are the chances of that happening?'

I run the test, the haemoglobin is 9.6 g/dl. Mmm, what to do now? Phone it through and confirm that the doctor still wants to transfuse two units of blood ... *or* let the sample stand on the bench for ten minutes until the red blood cells settle out and become a bit more concentrated? Yes, I'll do that. Test it again in ten minutes and the Hgb is 10.2 g/dl – result. Off to bed.

By the way, this is one of the mad laws of medicine. Junior doctors will always request a transfusion if the haemoglobin is less than 10 g/dl, which is nonsense – who came up with that rule? An idiot, that's who. Consider that a pregnant woman's normal haemoglobin could be, say, 11 g/dl, so that if she has a bit of a bleed and let's say loses around a pint of blood, this level could drop to below 10 g/dl. According to this 'rule', she will be transfused two units of blood. This is patently rubbish – I regularly lose a pint of blood when I donate at the blood transfusion donor sessions and all I get is a cup of tea and a couple of biscuits.

I believe that we should implement this in the NHS. Furthermore, if someone loses two pints: cup of strong coffee and a few chocolate HobNobs. Three-pint bleed? Here's a pot of Darjeeling and a packet of Garibaldis. Much cheaper, much more efficient and a damn sight safer.

There are small unexpected moments of joy that surprise you during the long endless nights on call – and one is when you test a haemoglobin and it's as low as 3 g/dl and no hot-beverage-and-biscuit combo is going to help, and you phone it through to the ward and then this happens.

Me: I've got the haemoglobin result for Mr Dawson.
Nurse: Okay, let me write it down. What is it?
Me: (*Resignedly.*) It's three grams.
Nurse: Oh wow! That is low.
Me: I know.

Nurse: What a shame! He's a Jehovah's Witness.

Me: Oh no, is he? Well, thanks then. (*I hang up.*) GET IN!!!!

(*Run round the lab with shirt pulled over my head in celebration.*)

TATT

OVER TIME, THE amount of test requests received in the lab sky-rocketed. I think this was due to two things – firstly, clinical judgement seemed to be a fading art; and secondly, the world now seems to be populated with hundreds, nay, thousands of time-wasting hypochondriacs.

We began to see more and more requests with the Clinical Details as 'Tired all the time. ? Anaemia'. Only about 10 per cent would be anaemic; the rest were tired. Go to bed earlier, exercise more, adopt a healthy diet and stop skiving! We got tired of typing the details into the system and so we invented acronyms. TATT = Tired All The Time. The doctors soon picked up on this and started to use it routinely themselves on requests, in addition to TATTD ('Tired all the time, doctor' – said in a wimpy, whiny voice).

As time went by and requests continued to rise, we invented more and adopted established acronyms to amuse ourselves and other hospital staff. These included:

NFB	Normal, For Bolton
FORD	Found On Road Drunk
FLK / FLP	Funny-Looking Kid / Funny-Looking Parents
TFTB	Too Fat To Breathe
PFO	Pissed, Fell Over
FTF	Failure To Fly (suicide jumpers)
WOFTAM	Waste Of F***ing Time And Money
LTBB	Lucky To Be Breathing
CTD	Circling The Drain (for patients who just will not die)
GFPO	Good For Parts Only

And from the wards:

TUBE   Totally Unnecessary Breast Examination
CODE BROWN loose-bowel-related incident

Patients with TATT also usually had a variety of accompanying vague symptoms. Backache, sore feet, mee-graines [*sic*] and very often 'depression', said in a pathetically weak voice over the phone. I'm sure that you have worked with or known some wimpy, work-shy, pathetic excuse for a human being who has been off for months and months with 'depression'. I get incredibly annoyed with staff who phone in sick with 'depression'.

Them: I won't be in work for a while. I've got depression again.
Me: Oh, again? Have you? That's three times this year, isn't it?
Them: Yes.
Me: Look, that's not depression, that's fed up, that's down-in-the-
    dumps.
Them: No. I can't get out of bed in the morning.
Me: Neither can I! Make a bloody effort, you lazy git.

Don't get me wrong here: clinical depression is a very serious and tragic disorder, and so I find it outrageous that these contemptible people belittle the condition by adopting it as their 'sickie'. The government are introducing means-testing for people on long-term sick and I put forward a test for people with 'depression'.

You get them in a room and sit them on a chair and ask them to be clear about the nature of their illness. When they say 'depression', you get a monkey on a bike to ride across the room in front of them. If they don't laugh, then they really are f***ing depressed because a monkey on a bike is the funniest thing in the world. Imagine a smiley monkey, wearing a red-and-white tank top, waving its funny little arms about and making monkey noises as it peddles furiously … it's double funny. If they don't laugh, they are depressed; but if they do, which they will, it's 'Get back to work, you malingering sod! And give me that walking stick! You don't need it, never have!'

We should have a national walking-stick amnesty. Bring all those unused sticks back into the hospital. All you malingering skivers who've pretended to use them when you're out shopping or going down the pub, just in case you bump into somebody from the social, give them back, you cheats! Think of the money that would save in disability allowance and walking sticks.

The Beautiful Game

FOOTBALL, LIKE LIFE, is often a story of disappointment illuminated by moments of unlikely triumph. It is for such fleeting glories that, every Sunday morning, tens of thousands of men and boys roll and stumble out of their beds, grab a sports bag and, with eyes barely open, head down to the park pitches. Come rain or shine, sleet or snow, this disparate collection of men and boys assemble with their teammates to brave muddy pitches, windswept parks, psychotic opponents and challenging shower facilities. In freezing changing rooms, where icicles hang from broken showers, they strip, shivering, and quickly pull on their team's shirt ... and in that moment become united. Throughout the land, they stand in strips of many colours on a multitude of rain-sodden pitches, like some massive abstract rainbow waiting for a whistle to blow. This is the strange and magical world of Sunday league football.

I played and loved Saturday and Sunday football for thirty-odd years. I played alongside and against a great assortment of men and boys; some of whom became lifelong friends, and a few who remain enemies. It is a wondrous world: the camaraderie, the craic, the satisfaction of a good team performance and the elation of winning against all odds during a hailstorm on a bitter cold January morning.

An enthralling aspect of this world is the diversity of the players you find within each team. I played for sides that had a rich mix: doctors, lawyers, accountants, brickies, printers, begger-men, thieves. Men who would never normally mix off the pitch (only because their social spheres would never collide), but who nevertheless became, in that instant of pulling on their team shirt in the wet, freezing park changing rooms, a band of brothers.

I'd always been reasonably good at football and when I started work in Haematology, Ken, one of the seniors, asked me if I fancied training with the team he played for, 'Harper Green', which was just down the road from the hospital. I jumped at the chance and soon became a regular for them. They played in the Mid-Lancs league, which was a reasonably good standard, and the lads were great down there. I only remember good times in the years I played for them.

A year or so later, someone from the regional health authority organized an inter-pathology football competition and we decided that we could get a decent eleven players from the department. We were lucky because our hospital had a good football pitch situated behind the psychiatric wards and we played a couple of games there. Sean was a good player, Glenn was pretty good, but the star was our boss Harold, who had played for Bolton Wanderers as a young man before his cruciate ligaments ruptured and his blossoming career was cruelly ended. He couldn't move about much on the pitch, and occasionally in the lab his leg would lock up and he'd cry out and then fall over behind the bench. One minute he was there, the next he wasn't. The thing was that although he couldn't run much, if you gave him the ball anywhere around the penalty area, he would almost always score.

We won the competition, which royally pissed off the lads from (I think) Rochdale Hospital, who'd organized it in the expectation of winning it, as you do. The highlight for us was beating the mighty Manchester Royal Infirmary on our pitch.

We decided that we had the makings of a good team and so decided to enter the Bolton Federation League the next season. It became clear that we would need reinforcements in order to turn out a side every week, to cover on-call cover and other commitments which would deplete our current squad. We drafted in friends and family and we did alright. It was great craic and we played together for many years. Because we eventually included two or three of the doctors in the team, there was the added benefit of retiring to the doctors' mess after the games for a few pints of Lees Lager (Loopy Juice). We had a goalkeeper, Dr Roy, who was exceptionally good – he had the chance to turn professional, I think, but chose medicine – and he was worth ten points a season with the saves he made. He was (and is) a top bloke and long-standing friend, who weirdly became my GP after he left the hospital.

Roy was (he's retired now) a fantastic GP. You could never get an appointment to see him, he was in such great demand. I once phoned for an appointment and Mrs Goebbels, the receptionist, told me that he had no appointments and she offered me a date ten days hence. I said with more than a hint of sarcasm, 'I might be dead by then,' whereupon she replied deadpan without missing a beat, 'If you are, can you make sure somebody phones in to cancel your appointment.' Roy would come in early before surgery if I had any health worries (and I have plenty, believe me); it is a bit weird though having a best mate feeling your balls for lumps and your stomach for bumps.

On pre-season tours, we visited Newcastle, Bristol, Nottingham and, er, lots of other places lost in the mists of time, where we drank a lot, laughed a lot and played a few of games of football.

I always roomed with Dave M on tour and we got on very well. Dave was quite a steadying influence on the team and the organizer who sorted out hotels and travel. Part of his remit included him wearing a traffic cone on his head and leading the rest of us in repeated choruses of 'We're off to see the Wizard, the wonderful Wizard of Oz' as we made our way back to the hotel after a drunken night.

Dave usually wore a suit, collar and tie on our nights out, possibly a legacy of his day job in the bank, and he had the ability to fall asleep on his bed after a night on the piss and not move an inch for ten hours. It was unsettling waking up during the night and seeing a well-dressed corpse laid out on the next bed.

The only time this didn't happen was in a grotty hotel in Nottingham, where the mattress overlapped the cheap base of the bed and he didn't get his balance right. I woke to discover that he had disappeared. This was so unlike Dave that I panicked a bit and started to search the room – only to discover him lying undisturbed on the floor in between the bed and the wall; still very smart he looked. Suit and waistcoat still buttoned and tie in a neat Windsor knot.

We didn't hit it off with the owner of the grotty Nottingham hotel, who resembled (right down to the handlebar moustache) and behaved in many ways like the late great Jimmy Edwards of *Whacko!* fame. That's *Whacko!* – a sitcom set in a boys' school – as opposed to Waco, an all-action drama set on a ranch in Texas. As he served us breakfast on the Sunday morning after a typically heavy night on the town, his voice boomed out across the small dining room, 'And with the dawn commeth full repentance.' Eleven sets of bleary eyes turned towards him and we all, as a man, replied, 'F**k off, Whacko!'

He tried to wreak his revenge later in the day after our game by announcing that he was shutting the hotel bar at three o'clock. This was in the days when all pubs closed on Sunday afternoons, but we expected, as residents, to be served in the hotel. Not unless we got back by three, he explained – and the game didn't finish until 2.30. We devised a plan, which was that Roy, as the fastest driver with the fastest car – a Triumph 2000; maroon, of course – would dash back after the game and order us in a couple of rounds, which should tide us over until some bars opened again at five-ish.

I decided to ride shotgun and as the final whistle went – I forget the score (as if that's important!) – Roy and I dashed to his car and raced away, pausing only to pick up a traffic cone at high speed, me leaning out of the open passenger door to achieve the impressive pick-up (yes, I know!). We got back to the hotel bar at about ten to three. 'Whacko', as he was now known, was serving a handful of customers dressed in their Sunday best.

Then it was my turn. I said, 'Sixteen pints of lager, seven pints of bitter ...'

Whacko interrupted, 'Sixteen?!'

'Yes please, and seven pints of bitter.'

'Is that it?!' he said.

'Oh, and a pint of mild,' Roy added.

Whacko stared at us for a second and then said, 'You are joking?'

So we exchanged glances and then Roy said, 'Alright then, make it eight pints of bitter.'

Listen to This

IT WAS DURING my early years playing Saturday and Sunday football for Bolton Hospitals and Ace Shutters (!) that I first noticed that maybe I had a talent for comedy. All those years listening to radio comedy on a Sunday afternoon after *Two-Way Family Favourites* with my mum and dad must have helped. *The Navy Lark*, *The Clitheroe Kid* and the fantastic *Round the Horne*; then early television comedy with Morecambe and Wise, Tommy Cooper and Phil Silvers as Sgt Bilko.

I loved Phil Silvers; he was a genius with his rapid patter, his caustic asides, his veiled piss-taking of his competitors and his amazing array of comedy 'looks' – he had this great range of comedic glances and pauses and double-takes. I've always thought that Eric Morecambe must have been influenced by Phil Silvers because he has a similar comedy armoury to add to his innate comic gift.

One of my happiest memories is watching Morecambe and Wise with the family and me and my dad laughing so hard that we could hardly breathe and sliding down the chair almost onto the floor together trying to get a breath in between the laughs.

I'll make an admission now that may lose me a degree of credibility: I never really thought Laurel and Hardy were that funny. I thought that all the situations and scrapes they got into, all those adventures and escapades, were very similar. I thought their dialogue in those situations was very, very samey and they didn't throw up any surprises for me. They both had their character and behavioural traits and repeated them over and over.

On the other hand, I really enjoyed Abbott and Costello, which was more the straight man versus idiot team, which is why I was also a fan of

Bob Hope and Bing Crosby, who were actually Abbott and Costello with songs and Dorothy Lamour.

Add into the mix a few Kenneth Williams EPs of my dad's, and the Goons, who (more points going here), apart from Spike Milligan ('Hello, I'm the famous Eccles'), I didn't really get, and then add the creativity and quick thinking I must have inherited from my parents – and suddenly I discovered, many years later, that I could make people laugh.

Not only that; it would appear that in most cases I was the quickest with a remark or a quip and, tellingly, my view on humorous events was slightly skewed and so more surprising – which is, of course, one of the major constituents in the practice of the art of comedy.

Of course, it helped that I was surrounded both at work and in the football changing rooms by colleagues and friends who were also naturally funny. In those circumstances, getting the laugh becomes a bit of a competition. Remember, in those days, we only had the news, early developments in popular culture and a mere four TV channels, which meant that we all had the same popular topics for comedy criticism and deconstruction in the staff room, the pub and the changing rooms. At work, Sean and Harold were very quick and funny, as were a couple of the girls, and at football there was Tony, who laughed louder at his own jokes than anyone else did.

My first foray into performing any sort of comedy came via the medium of the hospital pantomime. My friend Dr Steve, who I knew from football, somehow got involved in organizing this one year; for some reason, he wrote it in rhyme, which is of course quite limiting from a comedy point of view, however I went to see it and loved it! Loved all the hospital in-jokes (in rhyme) and the sound of an audience's spontaneous laughter. The following year, when Steve asked if I wanted to help him write the script, I jumped at the chance (as long as it wasn't in rhyme).

We wrote *Snow White and the Seven Dwarfs* and I gave myself a small part. I didn't really want to perform, but we were short of volunteers and, after all, we needed seven of the little fellers. Because of copyright issues, we weren't allowed to use the original dwarfs, so we made up some others. I played 'Cosmo', who was based on Les Dawson's slightly pervy character 'Cosmo Smallpiece', who was popular back then.

My daughter Jill, who was only about six at the time, came to see the show and was so impressed that she wrote about it in her 'news' book at school. Her teacher showed me the entry when I attended parents' evening. It said, 'Last night I went to see a pantomime. My dad was in it and he kept saying "knickers knackers knockers" and putting his hand up Snow White's dress.'

When Dr Steve moved on to General Practice, I took over the organization of the panto and drafted in Sean to help. I thoroughly enjoyed writing and directing them, and continued to have very little ambition to perform. Over the next few years, the shows increased in popularity and we had to hire bigger and bigger halls in which to perform. At the height of the popularity, we were selling out the main hall at Bolton Technical College for five nights in a row.

Of course, when you are directing someone who can't deliver your crafted comedy lines, patience runs thin on both sides and sooner or later a performer will say, 'I'll tell you what, stick your stupid panto up your arse,' and walk out. This happened only a week or so before one show and I had no alternative but to take over the role. I was a bag of nerves, not at all comfortable on stage, but once I got into it and the laughs started coming, I was hooked. I was used to getting a massive thrill from writing and directing and hearing the reaction from the wings, but this was way different; this was spine-tingling.

Sean and I were asked by Dot, one of the phlebotomists, to take small chorus parts in the Church Road Am-Dram panto one year and we jumped at the chance. Tony F directed the show (which was *Red Riding Hood*); a man with no discernable talent for comedy, who once stormed into the dressing rooms during the interval of one show and shouted, 'Listen, everybody! Less laughter onstage!' – in a panto!

The truth was that it was very hard not to laugh onstage, especially when one of the characters got out an electric guitar in the middle of a woodland scene, plugged it into an amplifier disguised (badly) as a tree stump and accompanied Red Riding in boring song and dance, while the rest of us 'Merry Men' stood around like lemons.

Sean and I decided the scene needed something extra. Backing vocals. So we suddenly joined in: 'Shooby doo wop a shooby do wap, do wap.'

A startled Red Riding Hood fell over, so we improvised a dance routine loosely based on the moves made famous by 'The Shadows' to distract the audience.

It was for much the same reason that we were thrown out of Bolton Premier Amateur Operatic Society's rehearsals for *The Boyfriend*. Too much laughter onstage! Humourless snobs, most of them. Most but not all.

In 1983, Bolton Royal Infirmary was celebrating its centenary – and we were asked to put on a show to celebrate. Sean took command and came up with the genius idea of producing the production as a time-travelling experience, jumping through the highlights of the past century. For instance, we could materialize in the roaring twenties, or the war years, or the flower power era etc.

Together with his brother Harry, he put together medleys from individual eras, which all the performers threw themselves into. In between the musical numbers, and to fill time to dress the next set and facilitate costume changes, we decided to perform hospital-based sketches, which were written by myself, Sean and Rick (who worked in admin and played football with us). We included a sketch set in a hospital Accident and Emergency waiting room, where Rick and I played two domestics in the Les Dawson–Roy Barrowclough style. We lampooned hospital culture, waiting times and private medicine, and the largely hospital-based audience lapped it up.

At one stage, the girls' chorus performed 'Cabaret' – without realizing that the chairs used in the routine had a hole at crotch level, which acted as a focal point when they straddled them in their leotards and fishnet tights ... Paula, a nurse, danced with Paul, a recent recruit in Haematology, in another energetic routine: he in shorts, headband and legwarmers; she in a very tight yellow leotard with no underwear. My dad was heard to remark, 'I'll never eat another custard as long as I live!'

Most of us had to have a stiff drink before getting onstage to undertake something so ambitious and I mean 'stiff' – 11 per cent 'Carlsberg Special' stiff. This did cause some problems; I ripped the arm off somebody's leather jacket during the 'Beat It' dance routine having thought (mistakenly) that, for a laugh, somebody had sewn up the sleeve.

What had actually happened was that I'd put my arm down the lining. I blamed Catherine and made her cry. Sorry, Catherine.

The show was such a huge success that we had to add a second week. Sean's production was inspired both onstage and front of house, where he had the idea of rigging up rope lights, a special projector that projected the passing years onto a curtain, synthesized music and usherettes dressed as air hostesses, who handed out programmes in the form of time-travel passports to the *Laser Train Revue*.

The show turned out to be Sean's swansong for Bolton Hospitals, as he surprised us all by leaving the department to take up a Chief Biomedical Scientist post at Huddersfield Royal Infirmary. His opportunities at Bolton in this rapidly expanding 'new' science were limited, and our loss was definitely Huddersfield's gain.

O Kay!

SOON AFTER I divorced, I started seeing Kay on a regular basis. We had been going out 'unofficially' in the months leading up to the divorce and she had ended her relationship with her boyfriend, Phil, around the same time. This was, of course, all very messy and unsatisfactory and people got hurt, and we both still carry some guilt about that, even though it was almost thirty years ago.

I'd actually known Kay since secondary school, although she was in the technical college and I was in the grammar. She had started going out with Peter, a great lad with whom I occasionally played football, when she was about fourteen, and they were an item until they both left at sixteen. They were married soon after; Kay had a daughter, Jenny, the following February. Then, by an absolute mad coincidence, she started work in the Department of Pathology at Bolton General almost exactly a year after I did. I remember walking past Blood Transfusion and thinking, 'I know her!'

We got to know each other over the next few years, but we really didn't like each other for ages, especially after she 'gave' me leukaemia – alright, I won't mention it again! I played football with her husband Peter quite a few times, and I remember he took coaching very seriously and invested in a book of Brazilian training methods. Believe me, we got some very strange looks from other teams training on Harper Green when he had us jumping up and at each other, banging chests for hours on end.

Having married at sixteen, it wasn't surprising that they grew apart. Peter began to work away and found a job in the Middle East, where he converted to Islam and found a new lady. Kay always speaks very highly and lovingly about him and how much he changed after converting and found inner peace. He died aged thirty-two in Dubai, after a choking fit caused heart failure. A terrible tragedy and waste of a good life.

When a new bloke called Phil M started working in the labs a few years before my divorce, I matched him up with Kay (d'oh! Idiot). They went out for ages before moving in together. Phil was a good bloke, and a great addition in the department and the football team, even though he came from Leicestershire somewhere – Melton Mowbray, I think.

By the time my marriage started to flounder – my fault entirely – I was working closely with Kay because she had chosen to take her Special Exam in Blood Transfusion and so rotated between there and the Haematology lab next door. I suddenly realized that I'd started to like her and that she was quite attractive. No, I mean, very attractive; and not only that, it seemed that the attraction was mutual. We started to see each other outside work.

When my divorce came through and I moved out of New Hall Lane and into my new house, we started to see even more of each other. We never had the 'Big Romance' thing because we had known each other for years and had become good friends first. This friendship had just blossomed into a loving relationship without any fireworks exploding, orchestras playing, torpedoes shooting or tides lapping the beach.

Me, aged eighteen months, with my wonderful mum and dad, practising 'stand-up'.

My dad was my hero.

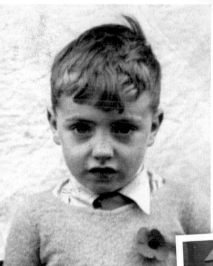

My childhood mugshot.

My family: (from left to right) Dad, me, my kid brother Pete, sister Joy and Mum.

Me and Sean 'hard at work' in the hospital labs.

Bolton Hospitals FC (I'm on the back row, fourth from left).

'Knickers, knackers, knockers': as Cosmo in *Snow White* (I'm in the blue costume).

The *Laser Train Revue*. From left to right: Sean, me, Pete, Rick and Harry.

Spikey and Sykey.

Nina MysCOW presents
me with the 'Stairway to
the Stars' award at the
Riviera Centre, Torquay.

With Rick on the 46229 'Duchess of Hamilton' steam train.

My fantastic children Stephen and Jill, with Bobby the dog.

My wife Kay and me, with Pippa.

My dad's last Christmas. From left to right: me, Joy, Dad and Pete.

With Cagney and Lacey on *Wanderer*.

A selection of our beloved pets from across the years. Clockwise from top: me with Lesley the chicken; Bertie, king of the garden; some of the dogs: (from left to right) Cagney, Whisky, Rosie, Lucy, Beau and Sammy; Billy the goat (centre), with Georgie and Henry.

I'm a big animal rights campaigner. Here Kay and I raise awareness for Animals Asia on a trip to Vietnam, pictured with the horrific metal corsets used on bears.

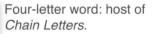
Four-letter word: host of *Chain Letters*.

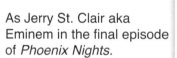
As Jerry St. Clair aka Eminem in the final episode of *Phoenix Nights*.

With Johnny Vegas and Iain McKee on the set of *Dead Man Weds*.

Meeting HRH Queen Elizabeth II backstage at the Royal Variety Performance realized a lifelong ambition.

On the set of *Parkinson*, with (from left to right) Katie Melua, Michael Parkinson, Rachel Weisz and Paul McCartney.

With my 'Performance of the Year' Award at the *MEN* Theatre Awards, with *MEN* editor Paul Horrocks. Winning this 'people's choice' prize was a career highlight.

I Name This Ship

KAY'S FAMILY HAD always been into canal boating and her parents, Albert and Alice, were part of the small band of boaters who, by sailing the canals in all weathers year round, navigating around rubbish tipped in the water, kept half the canal system open. We owe them a huge debt because our extensive national waterways are now a jewel in the crown of this country.

Kay's sister, Christine, had a narrowboat, the *Victoria Shane*, and the first holiday I took my kids on after the divorce was on that boat, cruising round the 'Cheshire Ring' of canals.

I was hooked immediately. I loved the pace of life on the 'cut'; I loved the fact that you could moor up in the middle of the countryside and open the doors in the morning to the peace and tranquillity of this beautiful country. I saw England from a different perspective, away from the hustle and bustle of towns and cities and the roar of the motorways and busy roads. Cruising at a maximum of 4 mph gives you the chance to take it all in, breathe it in.

The kids loved it too, helping negotiate the locks and open and close the swing and lift bridges. We sailed using the Nicholson Guide, which page by page illustrates the route of the canal, the position of the locks and bridges, the whereabouts of post offices and shops and the history of the towns and sites along the way. We also used the *CAMRA Guide to the Waterways*, which listed all the pubs along the way and the beers they served.

After the holiday, Kay and I had a chat about buying our own boat and came up with a plan, whereby I would sell my house and move in with her, thus freeing myself from a huge mortgage, which was crippling me.

I would then use any profit to pay off my rather large credit card bills and hire purchase contracts, and use the remainder of the money freed up to buy a boat.

We bought *Wanderer* (actual name!) from the boatyard at Worsely soon after. It was a fifty-foot 'Springer' design narrowboat. Although not the best make of boat on the canal by a long way, it was in good condition, was a good size and had been well maintained.

We painted *Wanderer* blue with red panels in the traditional style, and John, a professional narrowboat sign writer, added the name. She looked beautiful in her new livery.

We sailed on *Wanderer* for many happy years and all loved it. One of our favourite trips was up the Llangollen canal and over the stunning architectural masterpiece that is the Pontcysyltte aqueduct. Crossing this 1,000-foot-long aqueduct is an exhilarating and slightly surreal experience, as you are effectively sailing in a metal trough 126 feet over the Dee Valley with no handrail on one side, which creates the impression of sailing high up in the air.

The aqueduct was started in 1795 when the French Revolution was still raging, Beethoven made his debut as a pianist and the British captured Cape Town ... and today, well over 200 years later, it still stands as a monument to two great engineers, Thomas Telford and William Jessop. Even if you haven't got a boat, it is well worth the trip to see this masterpiece: you can, if you dare, walk across it on the towpath side. There is a day boat hire firm at Trefor, which is in the canal basin at the Llangollen end, and it's well worth a few of you hiring a boat and sailing across this and the Chirk aqueduct, which is a little bit further down.

A big part of travelling on the waterways involves, of course, the use of locks. As you probably know, locks are very dangerous – and I nearly died in one on the Wigan flight. This is an impressive flight of locks, which raises the Leeds–Liverpool canal over 200 feet through twenty-one double locks. These are huge locks, which were built to accommodate the big barges that used to ply their trade between these two great cities. The water pressure is enormous, and great care has to be taken when travelling up or down.

All would have been well if the idiot who had travelled up the flight before us had shut one of the top gate paddles after leaving the lock. I suppose we should have noticed, but with the gates being open, we simply sailed in and Kay and my mate Rick opened the bottom gate paddles and then strolled down to get the next lock prepared.

Everything was going well – until the water emptied below the level of the top gate paddles. The one that had been left open now admitted a torrent of water from above. This powerful spout hit me on the stern of the boat and knocked me clean into the turbulent waters of the lock – and I was on my own. Pam, Rick's wife, was on the toilet, but unless she felt the boat buffeting about now that the rope I had fed round a bollard to secure us in the lock had been ripped out of my hands, I was struggling.

The boat was swinging dangerously about and there was no way I was going to push a fifty-foot steel narrowboat away from me. I tried to clamber back on the stern, but it was too high and I only succeeded in cutting my leg on the propeller, which I'd left turning in order to keep the boat near the front gates. I shouted and shouted, really scared now because I could feel the suction of the water pulling me down towards the front gates where the water was pouring out. As if that wasn't bad enough, the unpredictable swinging of the boat in the turbulent water was threatening to crush me against the side of the lock.

Thankfully, Kay heard me and raced back up the hill to the lock. Without thinking, she jumped onto the roof of the boat, then onto the stern. She bent to grab my outstretched arm and tried to pull, but then, realizing that the boat was forcefully swinging towards the wall, she told me that she would have to let me go. I remember very clearly saying, 'Don't let me go!' as I was so frightened and exhausted.

But she let me go – she had to. I went under again briefly, before surfacing to see her grab the bargepole and jam it against the wall to keep the boat away. Once she'd done this, she jumped back on the stern and I asked her to throw a rope, which she did and I grabbed. Rick had returned by now and I shouted up and told him to close all the paddles – but, being a novice, he didn't understand at first and started opening others! No! Shut them all! He did; I was saved. It is very possible that Kay saved my life that day.

We cruised the waterways extensively during those years and were continually stunned and amazed at the beauty of the countryside. You sort of expect it if you are sailing on the Shropshire Union or Oxford canals, but one of the best views and the best stretches of canal for me is the length that takes you over the Pennines.

To get to it, you have to sail through the pretty grim industrial areas of Blackburn, Burnley, Nelson and Colne, until you get to a place called Foulridge. Legend has it that in the English Civil War, Cromwell faced the Royalists across the valley. When asked where he would like to engage them in battle, he said, 'On that foul ridge,' although this is probably bollocks.

There is a tunnel at Foulridge: as you sail through it, you leave behind the grey surroundings of the mills and warehouses. Almost a mile later – yes, it's almost a mile long – you emerge into the most amazingly beautiful scenery. It's like entering Narnia. The rolling foothills of the Pennines spread out in front of you and take your breath away.

A cow once fell into the canal on the Colne side of the tunnel some years ago and, being a cow, decided to walk through the tunnel. I would have loved to have been moored up on the Foulridge side to see the cow emerge, what a great moment that must have been. 'Odd-looking boat that, Jim ... Hang on, it's a cow.'

The cow was helped out of the canal and taken into the local pub, The Hole I'th Wall, and given brandy. If in doubt, give 'em brandy! They have pictures of it on the wall if you're ever passing – and I encourage you to do so.

There are some great pubs on the canals. Old-fashioned, never-been-touched, unmodernized pubs, which are listed in the guides. Our plan for these holidays was basically to sail to one of said pubs for dinner, and then to another one for an evening meal and overnight mooring.

We found a hidden gem, 'The Anchor' on the Oxford Canal, which according to the guide had been in the same family for generations and was completely unspoiled. We moored up outside and, being famished and thirsty after a long sail in the glorious sun, we went straight in. There were six of us – me, Kay, Jenny, Stephen, Jill and Jilly (Jenny's cousin). We ordered the drinks and I asked for a menu. Menu? No menu. I explained that we were famished and asked if there was anything she could rustle up.

'Toasties,' she said. 'Cheese toasties, cheese and tomato toasties, cheese and pickle toasties.'

'Excellent, we'll have toasties. Can we have four each? That's twenty-four toasties please and mix them up.'

We received the toasties over a period of hours. I think she only had a basic two-slice toastie-maker, and she kept peeping out of the kitchen, asking, 'How many have you had?'

'Sixteen.'

It was a memorable night and when everyone else had gone back to the boat, I was tempted to try a glass of 'Owd Tom', which was too thick to draw up the beer pipes and she had to go down to the cellar to pour from the barrel. Perfect end to a perfect day.

On another occasion, my daughter Jill dropped her ring into the canal as she was helping to moor us up outside The Crawford Arms at Red Rock, which is Standish/Blackrod way. She was upset and wanted me to get into the water and find it. It was November, it was cold, and the canal is not the cleanest around there. It was obvious that I should at least try, but what, seriously, were the odds of finding a small ring in the canal? I once knocked the boat's chimney off on a low bridge on the Llangollen canal and it was hard enough finding that. I remember standing in the canal for almost an hour searching for that chimney whilst other boats chugged past. There I was, chest-high in water, trying to appear nonchalant.

When Jill's ring fell in, Kay suggested that I get into a bin liner before entering the icy water (I'm pretty sure she didn't do physics at school as she seemed to understand little about water pressure). To please her, I got in the bin bag and lowered myself in the canal. The bin bag, of course, collapsed immediately, and I discarded it as I stood in the murky water.

We tried to calculate where the ring had fallen, but this was difficult because there's a lot of toing and froing during mooring. I had taken my shoes and socks off, risking listeria in order to feel around on the bottom of the canal – urghhhhh, there is so much shit in here – but I found the ring straight away! How the hell did that happen? Unbelievable. It was a sign of our good fortune during those years – some of the happiest of my life.

Spikey and Sykey

AN 'INTAGLIO' IS the opposite of a 'cameo'. It was also the name of the vocal duo that Sean and Harry put together after the success of the *Laser Train Revue*, in order to write and perform their own compositions. They were, in time, very good indeed and released a couple of excellent CDs. However, in those early days, they didn't have enough material to perform a full evening's entertainment, so they asked me and Rick if we fancied supporting them with some comedy sketches – and we did!

First things first, though: we needed a name for our comedy pairing for the posters and tickets. As people sometimes called me 'Spikey' (because of my hair) and because Rick's surname was 'Sykes' (and he was a bit mad), we came up with 'Spikey and Sykey'.

We wrote a routine about two Government Humour Inspectors who had travelled north to undertake a survey of Northern folk and their innate sense of humour, with the aim of getting to the bottom of how they kept smiling and laughing – no matter what shit Thatcher's government dumped on them. In the South, people were worrying about whether your glass was half full or empty, whereas in the North we just assumed your glass was too big. Get a smaller glass. We dressed in trench coats and wore dark glasses and were very much like Hale and Pace, without ever having seen the jolly fat blokes. We carried clipboards and ran through the various categories of humour in a very straight-faced, deadpan manner, ticking off the audience response to our presentation of slapstick, jokes, funny songs, observations, etc.

It sort of worked with the right audience. It wasn't a bad routine at all for the time, and quite a departure from the usual comedy double acts working in the North in that era. We also wrote a routine about two children's TV presenters reading a Dr Seuss-like poem to children, which was packed with innuendo about a bear in the forest having shit stuck to his fur every time he went to the toilet (or 'pit', as it was – which rhymes with 'shit', obviously).

Another sketch was about 'Mr Memory' (Rick), the man who never forgets, and his new routine, which involved his escape from the 'Trunk of Death' (which – ha, ha! – of course he'd forgotten to get in). As I revealed the trunk with a flourish and gave his escape the big build-up, banging on the sides and shouting, 'Mr Memory? Are you ready?' Rick wandered on behind me without his trousers, announcing himself as 'Mr Memory, the man who never ...' You get the picture. I asked him why he wasn't in the trunk, 'What trunk?' he replied, and on it went. You'll have to take my word that it was very funny. Rick was an excellent comedian and looked the part, very tall and thin, with great delivery.

There were two gigs with Intaglio; the second was at Golcar British Legion Club. Golcar is a small town near Huddersfield, Yorkshire, which boasts not only a British Legion Club, but also a collection of radio masts on the tallest hill in the area. I mention this because quite often the PA system in the club picked up random transmissions, which was very unsettling. If you can imagine Spikey and Sykey wowing the audience as stern Government Comedy Inspectors ... interrupted regularly by taxi transmissions: 'Anyone mobile in Halifax?'

Both gigs went remarkably well and we were encouraged to continue. We sought advice from a theatrical agency in Westhoughton, near Bolton, which was called 'Chance Promotions' because it was managed by husband-and-wife team Trevor and Brenda. (I personally wasn't convinced that this was a great name for an agency, as I imagined the slogan: 'Need an act? Take a Chance.') They came to see us and saw some promise: they suggested we perform at a club agents' showcase night and also arranged for us to do an open spot at the Comedy Store in London!

We did the audition showcase for Creeme Entertainments, the largest bookers for working men's and social clubs in the North of England, at Breightmet Labour Club a few weeks later – and we died on our arses. This wasn't the comedy of the local clubs. Where were the gags? Didn't we have a fat mother-in-law? Didn't either of us know a dumb Irishman? Had a bloke with a crocodile never walked into our pub? I think Creeme appreciated what we were trying to do, but they absolutely could not book us into the clubs.

Ah well, fair enough, it doesn't matter anyway – because we're off to London on Saturday to perform at the world-famous Comedy Store! (Believe it or not, this made the local paper: 'Bolton Duo Make the Big Time' or something like.)

We travelled down to London with a few friends and family, and had also arranged for friends who lived in and around London to get down there to witness the birth of a contemporary Morecambe and Wise. Lambs to the slaughter. We had no idea of the world of 'alternative' comedy; we didn't have our fingers on the pulse of contemporary comedy; in fact, we couldn't find a pulse in Bolton in 1986.

We got to the 'Store' on Leicester Square early on Saturday afternoon – way too early, obviously, but in our excitement we hadn't really established what might be required of us, when we would be performing, how a comedy club worked, etc. Kim Kinney, the manager and a lovely fella, let us put our Government Inspector 'costumes' in the dressing room and informed us that we wouldn't be appearing until the very end of the late show.

We were puzzled: 'late' show; there were two shows? We had seen the show advertised at 8 p.m. and assumed that not only would we be on that show, but that we'd also be performing early as we were the new boys. Idiots! Rule number one – do your homework. Here we were, excited, apprehensive and ready to go at three o'clock in the afternoon … and we would be onstage at what time approximately, Kim? Two a.m? That's a joke, right? Nope, no joke: we had eleven hours to wait; eleven hours in which to conserve our nervous excitement and evacuate our bowels completely.

We asked if we could watch the early show in preparation for our big night and Kim kindly agreed, and so we sat in the dressing room before the show with the most amazing line-up. Paul Merton, Kit Hollerbach, Punt and Dennis and the brilliant John Sparkes. We were amazed and impressed at how relaxed everyone was backstage. We could hear the buzz of the expectant crowd getting louder and louder – and there was John Sparkes reading the paper!

The show was fantastic and blew us away. It dented our confidence a bit. Mind, it was only a bit, because we'd polished our act over the weeks and were confident it would work.

The late show beckoned and nerves began to jangle. In later years, when the 'Store' had moved round the corner, 'open spots' would perform in both shows just after the interval, to give them the best chance to impress, but in 1986 and certainly on this night we went on at the end after this amazing line-up.

There was one other open spot that night: a girl whose name I forget, but who I often think about and wonder if she continued in comedy. She was on before us and she lasted about three minutes before the audience shot her down and she started crying. We panicked then because, do you know what? She wasn't that bad, in fact quite good for a newcomer, but by now it had become glaringly apparent that the destroying of open spots was an integral part of the Comedy Store's Saturday night show.

The compère, Ronnie Golden, introduced us with a certain amount of uncalled-for disdain and then we were on. I looked out and saw all our friends and family sat watching us, their faces exhibiting a mixture of apprehension, fear and concern. We started off reasonably well, but then the crowd smelled fear and began to heckle and jeer. Rick whispered, 'Let's get off,' but I wouldn't. We'd come all this way, we'd waited eleven hours to do our routine and we were going to finish it.

We didn't finish it – because the crowd got louder and louder, and the boos and jeers and offensive heckles saw us off a few minutes later. Ronnie Golden took us off with a few more barbed comments. We sat shell-shocked in the dressing room, worried mostly about facing our friends and family, who had witnessed our humiliation. Kim Kinney said some nice things, gave some constructive criticism and encouraged us to regroup and return.

Looking back now, I think that we knew then that we never would. That wasn't to say that we were giving up, though; rather, we had to find a different audience for our comedy. We decided to try to move forward. We'd been impressed by the acts at the Comedy Store, so we had a rethink about all our routines and tried to rewrite and refresh them, having been hugely influenced by the acts we'd seen on that night. We knew that we were never going to get much work in the working men's clubs, and we weren't aware of any northern 'alternative' comedy clubs, so we had to find another outlet.

My biggest influences in comedy were what you might call the folk-club comedians. Comics who had started out singing folk songs, whose stories were told in between numbers; but then those stories about their own life experiences had sort of taken over and become the main part of the act. Each region seemed to have its own folk-club comic: Scotland of course had the 'King' in Billy Connolly; Wales had the brilliant Max Boyce; the Midlands had Fred Wedlock; and in Lancashire we had Mike Harding, Bernard Wrigley (The Bolton Bullfrog), The Houghton Weavers with Norman Prince, and my particular favourite, Bob Williamson, who given the right breaks both on and offstage could and should have been a major player.

Inspired by these influences, I suggested to Rick that we give the folk clubs a shot; there wouldn't be any money in it, but it would help to sharpen the act, and so he agreed. As it turned out, because we didn't actually sing any folk songs per se, most clubs were not interested, but a couple were – and God bless the good people at Hindley Folk Club, who let us try our new and improved routines and encouraged us immensely.

We also did the odd talent show – partly to try to win a bit of cash, but mainly to work the act and try out new routines – but it soon became clear that most competitions were heavily 'biased', shall we say, in favour of the local talent. We once did a talent show at The City in Bolton, which is a smallish pub between Chorley Old Road and Church Road. The money on offer was only about £25 for the heat and £200 for the final, but we decided to give it a go. We were drawn second of the six acts and actually did really well and had high hopes of progressing to the final after seeing all bar one of the acts afterwards.

What we didn't know then was that the favourite act, the one they wanted to win, always goes on last. When we heard the MC announce 'Jimmy B from Elgin Street', we weren't particularly perturbed, even though he got a surprisingly loud cheer from the crowd. Then the MC pushed Jimmy onstage in a wheelchair. He was dressed as Elvis. Rick and I exchanged a resigned look before Jimmy started singing 'The Battle Hymn of the Republic' in the style of the King. By the time he got to 'Glory, glory Hallelujah', I was halfway back to Chorley.

The worst gig we ever did was at a London club in Mayfair that Trevor booked us into. I'd written a routine in which Rick and I played two male penguins. One male penguin was instructing the other in penguin-mating behaviour. It was all based on fact, but confused by another obvious fact: all penguins look the same. The mating routine, should you be interested, involves the male penguin picking up a pebble and laying it at the feet of a lady penguin. Should she be interested, she extends her neck heavenwards and emits a piercing cry, to which the male responds by doing the same. They then intertwine necks and repeat this call of the wild.

In the routine, one penguin (me) explains all this to other (Rick), who thinks about it for a while and then asks the question, 'What if it turns out to be a male?' to which the answer is: 'He pecks your bleedin' head in.'

We decided to include the sketch for the club date and thought – bizarrely – that we should have penguin costumes made specially, which we did, complete with big yellow swimming flippers. *Why*?! Why couldn't we simply have done it in conversation as ourselves? Why did we have to act it out?!

So we turn up at this London club in Mayfair and the manager shows us into the dressing room/storeroom and asks us what we need on stage. So we say, just two microphones please, and he stares at us and says, 'Why do you need microphones?' And we explain that we are comedians and he pulls this face. A sort of exasperated, raised-eyebrows look of comical surprise ... and we know then that it is going to be awful.

He disappears for a few minutes and then comes back to announce that there is only one microphone and that is the DJ's and it will just about stretch to the performance space, but we'll have to hold it because they don't have a stand. Did I say 'awful'? He said the speciality performance (us) usually went down well and that last week they had had a bloke who came out of a coffin, pierced himself with nails and ate glass. When we said that we would appear as two penguins, he just stared.

The rest of the night is a bit of a blur. The DJ announced us, we waddled on in full penguin outfits, I took the microphone from him and we made our way to just short of the stage, the extent of the lead. En route, I tripped over when Rick stood on one of my flippers. I looked out to the audience, who were stood on the various levels of the nightclub, and I realized that most of the assembled crowd were Arabs. Would they get penguin-based comedy? Nope, long shot when you think about it. Needless to say, the routine flagged. Afterwards, we got changed and sneaked out – luckily nobody recognized us without the beaks and flippers.

All was not lost, though, because Trevor Chance still believed in us, God bless him. He got us an audition for the new series of *New Faces* in 1987, which was to be hosted by Marti Caine. We auditioned with our Government Inspector routine. The producer, Richard Holloway, seemed to like it, but we stuck out like a sore thumb against all the other club-based entertainers.

A couple of weeks later, I took a phone call at work in Haematology. Trevor told me that they wanted us and not only that, they wanted us on both the non-broadcast pilot show and the first show of the series, both to be recorded at the fab Birmingham Hippodrome.

Then we did something incredibly stupid. Instead of playing it safe with our strongest routine, we took bad advice from various sources, who suggested that we should write a new routine which was more 'TV-friendly'.

In the excitement of the moment and bowing to far more experienced performers than ourselves, we were convinced. We changed the act. I'd had an idea that I'd been working on about a top Russian comedy double act, who were on a cultural exchange visit (so that while Little and Large were playing Vladivostock Conservative Club, they were over here performing). The comedy would arise from their poor grasp of English, their Russia-based jokes about potatoes and gulags, and their appearance. I also added a 'catchphrase'-type of thing, where at the end of every joke, they did a Cossack dance on their haunches while singing 'Hava Nagila'.

And do you know what, that's not a bad idea, and if we'd just had time to perform the bloody thing live a few times before showcasing it on national television (!), it could have gone down big.

Now add into the mix the bizarrely ill-judged transformation of the opening gag at the suggestion of the show's script editor ... and we have an accident waiting to happen. The original idea was that I would go onstage first and set the scene, worrying about where my partner had got to. Then Rick wanders on with a kettle on his head and I say in a dodgy Russian accent, 'Where have you been, Igor?' and Rick says, 'Before you are leaving the dressing room, you say, "Put kettle on."' Look, alright, I know! But it would have got a laugh for the visual, trust me.

However, this script editor suggests that a better 'misunderstanding' would be if Igor had heard me ask him to put the 'cattle' on, and, if we sourced a pantomime cow, he could carry that onstage for a bigger laugh. We were persuaded and so Rick sauntered onstage with this huge cow draped around his neck. 'You say, "Put cattle on!"' – not as funny as 'kettle', right?

To make matters worse – oh yes, they can get worse – the judges that night were Barry Cryer, Bonnie Langford and the acerbic Nina Myskow, and somebody (it might even have been me, I don't remember) suggested that I ask Igor about the cow he's carrying: 'Who is this?' And Rick replies, 'Is Nina,' and I go, 'Nina?' and he says, 'Ya, Nina MysCOW.'

We did the gag, it got a muted laugh from the audience and a sneering grin from Nina and then ... then ... instead of ditching the cow and making some clever comedy comment, Rick kept it on for the entire routine. Why didn't anyone suggest we dump the cow into the orchestra pit? That would have been funny. Or on the stupid script editor's head, maybe?

We did the routine and, to be fair, Barry Cryer was very positive, Bonnie didn't 'get' it at all and Nina was quite critical, but we got away with it. We didn't come last – but we were beaten by a whippet juggler from Todmorden and a Latvian plumber who played 'I've got sixpence, jolly jolly sixpence' on a selection of radiators. There was also a good impressionist, George Marshall, on the bill and a couple of decent girl vocalists. A Scottish piano player won it, and a three-girl a capella group who sang 'Mr Sandman' finished last. So not a total disaster. Just sit back and wait for more TV, radio and theatrical impresarios to come knocking.

Nobody knocked. Not even opportunity. By now, Rick was getting understandably disillusioned. He even broke his arm on purpose once to get out of a booking at a working men's club (he didn't, obviously, but I thought he might have).

As a last resort, I entered us into a talent contest in Scarborough, which had a first prize of £750! But as the day of the heat approached, Rick said he didn't want to trail all that way across the country for a talent competition, and so I said I would go and do it on my own and he said okay. And that was that. R.I.P. Spikey and Sykey.

It's Raining Dogs

KAY HAD A dog, a cocker spaniel called Lacey, and two Siamese cats when I first moved in. I'd always wanted a dog and we agreed that I could get one from Bolton Destitute Animal Centre; it would be great for us to rescue a dog and it would be company for Lacey.

We decided that we would let fate decree which dog we rescued by offering a home to the next dog due to be put down at the centre (they don't put healthy dogs down now, but they did then). I was on call at the hospital on the Saturday night and I said I'd pop into the centre on my way in. I nipped in and asked if I could home the next dog to be 'destroyed' – what an awful description. They told me that they had an Alsatian cross due to be euthanized on the Monday and I said I'd have her. They asked if I wanted to see her and I said no, I was late for work, I'd pop in first thing Monday.

We picked up 'Cagney' (obviously) on the Monday and she was a wonderful dog. I cannot believe or understand how anyone could have allowed her to be killed. We had Cagney for about fourteen years and she was just about the best dog that you could ever wish for. Loyal and trusting, loving and always playful, with the most perfect temperament with people and other dogs.

When they saw Cagney, Kay's mum and dad decided that they'd quite like a dog from the shelter too, so we took them down not long after and they chose 'Kim', a 'Cagney' lookalike, but not as dark and with floppy ears. While we were down at the shelter, I spotted a beautiful Rottweiler-cross puppy and Kay saw a small, black, timid spaniel-cross, which a bloke who worked there called the 'Iffy' spaniel because she had attacked him! We mentioned the puppy to Jenny, who immediately wanted her, so we went back to collect her ... but came away with two dogs because Kay couldn't leave the 'Iffy' spaniel cowering and shaking in the cage. The Rotty puppy was named 'Bo'; the spaniel was 'Lucy', and she was probably Kay's favourite and most loved dog of the twenty-odd we re-homed over the next twenty years.

I don't really have time or space to tell you about all the wonderful dogs we've re-homed over the years. They were all great characters and many had come through terrible experiences at the hands of their human owners with immense courage and resilience. They all were quickly accepted by the resident 'pack', who seemed to sense their history of abuse and neglect and welcomed them into the house and the gang. The most we had at one time was nine and they all lived in perfect harmony, which always amazed me considering their individual histories and experiences.

One of our dogs was Rosie, a cairn terrier-cross who was full of fun. She was probably the friendliest, most gregarious dog we had. When we took her out and about and down the pub, we could let her off the lead and she'd wander around, making friends of everyone she met.

She was also very intelligent and loved soft toys to 'savage' and throw about. In fact, she had this uncanny, almost psychic power, you might say, of knowing when we'd bought her a soft toy from the market. We might struggle into the house, laden down with shopping bags from a variety of outlets, but she absolutely knew if we had a toy for her in there and went wild with joy. How could she know?

We were all in the pub one lovely summer's day; Rosie had made herself at home under the bench seating beneath us. The pub was full and a young couple came in with a toddler in a pushchair and made their way into the back lounge. Rosie decided to go for a wander. As usual, we heard a lot of 'Aws' and 'Ahs' as she made her rounds.

About half an hour later, the young mother appeared from the back lounge and started looking around on the floor. Someone asked her if she'd lost anything and she said that her little girl must have dropped her teddy bear somewhere between the car and their table in the pub. Kay and I exchanged a look of dread.

Once the search had been called off, we slowly bent down to look under the bench – and there was Rosie, with the remains of what was once a teddy bear. She saw us, wagged her tail madly, and dropped a little furry arm at our feet. I quickly kicked it back under the bench, out of sight.

Sammy, meanwhile, was a beautiful bearded collie – a pedigree, probably, who'd been on the streets for months, years maybe. He was terribly malnourished, partially sighted and his back legs were so weak he could hardly stand when we got him. He'd been found after a storm under a pile of cardboard boxes, unable to walk. The staff at the shelter asked us if we'd take him for the last couple of months that they assessed he would live.

We took him and bathed him and groomed him and he was so handsome. He lived for two years and had the best time running with the girls (he was the only boy at the time). I say running 'with', but in practice this was running 'after' the girls. They would chase the stick or ball and he'd set off with them, but only catch them up when they were on the way back.

His back legs went after two years and we had to carry him everywhere and take him outside for his toilet. It was heartbreaking because he deserved longer. His brain was still active, his eyes still bright, but he couldn't walk. We thought about getting a contraption to put him in with wheels on the back, but we decided that this was just prolonging the inevitable by only a matter of weeks.

We arranged for the vet to come round the following morning and put him to sleep on his favourite bed. This is something we always did when the time came; we couldn't take our dogs into the vets at the end of their lives and leave them there, we owed them so much more than that. We had to sit and stroke them and talk to them as the injection was administered, so that the last thing they heard and remembered were our words of comfort and praise: 'Good girl, Lucy.' 'Good boy, Sammy.'

It always broke my heart when they died. Whether we'd had them for a matter of months or for seventeen years, they all touched our lives. They all had their own traumatic back story and they all deserved happiness and peace in their old age – and that's what we tried to give them. When you only take old dogs on, as we did, you also have to take on the accompanying heartache.

Kay was probably touched the most by Pippa. Pippa was a miniature Yorkie who had been fished out of a river in a sack with her brother. She was about three at the time and we took her on from Pet Rehome. She lived with us for over twelve years, but she never fully got over her experience.

Pippa was Kay's lap dog, and replaced Lucy to a large degree. She was a great little dog with the heart of a lion, who loved to run on the beach and adored the wind in her fur. She started to go blind and we spent thousands trying to save the sight in her one good eye. But the operation was really traumatic and she went into kidney failure and we had to let her go. We still blame ourselves a little, but she was an old dog, and when she went blind, she couldn't run on the beach anymore because she wouldn't leave our side.

Kay has Pippa's photo as a screensaver on her PC and phone. She was a special dog – but then they all were, in one way or another.

It's fair to say that I'm much more a dog than a cat person – although I did once take in a ginger tom from Feline Rescue. I don't know if you've heard about Feline Rescue, but they do a fantastic job: my particular cat had been pot-holing in Derbyshire without the appropriate safety equipment, there had been a flash flood and he was trapped underground, and Feline Rescue had gone in, with scant regard for the risks involved, got to him and brought him out.

They were a bit pissed off with him, actually, because apparently it was only two weeks before that they'd had to helicopter him off Snowdonia when he'd been caught in a blizzard wearing a light anorak and pumps. (Pumps! For climbing a mountain! But that's cats for you: just because they've got nine lives, they get a tad blasé about health-and-safety and risk assessments, and weather forecasts in particular.)

A Night at the Opera

THOUGH RICK HAD pulled out of the talent contest with the first prize of £750, I was still up for giving it my best shot. And so it was that I found myself travelling to Scarborough for my first ever solo stand-up gig.

The talent contest was held at the Opera House, Scarborough. The heats were held in the Circle Bar, and the Grand Final in the main theatre. It was an annual big deal in Scarborough and I turned up for my heat to find the bar packed for the show. I explained that it was just 'Dave Spikey' tonight, and the organizers were fine with that.

I had written and rehearsed my ten minutes in the days leading up to the heat. I'd decided to perform it as a character rather than straightforward stand-up, which to be honest scared me. I invented a vulnerable, put-upon, loser-type character and wore a balaclava and big glasses. I really didn't know what to expect, but I remember that I wasn't really nervous and I didn't know why.

So I went on, did my ten minutes, got a great reaction and came off, both relieved and exhilarated. And I won the heat! I was through to the semi-final, scheduled for two weeks hence, with the grand final only three days after that on a Sunday night. I met some lovely people on that heat night: wonderful Pat Helme and her lovely daughter Janet, who sort of took me under their wings and with whom I'm still in contact. Having their support meant so much at the time and has done ever since.

For the semi-final, Kay and I decided to take our newly acquired VW camper van and stay on a campsite. We were keen to explore the fantastic coast around there and take the dogs. We stayed on a campsite near Robin Hood's Bay, which has to be one of the most beautiful areas of the country. I did the semi-final on the Thursday, which was a new ten minutes specially written – and I won!

The final was only a couple of nights away so we stayed and explored some more and walked the dogs for hours in the pouring rain, before all cramming into the camper van at night. It was a great few days. I performed in the final on the Sunday to a packed house at the Opera House, which sadly is no longer there. I can't remember who else was on, it was all an excited blur because I won it! I won £750! I thought, 'I'm a natural, this comedy lark is a piece of piss.' And for a while it was.

I planned a similar campaign for the country's biggest talent show: 'Stairway to the Stars' at the Riviera Centre, Torquay. It was a long trek to the south Devon coast, but the first prize was £1,000. I went down for the heat and opened with a gag about Quasimodo, 'Look, once and for all, I haven't got your ball!' which went big (!) and then I put on half a pair of spectacles, which got a laugh, which increased when I delivered, 'Specsavers – I only get half an hour for my dinner' (if you remember, their slogan at the time was 'a pair of glasses in one hour').

I won the heat and drove the long haul home, elated. I won the semi-final too, a week or so later, and returned for the final later in the month. Kay came with me and we treated ourselves to a nice hotel with a swimming pool!

The place was rammed on the night and the judging panel impressive: Dora Bryan, Buster Merryfield, Larry Grayson and – ohmigod! Who's that on the end? It's Nina MysCOW! Will she remember the Russians?

She didn't and I won the final. I won £1,000 and drank to the early hours, listening in awe to the showbiz stories of Larry Grayson. What a great man he was.

Club Nights

AFTER MY TRIUMPH, I returned home, now a conquering hero in my mind. Then it dawned on me that I had the same problem that had plagued Spikey and Sykey. Where was I to perform? I reluctantly decided that the only route for me to progress was the working men's clubs; I'd have to tailor the act a great deal, but it was easier doing that alone than with the largely scripted routines of the double act.

Back to the Sunday agents' showcases. It never occurred to me at the time, naive fool that I am, why these agents booked their acts direct from a showcase, rather than through a reputable agency. It's obvious looking back that these guys ran small, rough, poxy little clubs, who wanted to pay the least amount of money for their acts. Showcases were a perfect arena for them because these were acts either just starting out or unwanted by agencies, and who were therefore desperate for work. I appeared in a few of these showcases and they were depressing experiences. I got a few bookings, but most of them were dreadful, demoralizing events.

I turned up at Blackburn Railwayman's Club on a Saturday night to be greeted with disdain by the doorman, who enquired, 'Where do you think you're going?' I said I was the 'turn' and he asked me what I did. I told him that I was a comedian and he said, 'Go on then, change colour,' which, I have to say, made me laugh. That soon stopped when he said, 'We don't get comedians here, this lot don't like them. They like singers and git-vocs [guitar-vocalists].'

I made my way despondently to the dressing room, the walls adorned by many of the stars of clubland; most of them strangely only having a letter as a surname: 'Johnny B', 'Jackie G'. I imagine that this is for security reasons – social security (boom boom). I once got hold of the North-West Concert Secretaries' monthly programme, which listed all the acts due on at all the local clubs, and I managed to get all the way through the alphabet with artistes' names. From the 'A Train' through 'Susie Q' to 'Billy Z'.

The concert secretary limped into my dressing room and announced with no warmth or friendliness – 'This is how it works. You go on at eight o'clock, do forty-five minutes, then you're off and it's supper, then bingo, and then you go back on to do your dance spot.' I told him I was a comedian and so didn't have a 'dance spot'. He said he didn't care, they always had a dance spot; I had to do one. Then he left.

I went on at eight o'clock and died on my arse. They didn't heckle, they didn't smile, they simply ignored me. I worked away for forty-five minutes and now and then a few people would turn away from their noisy conversations and look towards the stage with an expression that seemed to say, 'Is he still here?'

In the dressing room, the concert secretary was unhappy. 'What was that all about?'

I apologized and said that whoever had booked me had got it wrong and that I wasn't the right sort of comedian for this club. I offered to leave – without payment, just go – but he wasn't having any of that. I had to go on and do my dance spot, didn't I?

As I waited for what seemed an eternity for the pie and peas to be served and the bingo to end, I seriously contemplated escaping. There was no way out through the club because they'd see me, but I could see my car in the car park and I could climb out of the window. I didn't run, though; my pride got the better of me and so I went back on for my dance spot and did the same forty-five minutes I'd done before and they didn't notice because they didn't listen the first time. Nobody danced and they all ignored me again.

I once did a club where the concert secretary went on before me to make an announcement about a club member who had died suddenly. He requested a minute's silence – then introduced me!

I had another who said ...

Concert Sec: Ladies and gentlemen, we have had numerous complaints about the quality of acts that we have been putting on recently. People are saying that they are not of the required standard and that this club deserves better acts; acts of a higher calibre. I want to assure you that we have had a meeting of the committee and at that meeting, we agreed that the recent acts have not met the standard required and so we have decided that, in future, all acts will be booked through a reputable agent. (*Cheers from the audience.*)
So, that's from next week, ladies and gentlemen, but for tonight will you welcome Dave Spikey!

On another occasion I witnessed this extraordinary announcement:

Concert Sec: Ladies and gentlemen, we on the committee have received allegations that the finances of the club are being mismanaged, that the standard of acts has declined, that the quality of the catering has become unsatisfactory and that the ale isn't as good as it used to be. Now, I have to say that we have been hurt by these allegations; the committee feel they do a difficult job under the financial constraints, and allegations such as these are unhelpful. So I have called an extraordinary meeting of the members for Tuesday night and I want all the Alligators to attend in person.

I somehow got a booking for a corporate event in Wigan. It was the Brickmakers' and Concrete Fabricators' Awards night (next stop the BAFTAs). It was an all-male affair and I was due to go on after the final award – the Golden Trowel or something – and do my forty-minute set. It was a very subdued affair, which didn't augur well because the building industry had declined over the previous year and many of those present had been hit hard.

The awards went okay and then it was time for the Golden Trowel and emotions were running high. The chap who won it had been a brickmaker or concrete fabricator, I forget which, for thirty-odd years, and had just gone bust because of the downturn in demand. The chairman gave him his award and the bloke, let's call him Jim, made an emotional acceptance speech, during which I had to bite my lip until it bled in order to stop laughing. It went something like this.

Jim: I never meant to get into bricks. I fell into bricks. And bricks get in your blood. If you cut me in half, you'd find 'Accrington' written all the way through me. And, as you all know, I've been in bricks all my life until this year when I went . . .

(*Begins to cry a little. Stops to compose himself. Rousing support from the audience – 'Come on, Jim!'*)

. . . bust. This is a great honour for me and I'll treasure this forever because I don't think there's any way I can recover from this setback. I don't think I'll ever make another . . .

(*Cries again – audience crying too now, floods of tears – 'Good man, Jim.'*)

. . . brick. Who'd have thought it would have come to this, lads?

(*Not a dry eye in the place.*)

Thanks a million, I love you guys.

(*'We love you' echoes back, interrupted with sobs as he retakes his place at the table.*)

Chairman: Ladies and gentlemen – Dave Spikey!

(*I do my set to two hundred crying men. It goes slightly better than expected.*)

Animal Farm

A T HOME, IT became apparent that if we were to continue to increase our rescued animal intake, we should move to a house with a bit of land or a really big garden, and so we started to look in and around the Bolton area. We quickly realized that we couldn't afford anything so big in the immediate vicinity and would have to cast our net wider.

We got a map of Lancashire and drew a circle to include all areas within a twenty-mile radius of Bolton General Hospital. With our search area widened, I spotted a farmhouse that was up for auction in a place called Charnock Richard, the home of the 'Camelot' theme park, which boasted funfair, jousting and a show from Mad Edgar, the court jester, thrown in. (Mad Edgar was my very good friend Steve Royle, comedian and juggler extraordinaire, who should be a star.)

Kay was on call on the Saturday that the house was open for viewing, so I went to see it with my daughter Jill. We got there at the appointed time, but the house and grounds were deserted. After waiting for half an hour, we decided to explore. We tried the front door and it swung open with a creak like in all those horror films. We crept inside – like they do in all those horror films – to discover a weird arrangement of rooms and decor. The dining room and lounge downstairs were fairly traditional, but then we opened a door and found a really surprising gothic bathroom with sunken bath, all in dark marble and not quite finished off.

As neither of us had had a big axe implanted in our skull so far, we decided to push our luck and venture upstairs, where we found a long corridor with all the bedrooms off it to one side. We opened a couple of doors to find scruffy rooms in need of decoration, then opened the third door and there, in the bed, under the bedclothes was ... a body! The body groaned and moved and we stifled a scream and left, very quickly, and never went back.

On the way home, Jill suggested that we called into nearby Chorley to have a look at what the local estate agents had to offer because, if nothing else, we had discovered that it was a really lovely area. In the first estate agent's window, we saw an old stone house built in 1839 with a fifth of an acre of garden, which was well within our budget and situated in a nearby village. We asked for the details and the agent asked if we'd like to view it later in the afternoon. We said we would, he arranged it and an hour later we were walking up the small, private road towards the house.

Have you ever walked into a house and known immediately that you had to live there? That's what happened to me on that day. We had only seen the small, old, oak-beamed lounge and I absolutely knew and Jill agreed. The garden was a bit unkempt with the remains of a big aviary, but it had a mini orchard with various fruit trees, a massive Douglas fir and a few other big trees and numerous bushes. It was perfect.

We arranged to go back with Kay and Jenny the day after, and although Jenny loved it, Kay was less impressed – but I had to have it and it was three votes to one. I agreed that we should look around the area and meet a few locals before making a final decision, so we spent a couple of days doing this and realized that this was a dream location. Everyone we met was very warm and welcoming, the local pubs were very traditional and hubs of the local community, and our neighbours were brilliant; Ruth was a complete nutter and became an instant friend to Jenny, being as they were (and are) on the same wavelength – which is some way off the dial.

We bought the house and we've lived there for over twenty years now. Over time, we've ripped out nearly all the modernized aspects and tried to return the house to its original state, with flagged floors, beams, pine kitchen and a fantastic Lancashire range, which we discovered in a Preston junkyard. We luckily found someone who could reassemble and fit it, and even though it meant building a chimney and having a couple of missing pieces manufactured, it really was worth it. It's absolutely magnificent when the fire is roaring away in it and it acts like a giant radiator.

Having moved into our new house, we assessed the many changes we'd like to make. The garden was great, but the grass needed keeping down and neither of us are keen gardeners, so we thought that a rescued goat would be the ideal solution.

I went to Blackburn Auction Mart, a man on a mission. Kay wouldn't come as she thought it would be too distressing – and so it was. I saw a baby goat cowering in a corner, being poked and prodded by a group of men (I found out later that much of the 'meat' curry served up in restaurants is in fact baby goat). The goat was a brown-and-white baby boy goat – a Toggenberg – and he was a pretty boy, who had been taken away from his mother very early because they want the goat's milk to sell and boy goats 'aren't much good for anything'.

The kid was terrified and I had to rescue him. I paid twelve pounds for 'Billy' – come on, you don't get a choice of name – and I popped him in the back of the estate car and took him home. When I parked by the front door, Kay came out to see if I'd been successful, but he was so small that she didn't see him at first. Then he jumped up on his little back legs and she fell in love with him.

Because he was so young, he still had part of his umbilical cord attached. We had to go to ASDA to buy a baby feeding bottle and milk, and over the next few weeks we handfed him.

The dogs accepted him quickly and he ran and played with them. Throughout his long and happy life, I'm convinced he thought he was a dog. He was a handsome kid and we took him on holiday on the narrowboat with us; he'd run up and down the roof as we sailed. When we moored up for the night, you'd see people walking along the towpath, smiling at the sight of our three or four or five dogs … and then the smile turning to a quizzical look as they tried to identify the little brown and white 'dog' running with them.

When Billy was weaned off the baby milk, we introduced him to our lawn and said, 'Look, Billy! Lovely grass.'

Billy looked at it, unimpressed, and then looked around the garden at the many bushes and shrubs and trees and thought, 'Buffet! Good times.'

He never ate the grass, not once.

I'm Buzzing Now

I CONTINUED TO struggle to find gigs where I could improve and progress in comedy – until fate lent a hand. I saw in the *Bolton Evening News* that the Octagon Theatre was going to introduce comedy workshops in the studio on one Friday a month. Comedians and writers were invited down to chat about ideas and polish routines in the company of like-minded people. The course was the idea of the theatre director Romy Baskerville and was organized by a couple of local lads who had written stuff for the current (1991) hit series of *Spitting Image*.

I went down and discovered that these people were interested in the same comedy that I was. Comedy based on real life and the everyday things that happen to all of us. We chatted through various performers' ideas and routines and then we performed short five-minute sets. It went really well and I was immensely encouraged.

One of the participants was John Marshall, aka 'Agraman' – the human anagram – who performed his own poems. The poems provoked quite a mixed reaction, inducing groans and laughs in equal measure, with obtuse subject matter and awful rhymes, but I loved them for exactly that reason. John invited me down to a comedy club that he'd started in Chorlton, Manchester to perform an open spot. The club was called The Buzz and it was to become a legendary venue on the burgeoning so-called 'alternative' comedy scene.

I went down the following Thursday and took my son Stephen to see the North-West's first prestigious comedy club. I can't remember who was on that night, but I sat with Stephen on a table quite near the stage and lapped it up. Agraman was the compère, filling in between the acts with his unique brand of poetry, to which the crowd groaned along.

Then it was time for the open spot and I was introduced. Agraman gave me a nice build-up and then I was on. I did ten minutes to solid laughs and loved every minute of it, especially with Stephen being there, and when I came off, Agraman offered me a full paid spot a few weeks later.

I must have played The Buzz twenty or more times in those early years, and the venue and John hold a very special place in my heart. I had mainly good times there and propped up the bill when Lee Evans, Eddie Izzard, Jo Brand and many others appeared there.

Another pivotal moment at The Buzz came when I was performing at one of Agraman's special Comedy and Music nights. These were great nights and he always booked in the perfect mix of bands, singer-songwriters, poets, comedians and other performance artistes. I was on with a band called The Bosnians, who were being championed by a couple of local BBC radio presenters at the time. After the gig, the presenters approached me to take part in a variety show they were staging; I went on to appear in many shows for them all over the North-West.

The presenters were Eamonn O'Neil and Jimmy Wagg and they had (and have) an immensely popular Sunday morning show on BBC Greater Manchester Radio called the WOW show. Eamonn and Jimmy have been big supporters and good friends over the years, and in those early days they gave my comedy career a massive boost, with big shows at The Willows variety club, Tameside Hippodrome and, most famously, two shows in one day at Oldham Coliseum, where my son Steve was plucked out of the audience to play a guitar solo with the band to huge acclaim.

The WOW audiences were my sort of audience, and the gigs always sold out rapidly. I also guested on the radio show occasionally, which was a brilliant experience and a learning curve, as they also had a small studio audience and a largely phone-in-based chat show.

When Eamonn and Jimmy went on holiday, I filled in for a couple of weeks with co-presenters, most notably the legend that is Norman

Prince, ex-Houghton Weaver, a great presenter, funny man and all-round gent. I wanted to change the format a little bit because I didn't want us to be a poor man's WOW. I convinced the producer, after much persuasion, that it might be a good idea to include quizzes on the show that were actually impossible to do on the radio. She was sceptical, but I knew that the WOW audiences would go for this madness. I called this 'Quiz with a Difference' and sang a little jingle to that effect whilst accompanying myself on a kiddies xylophone.

The first week we did 'Name That Train', where I played a track from a sound-effects LP – and the phones never stopped ringing. Most callers played it for laughs, but as I'd hoped, a few took it seriously, which was even funnier.

'I think it's a Black 5 Class locomotive pulling the Settle to Carlisle express over the Ribblehead viaduct.'

Of course, I hadn't a clue what type of train it was or where it was going (how can you tell that from a snippet played on the radio?!).

Our main quiz, which required three contestants, was 'The Crossbow Challenge', in which callers aimed a crossbow held by me at a target in the studio – obviously this is impossible, but they went for it big time and we acted out the mayhem the game was supposedly causing in the studio. We also had 'What Happened Next?', where I played the recording of a 'South American' commentator excitedly commentating on a big football match and we stopped the commentary at a certain point. (My mate Rick provided the very dodgy soundtrack, screaming out random Spanish words: 'Santa Maria! San Miguel! *Patatas bravas!*' etc.) The callers queued up to provide the answers, which included a donkey running on the pitch and heading in the winning goal, and all sorts of other nonsense.

Another contest was 'Spot the Difference', where we acted out two almost identical scenes that I'd written for a murder mystery and then asked listeners to identify not only the three dialogue differences (easy enough), but also two scenery and costume changes.

I owe so much to Eamonn, Jimmy, the WOW listeners and the great Agraman, the human anagram. As a postscript, I once did a one-off comedy special with Agraman at Ronnie Scott's club in Birmingham –

and the crowd absolutely loved him. He went down massive and came offstage shell-shocked; he'd never had a reception like it. I reckon they recognized him as a true jazz poet. You know that old saying: 'He's a poet and doesn't know it.'

Compère and Contrast

I T WAS AROUND this time that I got a surprising opportunity by being in the right place at the right time. It was a Sunday night and Kay and I were literally putting our suitcases down after returning from a holiday when the telephone rang. Trevor Chance asked me if I could get to Blackpool in half an hour and I said, 'Just about, but why?' He explained that Cannon and Ball were playing the Opera House and needed a compère urgently and would I do it?

Would I? I loved Cannon and Ball; still do. Tommy is a perfect straight man and Bobby Ball is a comedy genius and until you see them live, you will not appreciate the breadth of his talent. And so it was that half an hour later I was stood in the wings of the Blackpool Opera House, being briefed by Stuart Littlewood, C&B's manager, with only three minutes to curtain.

He said, 'You go on and do ten minutes to warm them up, then introduce Shahid Malik, the illusionist; he'll do fifteen minutes, then you go back on and do five; then introduce Allan Stewart, he'll do fifteen, then you back on for another couple of minutes; then introduce Linda Lewis, Rock-a-doodle-doo and all that, then take her off and then it's the interval.'

Then the lights dimmed, the curtain went up and the band started, a proper good band I'm talking here, and they played a fantastic arrangement of 'Blow the House Down' by Living in a Box. (Every time I hear that song on the radio, it takes me right back to that precise moment in time.) Anyway, I had no time for nerves, I had no time to question, 'Why me, when I've only ever had a handful of paid gigs?'

(The answer to that was perfectly simple – I was the only comedian without a booking that night who lived within twenty-five miles of Blackpool.)

The stage manager announced my name and I was on – to a packed Blackpool Opera House, the largest theatre in Europe with every one of its 3,000 seats occupied!

I did a good ten minutes, got Shahid on, and then the rest of the half flew by and it was the interval before I knew it. I went back on at the top of the second half and did another ten, then brought Tommy and Bobby on and stood in the wings watching two of my comedy heroes. I must have done okay because I was asked back to host for the next three Sundays.

Stuart Littlewood rang me a few months later and asked if I would compère Cannon and Ball's big theatre tour – and of course I jumped at the chance. I toured with them on and off for three years, including a few dates in Northern Ireland during 'the Troubles', when we were escorted around by an army convoy. We stayed in a hotel in Belfast near the theatre and the windows had bulletproof glass and all the staff locked up at midnight and went home. A bomb went off some distance away while I was onstage one night, and I remember getting a laugh by saying, 'Bloody hell, everyone's a critic.'

In between the Cannon and Ball tours, I was asked by Stuart if I would tour with Max Boyce. I said, 'If you mean Max Boyce the Welsh comedy legend, I would be thrilled to tour with him,' and so I did. My dad and I were both massive Max Boyce fans and we'd watched all his TV shows and I'd bought his LPs, so to work with him was an amazing thrill.

The first show was at Bedworth Civic Hall, Coventry. Due to a traffic delay on the M6 (if I had a penny for every traffic delay on the M6 I've encountered over the years, I'd have about eight hundred and thirty-three pounds, give or take), I was late. I got changed quickly and Slim the tour manager ran through the show with me. There was only me and Max on the show, so I would go on and do half an hour, then it's the interval, then I'm back on for ten to warm them up and get Max on.

So Max's band strikes up and Slim announces me offstage, 'Ladies and gentlemen, will you please welcome Max's special guest, Mike Starkey.'

I stood looking at him, thinking, 'I thought you said there was only me and Max on,' and he's frantically gesticulating for me to get on, and I realize, 'He means *me*! *I'm* Mike Starkey,' and on I went.

At the start of the second half, I was waiting in the wings when Max appeared, resplendent in red blazer with a big Welsh RUFC rosette, white trousers, red-and-white scarf and, of course, his enormous leek. I was stuck for words, he was such a comedy hero, but Max was and is a wonderfully generous and encouraging performer. He praised me on my first-half performance, which thrilled me, and when I asked him how long a set did he want me to do before I introduced him, he just said, 'As long as you want; if you're enjoying it, don't worry about the time.' I did about ten minutes and got him on, and then stood and watched him from the wings, as I did most nights.

Max is a brilliant comedian, raconteur and singer/songwriter, and the only comic I know who uses the band to dramatize and complement his energetic routines, providing sound effects for thunder, wind and any other atmospheric conditions that will enhance his wonderful stories.

I toured with Max for a couple of years and loved every minute of it. I brought my mum and dad to see the show in Crewe, and Max arranged for them to have the Royal Box. He even had a good chat with them afterwards, when he was very flattering in his praise for me, telling my dad that I was a difficult act to follow. I wasn't, though – not for Max with his energy and passion and talent for comedy, and his skill for interweaving wonderfully evocative and poignant songs into his set. Top man.

I look back on this time with loads of affection and pride. Pride because I performed to vastly different audiences in that time and entertained them all very well, I hope. In one memorable twelve days, I appeared with Cannon and Ball on Sunday, Max Boyce on Tuesday, Jo Brand at my comedy club in Bolton on Wednesday, Jack Dee at The Buzz on Thursday, Lee Evans at a comedy night in Cheshire on Saturday and Eddie Izzard the following Thursday at The Buzz! Good times.

And the Winner Is . . .

S O, ON THE comedy scene, things were going well. A few more 'alternative' gigs opened in Manchester, and also through 'Laughing Gas', a comedy promoter in Chorley and Blackburn. I was picking up more and more gigs because the other big names in Manchester comedy, most notably Steve Coogan and John Thomson, had moved down to London to perform and voice *Spitting Image*.

But the really big name at the time was the brilliant Caroline Aherne, who was doing character comedy, first as Mitzi Goldberg, an oddball country singer, then as Sister Mary Immaculate, and then, of course, as Mrs Merton. I was lucky enough to work with Caroline a lot in the early years and she was always a brilliant performer. She had won the '*City Life* North-West Comedian of the Year' award in 1990 (an annual comedy contest which has become one of the most prestigious comedy prizes in the North-West of England) and Agraman encouraged me to enter it the following year.

The final was held at the Royal Northern College of Music and I went on last of eight, after the favourite, Dave Gorman. I won it, though it was not a popular win with the sponsors or the judges – but on the night I had a proper good one.

After my triumph, the next natural step for me was to get onto the London comedy circuit. Surely my win in the North-West Comedian of the Year competition would open some doors for me?

Oh no: one after the other, London promoters asked me the same question: 'The North-West what?' I couldn't get even open spots hardly anywhere – but then managed to secure one at the Comedy Café, about which I'd heard good things.

After working all day in the lab at the hospital, I drove, one Wednesday night, the three-and-a-half hours down to London, found the Comedy Café almost empty, and did my ten minutes to about twenty people. It went okay; no, it went good. I drove the three-and-a-half hours back home. I phoned the manager the day after, and he said that unfortunately he hadn't been able to get down to catch my act the night before, and could I 'pop' down again in a couple of weeks. It had to be done – and eventually I got a half-spot there, and months later a full spot.

The only person who gave me a half-spot over the phone without seeing me was a lovely girl called Monica, who ran the Meccano Club in Islington, and I went down and had a good gig. It was a great venue; all the top acts played there. I met Will Smith there – the comedian 'toff' Will Smith – who very kindly let me sleep on his couch for the night. It was an act of generosity that was representative of the comedy world at the time.

Other comics soon said I could use their names as recommendations for getting bookings. In the early days, John Moloney was very kind to me and I stayed with him and his missus at their flat in Balham. I started getting bookings at the best clubs – Banana Cabaret, Downstairs at the Kings Head, Ha Bloody Ha – and then Malcolm Hardee offered me a weekend at the legendary 'Up the Creek'. Although scared shitless by its reputation (it was the only comedy club I'd seen with bouncers!) and by his introduction – 'Next act now, all the way from Bolton, could be good, could be shit – Dave Spikey!' – I had a good gig. Malcolm was kind to me, as he was to so many up-and-coming acts, and his untimely death affected many of us deeply.

After a while, I decided I was ready to ask for an open spot at the best comedy club in the country, the club where so many years ago I'd suffered with Rick a death by a thousand heckles – the Comedy Store.

I did my first ten minutes on the late show (which could still be very intimidating, although they didn't throw you to the wolves at the end any more). I did okay and Don Ward, the owner, liked me and asked me back to do the early show, which also went well, and so I got a half-spot, which went even better – and then he asked me to bring my diary into his office in the interval. I did so and he gave me four weekends straight off.

I explained I couldn't do the Thursdays because of my hospital job and he was very accommodating and said I could just do the four shows on the Friday and Saturday (two shows each night).

I remember walking out of Don's office elated – I'd made it! I'd have my name on the listings outside the main entrance, alongside some of the country's best comedians; something I'd wished for for so long.

Bertie and the Chicks

KAY AND I stopped eating meat about twenty years ago, after we got stuck for twenty minutes on our way to work in a traffic jam, next to a lorry transporting battery chickens on their last journey. By the time we got to the hospital, we were vegetarian; and by the end of the day, they were mercifully dead.

When I say 'vegetarian', that's not strictly true: it didn't just suddenly happen; we had to wean ourselves off fish and seafood. During the next year, we worked our way down the evolutionary scale, until the momentous day when we ceased eating molluscs and threw ourselves off into the abyss of vegetarianism.

I have been veggie ever since, with the very occasional lapse early days, so that would be over twenty years now. I don't know why it took me so long to realize that this was the way for me because I've always loved animals and I consider myself a kind, caring, compassionate and fair person. It suddenly dawned on me that there is something terribly obscene about torturing and slaughtering a beautiful sentient creature in order that I might have a nice meal, which I will have forgotten about a couple of hours later, and yet for which an animal had to die, give up its precious life. Because life is precious and all of us animals of this planet have one thing in common, and that is the instinct for survival and the long, happy and healthy life that should go with it.

So, rant over, I suppose the natural progression for Kay and me was to take a more active role in animal welfare and rescue, which we did and have devoted a lot of time to ever since. We started off with chickens.

There's a bloke who comes in the local pub they call 'Chucky' (him, not the pub). They call him Chucky, not because he once used voodoo to transfer his soul into a doll, but because he runs a battery chicken 'farm'. So still evil, but a slightly different kind of evil.

I got some chickens from Chucky's place. He was sending a thousand off for slaughter and asked if I wanted some, and so I took two dozen and he charged me a pound each. A pound!

When I say, 'I took two dozen,' I understate the facts. What this actually involved was going up to the battery farm and choosing them. This wasn't an easy job. When you've got to choose twenty or so from thousands of sad, featherless, disorientated, beautiful animals bound for the great coop in the sky, it can be quite distressing. When I opened the first cage, one chicken made a desperate dash for freedom. Chucky dashed after it, caught it and roughly threw it back in the cage with a 'You don't want that scrawny thing'.

'On the contrary,' I said, 'that's one I do want, put it in the container.' I chose the others, trying hard not to make eye contact.

I took them home and released them into the garden. It was a wonderful moment; a moment that causes me to smile whenever I recall it. To these sad chickens, who until now had never had room to move about freely, the space was overwhelming; the grass under their feet alien after living their lives standing on cold wire mesh. The sight of these twenty-four chickens walking very deliberately, placing their feet down slowly and tentatively as they explored their new world, was funny and satisfying in equal measure.

Then the sun went down and the chickens froze where they stood (metaphorically, obviously – that's not how Birds Eye do it). This was because battery chickens never experience darkness; they are kept in constant light to stimulate the hormones responsible for high-yield egg production. Our chickens froze at each and every sunset until they eventually got the hang of night and day, which for me meant that for the first week or so, I had to go into the garden every evening with my torch and play 'hunt the chicken', pick them up and place them in the safety of their hut.

Watching their transformation over the next few months from featherless, bloodied, battered and tortured souls into happy, beautiful, proud and inquisitive birds was a heart-warming thing. Battery chickens are more intelligent than you would give them credit for, plus they know no fear; how could they?

So ... they wanted to play with the dogs and the cats. They wanted to ride on Billy's back and constantly followed me around as I undertook my gardening chores. It is surreally funny when stretching and turning after a session of weeding to find twenty-four chickens stood around you in a bunch, smiling as only chickens can (I've seen geese try and fail), as if to say, 'What are you doing? Can we help?' It is a constant delight to sit and watch the happy, funny chickens scratch in the soil, take a dust bath, sunbathe, or just mess about, dashing suddenly here and there for no apparent reason, genuinely seeming to be having a laugh.

What is especially lovely is that they care about each other. One of them, Lesley, broke her leg when Bertie fell in love with her and wanted her to have his babies. Who's Bertie? Where did he come from? I'll tell you ...

The Turkey Who Would Be King

IMAGINE MY SURPRISE when Kay announced that she wanted a turkey for Christmas. At first, the only explanation I could think of was that maybe she wanted the *Robin Hood: Men in Tights* DVD in her stocking. Not so, as it happens: she wanted a real turkey. A live one. One that we could release into the wilderness that is our back garden. I was overjoyed, not only because she had quelled my fear that she might be relapsing into meat-eating, but also because I wouldn't have to sit through Mel Brooks's filmic aberration.

I decided to go back to the Animal Auction in Blackburn – where I'd got Billy from – to see if I could buy a turkey, but when I got there, they were selling them in lots of six; and I couldn't have six!

Then I saw two small billy goats in the same pen that Billy had been in and went over to have a look at them. They were terrified by the prodding and poking of the surrounding crowd and it was quite upsetting. A man approached me and asked if I was going to buy them and when I said no, he seemed crestfallen. I asked him why he was so concerned and he told me that they were his pet goats that he had kept on his allotment. The council had compulsory-purchased the land and he had nowhere to keep them. He obviously loved the goats, which both looked about two years old, and he was in bits about them going for halal meat.

I bought the goats. I bid against a surprisingly angry crowd and got them both for twelve pounds. One was a white Sanaan goat and the other a beautiful Angora, and as I loaded them into the back of the car, a feeling of dread started to spread up my spine. My minor worry was that in the heat of the moment, I hadn't really considered the implications of introducing two more billy goats into a garden ruled by King Billy the big brown goat – could there be constant aggravation and bloodshed? My major worry was how Kay would react to me returning turkey-less but goat-ful – and would there be constant aggravation and bloodshed?

As I made my way to the driver's door, the man who had owned the goats before ran over to me – tears in his eyes, smile on his face – and gripped my hand with both of his. As he shook my hand, he blessed me for my kindness and compassion, let go his vice-like grip and walked away. I looked at my hand to find two pound coins he'd placed there.

Kay was at work until lunchtime, so I released Georgie and Henry (I went with the king theme) into the garden. Billy came to say hello, they sized each other up for a few minutes ... then went to eat a tree.

When Kay came home, things didn't go as smoothly. She went ballistic! I told her the story of what had happened: I showed her the two pound coins, I tugged at her heartstrings, I suggested that she could get an Angora jumper made from Georgie and she calmed down ... eventually. But she still wanted a turkey.

A few days later, I was driving past a farm that had a sign: 'Christmas Turkeys – Pick Your Own.' A stupid sign, I think you'll agree – how do you know which is yours? So I pulled in, saw the farmer and picked a turkey. He said, 'Shall I kill it and pluck it?' And I said, 'No, put it in the car' – but because it was a spur-of-the-moment thing, I had no room in the back, so 'Bertie', as he became known, sat in the passenger seat, and I drove him home. It was a long drive and Bertie wouldn't keep his seat belt on and insisted it was a left turn at 'Fredericks' ice cream, but, as I tried to explain, that takes you through Standish, which although it looks quicker on paper, has those lights near the 'Old Priests Hole' that take forever.

Kay loved Bertie and she released him into the garden with a 'Happy Christmas, Bertie!' He was greeted by twenty-four chickens, three goats, a sheep, eight dogs, six geese a-laying and what looked like some sort of duck in the pear tree.

I don't know if you know, but turkeys are bred in June to be killed at Christmas. Six months – not much of a life, but it meant that the young Bertie was no problem; he integrated well and was a lovable pet. No trouble to care for and in return provided endless hours of amusement for family and friends with his antics.

Then he got hormones. Puberty, chemistry, testosterone. An adolescent turkey is a different kettle of fish. Not your normal everyday kettle of fish at all; not cod, halibut. He'd grown very big and now looked enormous when he displayed. He was a magnificent sight with his feathers all puffed out and his massive tail-feathers fanned out.

He was also rather scary. My daughter's boyfriends all (all!) refused to go out to feed the goats and chicks because Bertie was now King of the garden. He would attack when you least expected it, usually from the rear, but I could see the signs, so when I turned round quickly in anticipation of an attack to discover him hurtling at me full pelt, he'd stop suddenly, almost bashful, and put his wings back down and stretch his neck and pretend to whistle with that 'What?' look on his face.

Then he fell in love with Lesley. I was having breakfast one morning when I noticed the chickens were all stood in a circle, surrounding an animated Bertie. When I went to investigate, it became clear that Bertie was making turkey love to Lesley, while all the other chickens stood round in a circle ('What's he doing?'). Lesley, meanwhile, looked around in desperation with a pleading look that said, 'If you could get him off me *now*, please?'

I chased Bertie away and discovered that he'd obviously broken Lesley's leg. He'd also pecked the back of her neck so badly that all the skin had become detached and rolled up her neck – exposing sinews and bone! I rushed the poor thing to the vet, who I thought would say, 'Brick it,' which is a technical term, but he didn't; he unfolded the skin and stitched it in place, then put a plaster cast on her broken leg. When I put her back in the run, away from Bertie's amorous advances, this lovely thing happened, which was that all the other chickens signed it, 'Keep your pecker up,' that sort of thing.

We decided that Bertie had to go. It wasn't fair on him, keeping him alone when he needed a lady wife – and it was becoming increasingly dangerous for the chickens. Luckily, through our animal welfare connections, we found a farm in Ormskirk that were desperate to find a stag turkey after theirs had recently died. As previously explained, mature turkeys are hard to find. We took Bertie up there and when we got him out of the car, the farmer and his wife could not believe their eyes. They said he was the biggest turkey they had ever seen and he was huge.

We left him with heavy hearts, but knowing it was the best thing for him. For years afterwards, they would send us pictures of Bertie with his many wives. What a great bloke he was.

Ungrateful Beasts

ONE DAY, WE got home from work to find that Billy, Henry and Georgie had eaten the kitchen. We had obviously arrived home earlier than expected and surprised the lads, who were just finishing off dessert.

The first thing we saw when we opened the kitchen door was Billy standing on a worktop eating the telephone. He stopped mid-chew when he saw us, the curly receiver wire dangling from his mouth, and gave us a look which said, 'You're home early!'

There was that second or two of stunned silence as we took in the devastation – and then Kay screamed and swore at them and they bolted for the sun lounge doors, which were swinging open. Then Kay was after them. In all the mayhem, she seemed to have forgotten that she was carrying a length of 2 × 1 timber that we had collected on the way home, which was intended as an extra perch for the chickens, and now there she was, chasing the goats round the garden, brandishing it and screaming like a banshee, 'I'll bloody kill you!'

The next-door neighbours, Ruth and Keith, who were having tea in their conservatory, witnessed the action and apparently Ruth said to Keith, 'That's the last time I park outside their house.'

In my *Crimewatch*-style reconstruction of events, I'm pretty sure that what happened was that Billy – who still thought he should live in the house – had leaned heavily against the somewhat flimsy sun lounge doors, and then shouted over to Georgie and Henry, 'I think these'll go if we put our backs into it.' And so they did, whereupon the three of them made straight for the kitchen, which they proceeded to eat.

They opened all the cupboards and ate as much coffee, tea, flour, cereal, biscuits, bread (insert here every other food in the pantry) as they spilled on the floor. They ate wallpaper, place mats, cushions – you get the picture: everything. They ripped down curtains and pulled over plants and vases of flowers; the soil mixing with all the above on the floor and work surfaces. They obviously didn't have time to go outside to the toilet because mixed in was a liberal amount of goat piss and poo. It took us days to return the kitchen to anything like its previous condition.

The goats laughed about it for years. We didn't; we had their knackers chopped off.

The noisiest animals we ever had were a peacock and some ducks. Peacocks shriek, you know? Proper shriek. In summer, they start at about four o'clock in the morning. Of course, cockerels crow to greet the dawn, but you can sort of register that and keep on snoozing, but when the bloody peacock starts, you've no chance. What does he want? Why does he keep doing it? What is the point?

Hang on, though! Maybe he's trying to warn us of something. Maybe he's a guard peacock. The first time it happened, I got out of bed and stumbled downstairs and out into the garden to see why he was shrieking. When he saw me, he just turned and spread out his massive tail and said, 'Look at me!' – and that's all they want. They are just showing off.

We once got some ducks and if you'll take my advice, you won't follow suit. Don't get ducks. Ducks do cabaret. I'm sure you will have experienced this if you've ever camped or caravanned near a country stream or pond, or had a canal holiday or sailed on the broads. The thing is that the cabaret doesn't start until midnight, just after you've drifted off into a deep slumber brought on by the tiredness induced by outdoor life. 'Oh, I'm tired. Are you tired? It's all this fresh air. You can have too much fresh air.' (It's nothing to do with the six pints of real ale you've had in the country pub.)

So there you are, sound asleep in your sleeping bag or your bunk, and the duck cabaret starts spot on midnight. The comedian comes on at about half twelve and begins, 'Quack quack quack quack – quack quack – quack quack,' and all the other ducks laugh loudly and hysterically, 'QUACK QUACK QUACK QUACK QUACK QUACK!', half the bloody night.

And the Winner Is ... II

I PLAYED THE Comedy Store for years, some nights cramming in three other gigs around London in between the early and late show. Then came a hosting gig that was to prove momentous. Fate was again waiting behind a bush, ready to ambush me.

The North-West Comedian of the Year competition was getting bigger, better and more prestigious year on year. It was a tradition that one of the previous winners would host the final – and it was my turn in 1997, when Johnny Vegas was the hot favourite.

I knew Johnny from playing his comedy club, The Citadel in St Helens, and I always remember the first time I saw him (well, you would, wouldn't you?). I was on the bill with Mark Hurst, whom I really rated. I went on first after Johnny's compèring spot. I did well and came off and met Mark in the dressing room. Mark asked me what Johnny was like and I couldn't really explain it! I think I said something like, 'I think he's shit, but if he is, I've never ever seen anyone with so much confidence doing such rubbish onstage.' Turns out, of course, that I was way off the mark: Johnny was and still is like nobody else. I very soon realized that he is a comedy genius – and I mean about half an hour later when he did his second compèring spot. I've been a massive fan ever since.

I had a gig at The Buzz the week before the North-West Comedian of the Year contest and Agraman asked me if I'd seen a young comedian from Bolton called Peter Kay, who he said reminded him very much of me. I hadn't seen Peter, but I met him early on the night of the competition because he'd got there *very* early. Agraman introduced us and we got on very well. I found out that he'd only done a handful of gigs after leaving college and was very nervous about the show. He was to get more nervous still when he drew the last slot on the bill, which looked like being about eleven o'clock – which meant that he'd have to hang around for another four hours.

There was a packed house for the show. After a procession of average acts, Johnny went on about sixth and ripped the place apart – 'Game over,' we all thought. After the next break, with the time approaching eleven o'clock and the crowd getting drunker and noisier, it was Peter's turn. I wanted to get him on as quickly as possible, but in hindsight I could have given him a better build-up than: 'Come on now, ladies and gentlemen, settle down, there's only one act left and here he is ... Peter Kay.'

Peter came on and took control at once. His confidence and composure was staggering considering his lack of experience. He may have been a bag of nerves on the inside, but his stage presence belied this and his comedy presentation was enthusiastic and absolutely effortless. I remember that for part of his short set, he sat down on the edge of the stage and just chatted with a few hundred drunk Mancunians and they loved him; the next minute, he was throwing himself around the stage re-enacting kids' antics at weddings. I'd seen John Thomson do something similar before, but Peter lived it. He was amazing.

The judges got together and arrived at a stalemate. They asked for my opinion. They thought that Johnny should win, but had a problem with the crowd's reaction to Peter's set. This was really weird; it was an almost identical situation to the events that occurred when I won the competition – when Dave Gorman was the favourite, right down to me going on last on that night!

I couldn't believe that they had a problem, though, because although Johnny had produced his trademark set of random genius, Peter had lifted the roof off the place and was the absolute outright winner on the night. They agreed and Peter was crowned the North-West Comedian of the Year. Who would have thought then that he would get so big?

Chain Chain Chain Chain . . . *Chain Letters*

'D STARTED DOING TV studio warm-ups about two years before I met Peter. It is without doubt one of the most intensive, difficult, unsatisfying jobs a comedian can do. There is a theory that it is a good career move as it showcases your talents to television producers, but I must say that, on the whole, they don't take much notice of your efforts. It can be a lonely and discouraging experience – but on occasion, when you are welcomed into the studio by a good crew and team and the audience are up for it, you can have a great time.

I did warm-ups for *Crosswits* and *Chain Letters* at Tyne Tees, where the experience fell into the latter, most enjoyable category. I did *University Challenge* and *Quiz Night*, as well as a few recordings of *Question of Sport*; and this was possibly the easiest and most enjoyable job of the lot. I am a massive sports fan and so meeting the superstars involved at close hand was amazing.

The shows were recorded on a Sunday afternoon at BBC Manchester and there was a tradition of sitting down to a formal Sunday lunch before the show. I clearly remember pinching myself as I joined Bill Beaumont, Sam Torrence, Ian Botham and Lynford Christie at the dining table. I was totally starstruck and wandered round in a bit of a daze – so much so, in fact, that I remember one Sunday seeing somebody I sort of recognized (maybe one of the BBC team?) walking down the corridor and so I engaged them in conversation.

Me: Alright?

Familiar-looking chap: Yeah – you?

Me: Great, thanks. So what are you up to at the moment?

Familiar-looking chap: Oh, just the usual, you know, still captain of Man United and England!

Me: (*Smiles stupidly.*) Good . . . see you later, then.

How could I have not recognized Bryan Robson?!

As mentioned, I'd done occasional warm-ups for the mid-morning quiz show *Chain Letters*, with various presenters, including Allan Stewart, Ted Robbins and Vince Henderson. It seemed tradition that every season had a new presenter. I'd always got on well with the crew, and the production team at Tyne Tees were always brilliant. Nevertheless, it still came as a surprise when Christine Williams, the producer, encouraged me to audition to be the presenter for the new series in 1997.

I had the advantage of knowing the show inside out, but I wanted to introduce more comedy into the format and consequently prepared an audition piece to highlight this. At the audition, the producers and the show's creator really seemed to like my take on the format. I knew I was up against some big guns and household names, but at least I had the satisfaction of knowing that I had given it my best shot.

A couple of weeks later, I was working away in the Haematology lab when the phone rang and Christine told me that I'd got the gig. They liked the added comedy element and wanted more of the same introduced into each show. She told me the dates of recording and that they would be filming forty shows, at five shows a day for the most part. I should come up a day early for a couple of trial runs and to pick a wardrobe from a local gents' outfitters. I was stunned and sat there for a long time trying to take it all in. What a break!

Before the appointed filming dates, I met Peter at the North-West Comedy Awards. After seeing his amazing performance, I asked him to help write comedy links for the top of the show and for my intro into part two after the adverts. I also used a few ideas from a good friend, Rob Dean, and from my son Steve, and they are credited on some of the shows.

During the meetings with Peter at which we wrote the links, we realized that we had a lot in common in our comedy influences, both writers and performers. We chatted about ideas and projects that we had in our heads or partly written and developed, and found a lot of common ground which we would later put to good use.

I took two weeks' holiday from the pathology department and travelled up to Newcastle to record *Chain Letters*. They treated me like royalty up there: I stayed at the posh Copthorne Hotel on the river and was kitted out with numerous suits and shirts and shoes ready for my debut.

During the rehearsals, I began to realize the enormity of the task. If I had been nervous and apprehensive beforehand, I was ten times as bad now that it had all become 'real'. There were six cameras and I had to remember which one to present to during the quiz, and although there was a fab floor manager – whose name I'm embarrassed to say I forget – who helped me brilliantly, it was a very alien world to me.

Add to this the fact that I had to remember all the rules, the order of play in each of the rounds and the validity of the words the contestants generated in various permutations throughout the game – all this without the aid of autocue or earpiece for direction – and you have a recipe for a nervous breakdown, especially for a person who was more at home trying to decide if a lymphocyte was normal or 'atypical'.

With all the pressure, I found that trying to insert the comedy moments was virtually impossible, as my brain was already thinking about round three and who was in the lead and who was to play first and how the round actually worked! And let's not forget that we were filming five shows a day with three contestants in each show, all with their own 'hilarious' stories to remember and discuss in a light-hearted and amusing manner ... and you can see that I'm making all sorts of excuses for my, at times, wooden performances, in which I do a passable impression of a rabbit caught in your headlights.

Me: Contestant 1, I understand you have a passion for ducks?
Contestant 1: Yeah! I love ducks. I collect them. Not real ducks: plastic ducks, plaster ducks, metal ducks – all sorts of ducks.
Me: How many ducks?
Contestant 1: Hundreds! I've lost count. I've got them everywhere. I've got some on the wall by the stairs that quack when you walk

past them, I've got some in the hall, I've about fifty in the lounge, I've even got some in the toilet! I'm mad, me!

Me: Yes, you are. So, Contestant 2? You collect Tin-Tin Annuals? (*And repeat* × *200* ...)

As it turned out, the team were all very pleased with the run-throughs and passed on many words of encouragement, which helped me a great deal. All in all, the shows went well and I reckon, out of the forty, I was a bit rubbish on ten, but I had a great time up in Newcastle, which I'll never forget. They've just started re-running my episodes on Challenge TV and I watched about a minute of one of them through my fingers the other day, as they seem so dated and I look so young and inexperienced.

My favourite show is the one where I wore a brown wig throughout without making any reference to it. It was the third of the batch of three afternoon shows the audience had had to endure. I was flagging a bit as I sat in make-up prior to the record, when I spotted the wig on a shelf. I asked the make-up lady if I could wear it for the show and she said no. She said she'd get in trouble if she put it on me without the producers' approval, but I said I'd take full responsibility and if Christine didn't like it, she could stop the show as soon as I walked in around the revolving 'Chain Letters' sign (a sign in which I once got trapped when I mistimed my entrance). So I wore the wig – an ordinary brown wig with a side parting, not a comedy wig – and stood waiting for the theme tune to kick in.

'Chain chain chain ... Chain Letters' went the tune, the sign revolved and I made my entrance. The response was amazing. The camera operators all looked around their cameras, questioning what they were seeing down the viewfinder, the floor crew all looked on open-mouthed, and the audience looked stunned and then, because they'd seen me present two shows already, wigless, started to laugh – low at first, then bigger and bigger.

I feigned confusion. 'What?' I asked innocently, while waiting for the floor manager to shout, 'Cut!'

She never did, so I just carried on – and was blessed with comedy gold when I asked the first contestant to explain the circumstances surrounding her recent ejection from a job interview. She explained, with a glazed expression which I couldn't immediately account for, that the manager interviewing her had the worst wig on that she had ever seen and that she couldn't stop herself from giggling every time she looked at it because it was perched at a ridiculous angle. I shook my head and gave Camera 2 (I'd learned by then) a despairing look, exclaiming, 'Why do people do that? Why hide your head under a wig, for goodness' sake?'

With that, I straightened mine a bit and moved on to the next contestant. 'So, Malcolm, I understand that something funny happened when you had an epidural?'

When we broke for the interval, I heard the unmistakable sound of Christine, the producer, descending the steps from the gantry. 'Uh oh!' I thought. 'I'm in for it now' – but no, she was smiling broadly. She produced a comb and said, 'Let's move the parting to the other side and see if anybody notices.' I did the rest of the show without mentioning the wig and it was definitely my favourite episode.

One of the great things about *Chain Letters* was that we largely dealt with four-letter words and that fact – combined with the contestants' urgency in moving rapidly from one word to the next almost without thinking – introduced another dimension of jeopardy which the studio audience loved.

Up would come a sequence starting with 'PAST': 'I'll change the "T" to a "S" to make "PASS". I'll change the "A" to a ...'

The audience are laughing because they are way in front of you, my friend.

'... To a, um, to a "U" to make "PUSS"?'

Sorry, no – not allowed; you should have stuck with 'PISS'.

The best of these was a taxi driver from Salford, who had won his way into the final and had to change ten words in sixty seconds (or something like that). He was struggling with 'PANT' and said, 'I'll change the "A" to a "U" to make "PUNT" ... Oh, oh! Now what? I'll change the "P" to a "C" to make "C*NT".'

Then he looked at me and I shook my head, as the audience dissolved into hysterics. 'No, you won't, mate,' I said – but then, unbelievably, I saw the floor manager urging me on: 'Carry on,' she mouthed.

So I carried on. Inevitably and magically, the cabbie was now struck dumb, so we were stuck with a massive 'C*NT' displayed on the *Chain Letters* board for the remaining ten seconds.

The production team had thought that 'C*NT' might be an acceptable Anglo-Saxon word. I said, 'Yeah right, but even so, you couldn't broadcast that before *Richard and Judy.*' So they had to give the cabbie, who had been failing miserably, another go. This time, he succeeded in getting all the way round the board to win the £1,000 jackpot!

I have often since thought that maybe, on that first attempt, he had clocked the time elapsed and knew he was going to fail – and so he seized the opportunity of securing another chance by chucking in a filthy word. If that is indeed the case, then every credit to you, my friend.

It's a good job that every other contestant didn't realize the potential of this tactic – no, hang on a minute, when I think about it, that would have been brilliant!

Strange to say, that was the last ever series of *Chain Letters*.

He's Behind You

MY GOOD FRIEND Eamonn O'Neil, who had given me a big break on his radio programme and WOW roadshows, gave me another opportunity when he became a producer at Granada TV. They had a new live Friday night show in the pipeline, which would showcase comedy acts, bands, actors and other celebs who would be soon appearing in the region. The show was called *What's New?*

Eamonn was to co-present and had persuaded producers that they would need a comic to fill in between the featured acts and in the gaps caused when bands had to set up after a comedian etc. I did an audition on camera – filmed in the Granada car park! – and got the job. This was a surprise because my audition piece was a bit shit and involved me wearing a sombrero at one point, but I can't remember why (although I might have sold it on camera as a misunderstanding, as I thought that they wanted somebody on the show doing 'tropical' comedy and Mexico's in the tropics, right?).

It was a great gig, but very nerve-wracking because it was totally live and I had to be ready to fill gaps as they arose, sometimes for twenty seconds and sometimes for three minutes. Many times, I had to stop routines halfway through and think of a way to get out of them. Because it was a variety-type show, I also threw in some rubbish magic, mind-reading and juggling, and it all went well, thank the Lord, and was fantastic experience. It was a great show with all the top bands and comics of the day, and celebrity interviews thrown in too – so I'm talking Georgie Best, Les Dawson and Wet Wet Wet, oh aye!

It was around this time that I dipped my toe into acting again (of sorts). Eamonn had starred in the pantomime at the Gracie Fields

Theatre in Rochdale; the following year, they asked me if I fancied it, and I thought I might. It would mean taking a chunk of time off work for rehearsals and matinees, but although the money wasn't great, I judged that it would be a good experience.

The panto was *Jack and the Beanstalk* and was directed by Colin Meredith, who is an accomplished actor. Jack was played by Ginny Buckley, who is now a top television presenter, most notably on BBC1's *Holiday*, and the fairy was the lovely Kathryn George, who is a fab actress and is probably best known for her role in *Hollyoaks*. I was the 'Silly Billy' character, the kids' friend (I hate kids), and I was the only character given any leeway with the script, in order to warm up the audience with ad-libs and get the kids going with some audience participation and all that.

I ran on after the opening number with 'energy' (which is how you must always enter and leave the stage) and launched straight into the 'Alright – Okay' game. I shout to the kids, 'When I shout, "Alright?" You shout, "Okay!" When I shout, "Okay!" You shout, "Alright!" Alright?' The kids shout, 'Okay!' and we're off. (I once tried this approach when I was doing the studio warm-up for a children's TV show in Liverpool and it went horribly wrong. This was Liverpool, after all. I ran on, did the whole spiel, 'When I shout, "Alright?" You shout, "Okay!" When I shout, "Okay!" You shout, "Alright!" Alright?' and a little kid on the front row said, 'F**k off.')

The cast and crew were lovely to me and the panto was good fun, although I hated the dancing because I'm rubbish at learning the steps and routines; I can't even sway in the same direction as everyone else. I had to do a big dance routine with the children's chorus, which involved me doing a bit of mopping and singing, 'You've got to S-M-I-L-E to be H-A-double P-Y' – and I wasn't! It was hard enough remembering the routine without Kath and Ginny stood in the wings, trying to put me off.

I'll always remember the brilliant time I had. I returned the year after to play the part of the 'Big Bad Wolf' in *Little Red Riding Hood*, but I haven't appeared in panto since, even though I do get offered them on a regular basis.

In fact, it wasn't until December 2009 that I was tempted back onstage, when I was offered the part of 'Narrator' in *The Rocky Horror Show* at the Manchester Palace Theatre. My first instinct was to turn it down because I didn't know the show and I'm not really into the spoof horror genre. The thing was that everyone I mentioned it to, friends and family alike, said, 'You've got to do it! It's an iconic piece of theatre and a massive cult hit!' I trusted their opinion and agreed to take the role.

In preparation, I went to see the show at the Liverpool Empire. I sat there with my jaw on my chest for the whole performance as the audience, dressed as characters from the show – blokes in golden hot pants, girls in saucy maids' outfits, and both sexes in variations on the basque-and-suspenders look – heckled the cast for the duration, with the Narrator bearing the brunt of their 'contributions'. I loved the show; it had so much energy, stunning performances all round, fantastic sing-along songs and the almost deafening encouragement of the audience, which was stirring and daunting in equal measure. I came away thrilled, but also very apprehensive about taking this on in a couple of weeks' time.

I had a three-hour rehearsal the week before, a run-through on the day … and then I was on! In a way this helped because I didn't get much time to think about what lay ahead. Adding to my nervousness was the fact that the opening night was Press Night, and also the night when the most hardened and devout Rocky Horror fans attended.

I went to the toilet about a dozen times in the hour before, and then donned my costume and stood in the wings with my Narrator's book, listening to the audience come into the auditorium. They were noisy and excited, and now and then a massive roar would go up as a particular punter entered in an outrageous costume.

The opening number is fantastic – 'Dammit Janet' – and as it ends, the lights dim and I enter through smoke from downstage. The spotlight picked me out and a huge cheer went up, which gave me such a lift and helped carry me through the chorus of obligatory boos that the Narrator always receives.

I began with, '*I would like if I may …*' A dozen or so people shouted out, 'You may!' and I responded graciously, 'Thank you,' and then, 'It's a good job, really, otherwise we'd be f**ked.' I got a big laugh and continued, '*… to take you on a strange journey.*' A hundred people shouted, 'How strange?' and I said, 'Very strange; stranger than dancing with a beautiful woman and feeling an erection start … and it's not yours.'

There are certain places in the script where you know you will always get heckled and so you leave a gap to let the audience in. One such line regarding Brad and Janet should read: '... *had left them feeling both apprehensive and uneasy.*' I intentionally paused after '*had left them feeling*' and every night someone would shout 'Horny!' and I would agree with, 'Oh yes, hornier than Tiger Woods approaching the second hole,' which was topical at the time and got a massive laugh.

Another favourite was, '... *but it was too late to go back now. It was as if she was riding a giant ...*' They all shout out 'Cock!' whereupon I consult my book and say, 'I've got "tidal wave" here – but I will accept "cock". Well, when I say "accept" ...'

Sometimes, I would engage in a bit of banter with the hecklers, some of whom could be quite persistent.

Bloke: (*Shouts out something indecipherable.*)

Me: It's like being heckled by Scooby-Doo! Bit of advice, mate, try putting a few consonants in there, all I'm getting is 'euuuaaaooo ...'

Bloke: No neck, no neck.

(*A rubbish heckle which refers to the Narrator in the film version, so doesn't make sense.*)

Me: You're very quick, aren't you? You know who told me that? Your wife. Well, I think that's what she said, but she had her mouth full at the time. And ... it might not have been me she was telling because there were a few of us there.

Bloke: Tell us a joke.

Me: God, he's like one of those turds that won't flush away! Alright then, a joke: an Englishman, an Irishman and a Scotsman walked into a pub and they all agreed that you are a bit of a twat.

GAME OVER

The show got five-star reviews, we had great audiences for the run, I got to sing and dance on stage ... and I enjoyed it! I led the 'Time Warp' from up a ladder and had the best time. I worked with some amazingly talented people, and along the way learned a lot about stagecraft and, more importantly, about myself, and how essential it is to get out of your comfort zone now and then, and to test yourself.

A6 in a Camper Van

THANKS TO MY increasing experience, and my continuing regular London gigs, I was doing well on the comedy circuit. After one show at Jongleurs Camden, which was a fantastic gig early days, a lovely girl called Lisa White asked if I'd consider joining her agency and allow her to represent me. We had a quick chat as I had a train to catch; I liked her a lot and agreed, and she started to get me gigs with Off the Kerb and other big agencies.

I'd been with her a couple of years, I think, when she phoned and told me that she'd got an associate producer's job on a new television stand-up show called *Gas*, which was to be hosted by Lee Mack and which would be a showcase for brand new comedy talent. They were auditioning in Manchester the following week and she had a list of up-and-coming comedians that had been submitted by a Manchester agent that she wanted to run by me.

I gave my opinion on the mixed bunch, and then expressed my disbelief that Peter Kay wasn't on the list, as he was potentially a huge star and already in a different league to those she'd got on the list. She made a few calls and Peter was added to the show. A few weeks later, he had a great gig on *Gas*, then joined Lisa's agency and was on his way. To my surprise, a few months later, so was I.

In time, Peter became hot property and Granada TV asked him to submit a script or idea for development. We'd been writing a few things together since we met – including a script for a sitcom/sketch show called *It's Dick Martin*, which revolved around the writers' room in a TV studio, as the writers turned out scripts and gags for the elusive 'Dick Martin', a smarmy, greasy yet hugely popular chat-show host.

The writers were a diverse bunch, ranging from the old school to the new breed, which generated the tension and friction that is essential in every good sitcom. The added dimension was that every time the writer(s) left the office, they would enter a sketch, which had nothing to do with the main storyline and was standalone but funny. The characters in the sketches would be played by the same actors, disguised by make-up, costume, gender, as in all good sketch shows, and would return every week. The script and sketches were written, but nobody took up the idea – idiots. I suspect they'd have been all over us a few years later when *Phoenix Nights* was breaking.

Anyway, Granada were going to produce a series for up-and-coming comedians, which was to be called *Mad For It* – and so the comedians or sketch groups had to come up with a 'Mad for … whatever' idea. Peter was approached to provide one of the episodes, and he very generously said he would do it if I could be involved, which they eventually agreed to.

We had conversations about suitable topics and Peter and I thought that 'Mad for the A6' might be fun. There had been programmes about Robbie Coltrane travelling along Route 66 and Billy Connolly (or was it Lenny Henry?) motoring down some other famous US highway, and we thought it was about time that the main arterial road going through our region got its deserved recognition. Peter thought it would be good if we started at the bottom of the Granada region in Buxton and drove north until we 'lost' signal and the picture started breaking up in the Lake District. He also thought it would be funny if we had just one cameraman, a lighting guy and a sound engineer travel with us in a VW camper van.

We had one dry run, where we basically noted any significant landmarks or signs or buildings/pubs etc. along the way, while Peter taped our improvised comedy views, and then we did the drive for real. He wrote odd scenes, like the one where he visits Manchester Apollo, while I wait outside making cars crash by pointing a hair dryer at them in the manner of a speed camera. Neil Fitzmaurice (who later co-wrote *Phoenix Nights* with us) features as manager or techie at the Apollo in a very funny scene, which Neil may have had a hand in writing.

Peter met Neil on the North-West comedy club circuit and had recognized his huge talent for comedic performance, impressions and writing. I had moved on to the London and national circuit by then, so hadn't seen him, but Peter rated him highly and he wasn't wrong. Neil is a great bloke, immensely talented as a writer, actor and comedian. He's reluctant to perform stand-up these days as he doesn't really enjoy the experience, much preferring to concentrate on his acting and writing instead.

En route on the A6, we stopped by a field and I did a routine about cows knowing when it's going to rain way before we do, and we got the sound guy to put a plastic rain-mate hat on a cow. I remember Pete pulling the van over in Chorley, and me stopping a woman to ask, 'Is this the way to Amarillo?' She didn't really know, so I tried to help by asking if she knew Marie, who was waiting for me? No. 'There are church bells ringing?' 'Sorry, love, no.'

We picked up a hitchhiker, who was a friend of Peter's called Barrington, who was a children's entertainer/magician. I'd fallen asleep and woke up to find this crazy man making balloon animals and acting unbalanced in the van. We dumped him somewhere around Lancaster.

Peter went crazy after eating a family pack of Opal Fruits and overdosing on the mountain of E numbers contained therein – and I mean proper crazy. We stopped as dusk was falling and parked on a pub car park that had a great view of the Reebok Stadium in the distance. We sat on the roof of the camper van and Peter went off on one – I paraphrase – 'Concrete and Steel, Man's achievements, towering, rising magnificently,' he raved on, inspired for minutes, pointing into the distance, where I missed the focus of his eulogy.

'ASDA?' I asked.

It's quite a nice little programme, but a lot of the comedy was sacrificed in the edit for sweeping, moody, panoramic shots of the beautiful Lancashire and Cumbrian countryside. I think I've probably got one of the few copies of the programme still in existence.

That Peter Kay Thing

PETER WAS ASKED to take part in Channel 4's *Comedy Lab* and he'd had an idea that he'd like to write a spoof documentary set in a motorway service station. This, of course, went on to become *The Services* and was the first time that we got to see Peter's remarkable acting skills.

A group of us went on a fact-finding mission to the services at Rivington, which involved sitting in the restaurant and eavesdropping on conversations, observing the punters and bouncing ideas about. Peter also canvassed ideas from family, friends and colleagues to add to the research and his own pile of ideas. While lying on a beach on holiday in Greece, I had an idea that the boss of the services should be a woman called Pearl. I had this line in my head which was in typical documentary-speak and was something like, 'But they were only a cloud on Pearl's horizon.' (I think the 'they' were a group of French tourists whose coach, I suggested, should stop off on their trip to the Lake District, before setting off again – with a couple missing). Peter was reluctant to drag it up as Pearl, initially thinking it might be too Dick Emery and that it should feel real, but I remember saying that if it was played 'straight' and the make-up and costume were top class, he'd create a great character, which he did.

There's so much to like abut *The Services*, from the Chorley FM DJ in the car park (it was originally to be Bolton FM) to the country-and-western-obsessed coach driver. I remember that when it aired, the late great John Peel wrote a great review in the *Radio Times*, and even though I'd only contributed a little, I was really chuffed – and thrilled for Peter, who wrote the bulk of it and was brilliant in it.

Channel 4 unsurprisingly loved *The Services* and asked Peter for more of the same. He suggested a series of stand-alone spoof documentaries in the same style, and they commissioned what was to become *That Peter Kay Thing*. The title was chosen because people would often forget the name of a programme they had recently viewed and would refer to it in this way – 'Did you see that Peter Kay thing last night?'

He had most of the ideas in his head – and they included an ice-cream van war, a lad who worked in a bingo hall, another who worked as a steward at the MEN Arena (from his personal experience), Leonard, the oldest paper boy in Britain, and a talent show at a working men's club. The final episode, 'Lonely at the Top', arose out of the 'In the Club' episode and documented the rise and fall of the vocal duo Park Avenue, who won the talent search in the first episode.

Peter formalized the writing partnership, asking Neil and I to co-write the series with him. Peter gave us the briefs and we went away and created characters and storylines and dialogue. Neil sent his on disk and spoke to Peter by phone, while I spent nearly every lunchtime round at Peter's house, which was only a five-minute drive away from the General Hospital (yes, I was still working there full-time!). I typed up all my ideas and dialogue and we discussed them over a brew, and once he had collated the material, he assembled it into an episode and we would revise that until we were happy with it.

We all contributed in different measure to each episode. I didn't have a lot of stuff in the 'Ice Cream Cometh' or 'The Arena', but contributed a good deal in terms of ideas, character and dialogue to 'Leonard', 'In the Club', 'Eyes Down' and 'Lonely at the Top'. My favourite episodes are 'Leonard' and, maybe surprisingly, 'Lonely at the Top'. I loved the songs we wrote for Marc Park: the insensitive, crass 'African Tears' and 'Christmas 2000'.

I really enjoyed this creative process, especially having the luxury of knowing that the show had definitely been commissioned and was going to be made. As well as collaborating on the writing, Peter and I went out on fact-finding missions. We spent an evening at Gala Bingo, Chorley and visited quite a few working men's clubs, including a couple of really big ones – Horwich RMI and Deane Conservative Club (or 'Connie Club', as they're known round our way). I also managed to wangle us an invite to a regional concert secretaries' meeting, which turned out to be a brilliant source of material. We gathered loads of information here, which in turn generated a massive amount of ideas, which we included in the show. All helped to mould Peter's character Brian Potter.

Once we'd finished the series and Channel 4 had accepted it, Peter had to assemble a production team. He got Ivan Douglass on board as producer, Lisa White as associate producer and Andrew Gillman as director. Peter then surprised me by asking me to play the part of club compère Jerry 'The Saint' Sinclair.

I was reticent at first, because I'd never acted outside pantomimes and a few appearances with the Church Road Am-Dram group (which later became known as Phoenix Theatre – how weird a coincidence was that to become?) in Bolton. He persuaded me that I could do it and, having given it a little thought, I agreed – mainly because I loved the character that we'd created and I felt I 'knew' him, both from helping to develop him on paper and having seen various incarnations of him on my travels through the wonderful world of the working men's clubs.

Channel 4, however, were less convinced – and insisted that I audition for the part. I was deflated at first, but then common sense kicked in and I thought it was a good idea. I didn't want people to think that I'd got the part because I co-wrote the show, plus I still had an element of self-doubt. Auditions were held at a hotel in Bolton. I turned up at the appointed time and auditioned for Jerry ... I got the part and surprised myself.

At least I wasn't the only one on set with limited acting experience. Peter had the inspired idea to cast most of the main characters from friends and fellow stand-up comedians from the Manchester circuit, most of whom had never acted before. The result was that the cast produced raw, 'real' and believable performances.

'In the Club' was the first episode to be filmed. We took over Farnworth Veterans' Club, which wasn't too far from the hospital. It was a fantastic experience and worked really well in the mockumentary style, as it featured the run-up to and performance of the 'Talent Trek' final, 'the biggest talent show in clubland'. The talent show was typical of all those I'd seen in my time, especially contestants Mark Park and Cheryl Avenue, who together were 'Park Avenue'.

Jerry was 'the compère without compare' and it was a big night for him – even more so with the film crew in attendance. He arrived from work, still wearing his dusty overalls because Jerry worked in bricks. He never meant to get into bricks; he fell into bricks. And bricks get in your blood; if you cut him in half, you'd find 'Accrington' written all the way through him – guess where I got that from?

Jerry sang with typical club backing of keyboard and drums. Singing was a real test for me because I hate singing in public, even karaoke, so having to get onstage in front of the crew was nerve-wracking enough, quite apart from looking the part as Jerry and carrying off the performance in front of the audience. Now, yes, I do know that Jerry isn't the best singer in the world, but he had to be a half-convincing vocalist/compère and I think he pulls it off … just. Backstage, Brian Potter and Jerry reflected on the many acts they'd seen come and go through the club and how they'd changed when they'd achieved stardom: 'The higher a monkey climbs, the more you can see its arse.'

The series was very well received and we couldn't have asked for better reviews; Alison Graham in the *Radio Times* became a huge champion of the series, which helped a great deal. It was all a little surprising, really, because when you become involved in the creation of characters and storylines and commit yourself to the research and writing, it sort of becomes a job, if you know what I mean. You do it the best you can and don't give much thought to how it's going to turn out. This was especially true in my case because this was the first big thing I'd helped to create, and when I saw it brought to life on the television and recognized how good it was, for so many reasons it was a shock to the system. A huge, pleasurable, emotional, 'ohmigod!' type of shock.

We were all so proud when the series won a British Comedy Award in 2000 – for Best New Comedy. The three of us went down to London and stayed in a fancy 'boutique' hotel (i.e. small and pricey), and dressed up in black tie as advised for the event. Peter made his entrance in a bright purple suit that was to become a bit of a trademark, with a 'How are you?!'

Looking around the room, I saw most of my old and new comedy heroes, together with many other stars from the comedy world. Caroline and Craig and Sue Johnston from *The Royle Family* were on a nearby table; there was Rob Brydon, Alistair McGowan, Ronnie Barker – I sat on the next table to Ronnie Barker! Victoria Wood was there and the brilliant Alan Bennett; Bruce Forsyth walked by my table and I was such a fan, I had to speak to him. I stood up abruptly and said, like a complete nerd, 'I just wanted to say how much of a fan I am and thank you for all the enjoyment you've given me.' He was very gracious and thanked me and walked away. I sat down totally happy – until I realized how cheesy that sounded.

When we were announced as Best New TV Comedy, I couldn't breathe, I couldn't feel my legs – but we had to go on stage to collect the award from Richard E. Grant. Peter made a speech, Neil said a few words … and I said another gushing, nerdy thing to Richard E. Grant about *Withnail and I*, and he smiled.

At the aftershow party, I was totally star-struck – and although a lot of nice people said lots of nice things, I answered in a stunned, monosyllabic fashion. It was quite a surreal night and it all went by in a happy, crazy blur.

Decision Time

AFTER THE HUGE success of *That Peter Kay Thing*, Channel 4 naturally wanted more. They suggested that we develop one of the six episodes of *That Peter Kay Thing* and turn it into a full series.

The show that stuck out as having the most potential was 'In The Club', being as it was populated by a great mix of characters, ranging from the officious Brian Potter and his stooge Jerry, through Holy Mary, to Les Alanos and Max and Paddy the bouncers. Add in a couple of 'Kennys', one young and a bit dim and the other older and a habitual liar, and introduce a mullet-sporting Neil Fitzmaurice as the fab DJ 'Ray Von' and his catchphrase 'Shabba' … and potentially you have comedy gold.

Personally, I now had a major decision to make. I thought that it wouldn't be fair to take my annual leave from the hospital in regular blocks of half-days in order to write and appear in the new series (as I had done for *That Peter Kay Thing*), as it would disrupt the smooth running of the department – and so what were my options? At first, it seemed a black-and-white decision. I could continue with my successful career in Biomedical Science (by now I was a Chief Biomedical Scientist) or I could gamble, sacrifice my thirty-two years of hard work and dedication and give it all up for a career in the volatile world of light entertainment. One thing was clear: I couldn't do both – or could I?

A thought struck me. One of the senior staff in another lab had recently been granted a one-year career break to travel the world, with the guarantee that his job would be kept open for him to return to in twelve months' time. I took my copy of Personnel Policies down from the shelf and turned to the relevant chapter – and there it was. Senior staff with so many years' service could apply for a career break, with the guarantee that their job would be waiting for them after the agreed period.

I arranged a meeting with our personnel officer for clarification of the rule and any conditions that might apply. I told him exactly what I wanted to do in my year off and he confirmed that if I obtained approval from both my Consultant Haematologist and Senior Chief Biomedical Scientist, there were no obstacles in my taking the career break as outlined. He wished me the best of luck and I quickly sought meetings with my bosses and both my Consultant and Senior Chief approved the career break. Result! I handed in my required letter of notice.

Hang on, though, what's that coming over the hill, is it a monster? No, it's a Clinical Director and he's a Biochemist – smell the Old Spice? Note the corduroy and the balaclava? He informs me that he is rejecting my application for a career break because taking a year off to perform comedy is absolutely not the reason the scheme was implemented. I tell him that my Consultant and Senior Chief have approved my application, which has now been approved by Personnel. He says that he can override the decision and that my application is officially rejected.

I have to make an urgent decision, and so I contact Mick Coyne, my brilliant union rep, and discuss the situation with him. He talks to my bosses and an investigation is launched. Mick warns me that this could take months, but as I don't have months before we need to start writing *Phoenix Nights*, he suggests that I hand in my notice and leave on the agreed date, as this will not affect the outcome of the inquiry.

I take the chance and hand in my notice. One month later, I pack my things, say my goodbyes (maybe only temporarily) and set off down the yellow brick road – well, Minerva Road, Farnworth.

The grievance hearing is convened some ten months later (!) and I attend with Mick Coyne. A senior hospital administrator chairs the session and is accompanied by a representative from personnel. The Clinical Director is asked to explain his decision to reverse the approval of my career break and after he attempts to do so, Mick Coyne slowly and methodically destroys his argument. I have waited ten months for this moment and it is everything I'd hoped for and more. A wrong is righted and in spectacular fashion! I still smile today when I think about it and very occasionally I read the written decision of the panel, which confirms the reinstatement of my career break and my job still there for the remaining two months of the agreement.

With a month to go, I handed in my official notice – because the comedy career was taking off and I didn't want to return to work under the current regime. I knew this before the tribunal, but I'd wanted my day in court.

With my long hospital career formally ending for good, I applied for an official leaving party, to which I was entitled – but guess what, my request was denied! No surprises there. Nevertheless, I wanted to say goodbye to everyone, and so I invited all my colleagues from all laboratories and departments to the staff room at lunchtime on my last day.

Everybody came – and more than that, they brought food and drink to stage a grand unofficial leaving do. It was a very moving farewell after thirty-two years of loyal, dedicated and important service.

Now I could concentrate on more serious issues … like transforming myself into a giant berry.

Phoenix Nights

WHEN IT CAME to writing the first full series of *Phoenix Nights*, we had garnered so many stories and ideas on our visits to the clubs that we weren't short of material – although I did visit Chorley Labour Club to try to add to the pile.

The concert sec there told me a few good anecdotes, which included details about an Ann Summers night he occasionally ran. He gave me the contact details of the girl who organized it and I phoned her to find out more. She told me some great stories! (You can imagine.) I asked if I could attend her next event, but she said that men weren't allowed. So, I hatched a plan to send Kay and Jenny to observe the presentation.

This was held at the Railway pub in Chorley. I drove them up, then sat outside the function room with a pen and pad at the ready. I didn't make any notes – because from the moment the event started until it finished, all I could hear was constant screaming and hysterical laughter.

Luckily, the girls picked up a few nuggets of comedy gold, which all came in useful when the Phoenix had its first ladies' night. The brilliant Kate Robbins played the part of the rep, delivering a host of great lines, including one about love-eggs: 'Pop them in on the way to work and you'll come before the bus does.'

It was decided that the spoof documentary style was too restrictive for a full series, and so the series was written as a straightforward sitcom. The three of us wrote the first series in much the same manner as we did *That Peter Kay Thing*, with Peter collating Neil's and my work, and then the two of us sitting down with all the notes we'd made on our club visits. We had picked up some fantastic ideas from these visits, purely by listening and observing the day-to-day running and organization of the club, and by speaking informally to club members and the committee. (When they actively sought us out to tell us something funny that had happened, it was never funny.)

The first series was 'hidden' away by Channel 4 late on a Friday night, which was initially disappointing, but ultimately worked in the show's favour – as viewers 'discovered' this comedy gem, and people love discovering stuff, being the first person on the block to find something and then bring the good tidings to others. That is how 'cult' shows arise, I think. That, together with great characters and the kind of sparkling dialogue that inadvertently spawns catchphrases.

One of the strengths of *Phoenix Nights* can, I think, be attributed to having a team of writers. We would never leave a scene unless all three of us were happy that we'd wrung the last ounce of comedy out of it, and I think in so many other television comedies, this is so obviously not the case. It seems to me that writers finish a scene and think, 'That's good, that'll do,' and quite often it won't do.

Another element that contributed to its success and realistic portrayal of the world was without a doubt the club audience. We used a different club than the one used in 'In the Club' for *Phoenix Nights* because Peter wanted it to look a certain way from the exterior. St Gregory's Social Club down the road in Farnworth was the perfect setting, on a side road off the main street with its own big car park and the west Lancashire moors in the background. We would film the cast's performances onstage during the day, and then the local club audience came in at night, dressed up to the nines, to see 'the show'. All the cameras were turned on these wonderful people to capture their real, spontaneous reactions to whatever was happening on or around the stage.

I have so many wonderful memories from filming the series that they have all merged into one, and I have difficulty in identifying what happened in the first series and what happened in the second.

Wild West Night was inspired out of the aforementioned 'Mad for the A6', when Peter and I stopped off at a club in Wingates to witness, film and participate in such a night, complete with fastest draw competition. I loved the outfit. Wild Bill couldn't control the horse – well, he couldn't control anything, the crowd, the microphone … I remember him shouting something nasty at the horse and Janice Connolly (Holy Mary) shouting out, 'Oh, no need!' The gunfighters (who lived on the car park in a caravan flying a confederate flag during the shoot) hated the line dancers, and the little bloke who was supposed to hit me 'couldn't knock the skin off a rice pudding' as my dad used to say. The horse wasn't that keen on mounting the bronco until the trainer gave it a hand (in more ways than one – you wouldn't believe me). Brilliant.

A big episode for me featured Jerry hosting an 'alternative' comedy night and getting heckled by a group of aggressive students. The regulars feel his pain as he sinks beneath the barrage, offering little resistance, and there comes a moment, a pivotal moment, where he will sink or swim. He leans his head on the microphone, sweat running down his brow, then there is a momentary squeal of feedback, which signals his fight back.

This scene was largely improvised around the old gags that Jerry would use, together with some surprises. Jerry says, 'What's your name, son? Any idea?'

'Stu,' the lad says.

'Is that short for Stupid?' Jerry asks, but quickly moves on. 'Here's something that will surprise you.' He pauses for half a beat, then jumps off the stage to land almost on top of Stu, who spills his pint. Then the Phoenix troops rally to Jerry's call and there is a fantastic ending as all the club regulars and members stand strongly together and banish the foe from their midst. Wonderful.

Other memories? Well, I loved the singles' night episode. I thought the scene in the toilets where Jerry was giving Brian advice was very funny – 'covered in piss'. Peter and Jo Enright were just brilliant; the romance montage and the scene on the chairlift was classic (the ducks on the wall actually 'quacked' when you passed them, and the original idea was that when he made her leave, after she'd revealed her work for the DSS, she went down on the chairlift and that very tender, poignant moment would be broken with the sound of ducks quacking). In the singles' night, I had a scene cut where I was chatting a young girl up, which rather showed Jerry in a different light – it was funny, but a bit creepy, and that's why it was edited out.

What else? Tim Healy and Half a Shilling – brilliant – you had to be there. Daniel Kitson as Spencer: inspired. The lovely Janice Connolly, who was just perfect as Holy Mary ('God loves you, Brian.' 'Does he? Well, He's a funny way of showing it.'). The Das Boot machine at the Captain's funeral (Brian – 'I ordered the Matrix'). When filming the captain's funeral reception, one of his old comrades had to make a speech, and on the day, the actor kept cocking it up. He was supposed to say, 'And halfway up the beach, they got him, the bastards,' but he kept saying, 'And halfway up the beach, the German bastards got him' ... very funny.

Last but not least, a character that the viewers loved because of his shock revelations was Psychic Clinton Baptiste ('I'm getting the word "nonce"') ... played brilliantly by Alex Lowe.

I'd had some below-the-waist problems in the months prior to *Phoenix Nights* and we included almost exactly my experiences of having a barium enema. We cast a friend of mine, Brian Hough, as the doctor undertaking the procedure. Brian is a printer by trade, but delivered the line, 'Nurse, it's filthy, give it a wipe' (referring to the monitor and not, as Jerry thought, his arse) perfectly.

Around that time, my wife Kay had started learning saxophone and started sitting in with a big band in a working men's club in Preston one night a week. We used the band to provide the music that underscores the scenes featuring an elated Jerry after he is given the all-clear later in the series. (Much to Brian Potter's dismay, as he has told everyone that Jerry's dying; he therefore insists on him wearing a baseball cap during that night's show.)

Series two came out about a year after the first and after series one had become a cult hit. As such, it was eagerly anticipated and we worked hard on making it every bit as good as the original. We decided to get a proper office and establish a structured writing schedule, and after viewing a few places, we found a space at Bolton Enterprise Centre.

It didn't work for us. Somebody was always late, Peter was always hungry and nipping out for food, and most of the time we just sat staring at an empty screen. Occasionally, we'd start and write half a page, and then scrap it because it was rubbish. We'd fight over the stupidest things, such as which is a funnier pie, chicken and mushroom or cheese and onion? Well, obviously chicken and mushroom, but would Neil agree? No. But what does he know about pies anyway? He's from Liverpool and there's no pie culture in Liverpool. Thankfully, in time, we reverted back to established working protocol and peace reigned once again.

Peter had decided to direct this second series, and so he scheduled everyone else's big scenes for the first week of filming, so that he could concentrate on directing rather than acting. Jerry had several really big scenes to do and I was worried about them because they were more ambitious than any in series one. There had been a big gap between the series, too, and I felt that I needed to ease into the part again, but I wasn't going to get that chance.

Possibly my biggest series of scenes were the ones where Jerry burns his hand on some fake merchandise from the recently burned-down club (Brian Potter had Ray Von burning ashtrays on a fire at the back of the club). Jerry takes powerful painkillers, then mixes them with his herbal remedies (he is by now a major hypochondriac) and then, just as the mixture starts to generate bizarre behaviour, he washes down some pills with what he thinks is a glass of water, but which turns out to be saki recently brewed by the illegal immigrant Chinese lads (Ant and Dec) that Potter has put to work in the kitchens.

Jerry becomes weirdly aggressive in the bingo, freaks out in the dressing room, then goes on stage to sing a manic version of 'Chitty Chitty Bang Bang', before shouting 'Catch me!' and stage-diving into the audience of stunned pensioners, who do not, of course, catch him. He then staggers into Brian's event promoting a Japanese lager (Kami-Kaze) dressed in drag, faints and pisses up in the air. It took quite a bit of doing and involved a large amount of improvisation, but, encouraged by suggestions from Neil and Peter, I went for it, and I'm very proud of how it turned out.

I can't leave this *Phoenix*-fest without mentioning the episode that has haunted me ever since (in a good way). The 'Phoenix Fun Day' was held to generate funds for repairs after the fire and included a parade and a funfair and jumble sale on the car park. Ray Von was in charge of the kiddies' roundabout ('Hold tight or you may die') and Justin Moorhouse as 'Young Kenny' had his face painted as a tiger in acrylic paint by a dodgy-looking bloke with long hair and a beard. If you remember, he couldn't get the paint off and spent the rest of the series as a tiger; he had to spend a ridiculous amount of time in make-up! I did suggest that it would be implausible that only Young Kenny had been on the receiving end of the facepaint scam and that many local kids would have been adorned with some animal or other. I thought it would be funny if we saw an occasional one during the series. It didn't happen, but I still like the idea.

There was Bernard Wrigley 'The Bolton Bullfrog', playing the bloke who brought the bouncy castle, which Potter had got cheap. (Turns out it was cheap because it was from a porn convention in Holland and was actually an inflatable 'cock and balls'. There was a great follow-up line, which went largely unnoticed, which was something like, 'It's one of a pair; I've got the other one on the van,' Brian Potter: 'No, thanks.' We strapped the 'love length' down and called it 'Sammy the Snake', with the testicles passed off as snake eggs.)

Bernard Wrigley's character was the same one who brought the Das Boot fruit machine in series one – the machine that played the German national anthem when somebody won the jackpot, much to the consternation of the old soldier members of the club, including 'The Captain', who later died during Ray Von's disco. The actor who played the Captain, Ced Beaumont, created a wonderful moment when, as we all gathered round him, he let his dentures slide out of his mouth – brilliant!

Anyway, back at the fun day, I was, of course, 'Jerry the Berry', dressed in a huge spherical berry costume, set off nicely with a stalky hat-type contraption. I sang 'Walking on Sunshine' on the back of a lorry – until Sammy the Snake broke loose and raised his ugly head (helmet, that is) behind me. Kids rolled me down a hill and I had all my clothes sold on the jumble sale, leaving me only a tatty old fur coat to wear. Sammy the snake exploded and Kenny Senior delivered the great line, 'One of his balls went over next door and they won't give it us back.'

The final scene, where Jerry is totally pissed off at 'being rolled round the car park as a giant hernia', is a great example of the benefits of having the writers on set. The scene wasn't quite working as well as it should have because the pay-off line wasn't strong enough. In between takes, as we sat in the make-up van, we racked our brains for a better ending. It was Neil, I think, who came up with the brilliant line for Jerry: 'I'm stood here looking like a gay Satan' – and in it went.

While I mention Kenny Senior, I must just say that his character, brilliantly played by Archie Kelly, is my favourite (apart from Jerry, of course). It is a well-written role, but Archie takes a lot of credit for his inspired interpretation of this inveterate liar, whom all of us must have met at work, down the pub, as neighbours.

His creation was a collaboration. Neil knew a bloke like him in Liverpool, who was obsessed with the Triads; and I knew a bloke from our pub who told the most outrageous stories about his life. The sad thing about these people is that not only do they expect you to believe the nonsense they spout, but they somehow (how?) convince themselves that it's true, that it *really* happened. I told Peter and Neil about a particular story which my bloke in the pub told, and it goes like this. This is an absolute true account of the incident. I might as well call him Kenny for the purpose of the story ...

Scene: The Pub. All the lads present. KENNY enters.

All: Kenny!

Kenny: Evening, all.

Me: Had a good day, Kenny?

Kenny: It's over, let's leave it at that.

Me: What happened?

Kenny: Cardiac arrest. (*To barmaid.*) Pint of bitter please, Mary.

Me: Who?

Kenny: Me.

All: What?!

Me: So you've been in hospital and had all the tests and that?

Kenny: No time for that.

Me: What do you mean?

Kenny: Well, I was doing my ironing and watching *Loose Women* when I got these pins and needles in my arm and my chest went all tight, like, and I recognized the symptoms straight off because I watch *Holby*.

Me: So you rang for an ambulance . . .

Kenny: No time! You've only got three minutes when you go into arrhythmia.

Me: So what did you do?

Kenny: (*Taps his nose knowingly.*)

Me: You snorted cocaine?

Kenny: No! I ripped the wires out of the iron and stuck 'em onto my chest. (*Performs the action.*) Zzzzzzzap, zzzzzzap – got it ticking again. (*To barmaid.*) Mary? A bag of pork scratchings, please, love.

(*We sit open-mouthed: does he really expect us to believe this shit? Yes, he does.*)

And Kenny Senior matched him in spades with, 'Turned over in bed this morning and guess who was there? Bonnie Langford, nearly broke her back.' His stories about the Triads and playing swingball with Robert de Niro feature in my highlights of the show; not to mention his brief but hilarious exchange with Roy Walker at the Phoenix Club's Gala Opening and his appearance at Brian Potter's trial wearing a chestful of medals: wonderful stuff.

One of the highlights for the viewer, so I'm told, were the auditions that were held over the end credits. We resurrected this idea from the sketch show that Peter and I had started writing (*It's Dick Martin*), in which two of the returning characters were theatre producers, who sat in theatre stalls in deep conversation, while a succession of acts trooped on and off the stage to audition – only to be halted by a loud 'Next!', sometimes even before they started. On *Phoenix Nights*, they ranged from the revolving spaceman, through the female magician who inadvertently threw a dove into the extractor fan, to the legendary Bolton comedian Bob Williamson, who appeared twice beside mechanical dancing toys. Along the way was a one-legged Elvis ('Blue Suede Shoe'), an inept escapologist, a beautiful girl contortionist who 'shot' ping-pong balls at the stunned committee, and the fabulous 'Rumbergers', the old couple who danced the paso doble in extravagant and extrovert style.

John and Marion were their first names. John, bless him, died recently after providing years of hilarity for all of us who were lucky enough to see them dance. The genius of the Rumbergers was that they appeared to be totally serious about the dance. As Marion wound herself up to perform a high kick, John would give her a disdainful look and throw in an occasional 'Hai!' in matador pose. You had to see them live to catch and appreciate all the wonderful little nuances that they had built into their routines. The beauty of their performance was that people didn't know how to react at first. Should they pity this old couple who were making fools of themselves; try not to laugh at them, even though it was all quite embarrassing until … Hang on! They know what they're doing! Massive relief; we can laugh.

During filming, we did two rehearsals with them and about five takes, and I can honestly say that we were still laughing as loud and hard at their final performance as we were at the first. Genius and lovely people, who appeared on a few of my solo shows later.

Another honourable mention must go to Ted Robbins for his faultless performance as Den Parry, Brian Potter's nemesis from the Banana Grove club down the road from the Phoenix. Ted's performance established him as one of the country's top comedy actors, to add to his existing reputation as a great stand-up comedian, first-class radio presenter and all-round good bloke.

Phoenix Nights was nominated for several awards, including a BAFTA, where we lost out to *The Office*. We gained our revenge over the brilliant Gervais and Merchant comedy by winning Best Comedy at the Royal Television Society Awards. We also won a People's Choice British Comedy Award over *The Office* by a landslide on a phone vote, which was incredibly pleasing. Along the way, I lost out in the 'Best Newcomer' category to the lovely Kris Marshall from *My Family*. (Nominated as 'Best Newcomer' at fifty-odd – not bad, eh? 'Best newcomer'! In all seriousness, it was amazing to be nominated for such a high-profile prize, especially in a performance role, and I was really proud of the accolade.)

Peter was also awarded and accepted the 'Writers' Guild of Great

Britain' award for best writer for *Phoenix Nights*. Strange, this – since there were three writers. I did have a thought that maybe he would go away and think about all the hard work that Neil and I had put into the series – the hours and hours of research, the ideas and characters we came up with, the great storylines and the dialogue we wrote – and that maybe he might change his mind, but he didn't.

Even in the wake of this, I think we still expected there to be a *Phoenix Nights 3*. We had a drawer full of ideas and it would have worked, but Peter didn't want to carry on. He announced that he wanted to take Max and Paddy away on a road trip and we said absolutely fine, foolishly assuming that he'd retain the writing team. I got on with it and wrote reams of dialogue for the bouncers and outlined suggested storylines and plots. I filtered them through to Peter. After about a month of hearing nothing, I phoned him – to be told that he'd changed his mind and intended writing it with Paddy. Fair enough, but I thought that he could have told me earlier. And that was that.

The production company phoned me a few months later and said that in one episode of the new show, there was to be a scene at the Phoenix Club, and would I be interested in appearing. I asked for the relevant scenes to be sent. When I saw them, I declined the offer – because the appearance was basically Jerry and the other regulars stripped naked standing against a wall while being hosed down by the fire brigade in a storyline about an anthrax scare, I believe. That was it, that was the scene, no dialogue just decontamination, so I didn't fancy it.

The scene is in the show. I have a body double and over the Phoenix Club entrance is a banner advertising 'Jerry's 60th Birthday' for some reason. Hilarious.

My Dad

M Y DAD'S HEALTH took a turn for the worse in the early nineties and he was diagnosed with Congestive Heart Disease (CHD). At first, it didn't incapacitate him too much, but he got progressively worse over the following years, developing oedema in his legs and other circulatory problems.

Around the time of *That Peter Kay Thing*, he was suffering and his condition had deteriorated. I remember him struggling to walk from the kitchen one Saturday and saying, 'Look at the state of me. This is what it's come to.' It was heartbreaking seeing him look so sad and dejected by this incapacitation.

His worsening illness coincided with Kay's daughter Jenny being appointed as a Senior Technician in the Cardiology Unit at the Royal Albert Edward Infirmary, Wigan. She suggested we send him there for assessment by her consultant, because something about his condition didn't sit well with her under the heading of CHD. Her instincts were right – and after various examinations and cardiac testing, it was found that he didn't have CHD at all, he had a very rare condition called constrictive pericarditis – trust him! In this disorder, the pericardium around the heart calcifies and inhibits heart function. It was, in some ways, a boost for us all, but also, in many ways, a source of anger and frustration, knowing that my dad had suffered all those years misdiagnosed and undergoing incorrect treatment.

On the positive side, the condition is treatable and, if the patient is fit enough, the pericardium can be removed surgically, freeing up the heart to function normally. The question was, was Dad fit enough to undergo such invasive surgery? He was only seventy-one, but the years struggling with the disorder had taken their toll. He went for a barrage of tests. It was lucky that I had finished work at this time, as I could ferry him from hospital to hospital for consultations, examinations and tests. They found that his liver enzymes were raised and weren't too happy about operating until they'd got to the bottom of why and so sent him for further tests.

Neil, Peter and I had gone up to St Gregory's late one afternoon to observe a 'Free and Easy' function, which is a bit like karaoke, but with the club backing band providing the music and with no screen for the lyrics. Anyone can get up and sing a song. It's good fun and we used the idea in *Phoenix 2*. While there, I took a call on my mobile from the cardiologist at Wigan, who told me that my dad had got liver cancer. He asked me for my guidance on whether he should tell him or not, or whether I wanted to take responsibility for doing it.

I didn't hesitate; I thanked him for all his brilliant efforts on behalf of my dad and said that I would do it. I wasn't sure if Dad wanted to know the truth, though, so I decided to ask my mum what she thought. I drove straight up to their house to see them. My mum didn't think we should tell my dad, and I respected her judgement. He knew, though, I'm sure of that. He'd retained a degree of knowledge regarding biochemistry tests and he must have known what his rising levels of liver enzymes indicated. This was in October/November time. All the family gathered at Mum and Dad's for Christmas and there is a great photo of him with us three kids (you can see it in the illustrated section of this book).

It was a Sunday evening in January and I was in the pub with my mates when I got a phone call from my ex-wife Julie, who said that I should come down to Mum and Dad's. I asked how bad he was, and she said that there was no hurry, and I knew then that he was dead. Although we'd all expected it, I was shocked because I'd been to visit him on Saturday afternoon as usual and although he'd looked poorly, he'd not seemed that bad.

Kay and I drove down to Bolton. By the time we got there, Julie and Stephen and Jill were there, together with my brother Pete. My wonderful father was lying on the bed that he'd had brought downstairs months earlier. He looked very peaceful and I sat with him, stroking his long grey hair, for a long and last time.

I have so many vivid, wonderful memories of him. So many that I could fill another book with his amazing life story; I've just realized that I've not even mentioned his venture into greengrocery!

I haven't said much either about his love of horse-racing, which he inherited from his father and passed on to me and my brother. I haven't dwelt on the traditional Saturday afternoons, when we would all gather at Mum and Dad's to pick our horses and discuss form, and Dad would trot out his latest theory – 'Always back Henry Candy on a Saturday' – then we'd go down the road to Ladbrokes and put our bets on, and in between races stroll across to the King's Head for a couple of pints and a catch-up on how our weeks had been. I remember arriving late one Saturday and going straight to Ladbrokes to join the queue for the cashier. A head turned round down the queue and our Pete smiled, and then he indicated further down the line and there was my dad, and right at the front was Grandad – makes you proud, three generations united in throwing money away on a horse called 'Lame Boy' in the two-thirty at Uttoxeter.

Dad used to shout at the screen in despair at tactics employed by the jockey. He hated his horse leading the race and would moan loudly, 'No! What is he doing?' Mind you, he'd do the same if his horse was dropped out last of the field in the early stages. And he would never, ever back Lester Piggott.

This position dated back to an incident that arose when I was a toddler and my dad was working at Walkers Tannery. It was Friday and pay day and there was an evening meeting at Ascot. Dad had a tip for a horse ridden by Lester Piggott. This was a seriously strong tip and so (and I think alcohol may have played a part ...), he bet his whole week's wages on this horse. So that was the mortgage money, the household bills money, my tooth fairy money – you get the picture.

The horse won at three to one! He'd trebled his money and he'd be coming home with the equivalent of near enough a month's wages. As he celebrated, there was an announcement – 'Steward's Enquiry' – and all went quiet. You have to remember that this was in the days before televisions appeared in bookies; the commentary was audio only and so nobody knew exactly what the enquiry was about until, 'Second objects to the first for taking his ground in the final half furlong.' How he must have sweated on that result, which came after five minutes, 'Objection granted, the placings are reversed'; he'd lost all his money and he never bet on 'that Lester Piggott' again.

I know that Dad was incredibly proud of his three children. I had had a successful career in the hospital labs and then in comedy; Joy was a gifted artist and had travelled the world; and Pete had overcome all odds to forge a successful career in IT. Dad said to me and Mum in a moment of reflection just before he died, 'Where did we go wrong, Marian? Our three kids have had successful careers, they all live in lovely big houses and drive nice cars, and look at us, back where we started, in a little terraced house just up the road from where we were born.'

And I said, 'You didn't go wrong, Dad, your children are testament to that. All those things you just said about us, all the achievements we've had in life, all the good things we enjoy and our children enjoy, are because of you and Mum. You didn't go wrong at all.'

He didn't live to see *Phoenix Nights 2*, but when we were filming it, Peter let me take up the tapes to show him and he loved them.

This is a short extract from what I said about him at his funeral …

I know a lot of people think that they've got the best dad in the world, but we never thought that. We always knew for sure that we had the best dad in the world. The greatest thing, the most precious gift we got from him were not presents, not toys, nothing like that; it was that we always felt loved, and still do.

He inspired us, and later his grandchildren, in so many ways – and he did it simply by setting us a good example. He was a good man, a kind man and a loving man. He was an exceptionally bright and intelligent man, and without his inspiration, none of us, his children, would be where we are today. The depth of his knowledge was amazing, yet he never boasted about it, never lectured us or imposed it upon us; he just used to beat us hollow when we watched University Challenge *every week.*

When he died, I found on his table near his chair books on art, the Bible and a volume by Dietrich Bonhoeffer, the theologian who was martyred by the Nazis. In his bookcase were many of the great works of literature, poetry and philosophy. He could quote Nietszche and Kierkegaard, Plato and Marcus Aurelius with authority. There were books on his favourite artists – Renoir, Degas and Van Gogh – and his record collection featured all the well-known classical works, as well as some of the more obscure works of Mahler, Schubert, Beethoven and Mozart. And as we all know, the amazing thing about all that is that he was self-taught. He left school with no qualifications apart from a twenty-five-yard swimming certificate, which he must have cheated to get because I learnt at a very early age that he always had one foot on the bottom.

I could go on for hours talking about my dad, but the bottom line is that if I am half the man he was, I'm more than happy because he was a very special person and my best friend. I can't begin to tell you how much I miss him.

On the night he died, I asked him for a sign that he was alright and he sent me one; so don't worry, he's okay.

Mayday, Mayday

KAY PROPOSED TO me a few months later. I say 'proposed', but what actually happened was that we were sitting in the back garden on a Sunday morning and she was reading the paper when she suddenly said, 'Do you know that if you die, I don't get your pension.'

We arranged the wedding for June 2003, but kept it a secret, and nearer the time invited friends and family to a barbecue at our house. We booked Salmesbury Hall for the wedding as it has a lovely little chapel for the ceremony and a old banqueting hall complete with massive fireplace for the reception. We left it until the last minute before telling everybody that we were having a wedding and not a barbecue.

We were blessed with the only sunny day in June 2003 and everyone turned out in their finery. We had a jazz trio playing on the lawn – musician friends of Kay's – to welcome the guests. Our daughters were bridesmaids, my son Steve was my best man, and Kay walked down the aisle to 'You Belong to Me'. When she got to the front, we had a little dance, which sounds a bit cheesy, but sort of worked. It was only a short civil ceremony, but I got quite emotional and struggled to hold back the tears.

After the ceremony, we had all the photographs to take and another friend of ours, John, did the honours. We'd had this idea that while we were occupied with the photos, the jazz trio should play and the guests would be served a cocktail of peach schnapps, vodka and champagne. We'd not really thought that through, had we?

As we walked back across the lawn towards our guests, I said to Kay, 'Is it me or do they look blurred?' When we had left them a mere half an hour before, they'd looked smart and sensible – and now they were all a bit wobbly and giggly. Some of the men had the ladies' hats on at a jaunty angle and some ladies had lost their shoes. They all looked ridiculously happy.

After the meal, I made a short speech, during which I had to stop a couple of times when talking about my dad, and then Steve made a brilliant best man's speech, funny and touching in equal measure. Other friends joined us for the evening 'do' and Archie Kelly sang 'Me and Mrs Jones' for our first dance.

I'd chartered a yacht on a Turkish flotilla for the honeymoon because over the past couple of years we'd become interested in sailing – don't ask me why, I have no idea, except that I've always been drawn to the sea. (I need to go back to Vinegar Vera to find out why, unless it was the Noah's ark period.)

We began our new hobby by going with our friends Tony and Barbara on a 'learn to sail' holiday around the Ionian islands. This was a big deal for Kay, who gets travel-sick big time, but it was something I'd always wanted to do, so she got some special seasickness tablets on prescription, bless her. When she was a child, her parents left her behind with her gran when they went on holiday because she was always sick for the whole trip. A year or so before, when I'd got a gig in Singapore, she got sick in the taxi going to Preston station!

As it turned out, we loved sailing and at the end of the week we got a certificate, which proved to be meaningless. We sailed to Lefkas, Ithaca, Megannissi and Kefalonia and even took part in the Ionian Regatta, which was a brilliant experience and in which we came second in class, thanks to our skipper Joel, who was a fantastic sailor. Mind you, it has to be said that he fell into the harbour most nights when he came back from the taverna worse for wear, managing somehow to miss the boat completely when trying to board!

We decided that we wanted to sail more, but we also wanted to gain the qualifications that would allow us to skipper our own yacht, and so we enquired of the Royal Yachting Association (RYA) as to the nearest college that ran a RYA Day Skipper theory class. Unbelievably, it was in Horwich, Bolton – about fifteen minutes down the road from us! So we signed up and studied yacht design and layout, navigation, chart plotting, rules of the 'road', sail trimming, safety procedures, meteorology, tidal charts and many other seafaring topics. We both passed and Kay went on to do another year and gained her 'Coastal Skipper' certificate.

And so it was that we arrived in Bodrum, Turkey on our honeymoon and took charge of our thirty-five-foot yacht. The yacht was very new and the layout of the ropes ('sheets' to be accurate) and mainsail and foresail (genoa) was completely different to the old yacht we'd learned on almost two years before. It was part of a small flotilla, accompanied by two other (much bigger, much faster) yachts (both skippered by very experienced sailors), plus the lead crew's yacht.

We nearly died in the very first hour. After showing us the charts of the area, helping us plot a course for our first port of call and giving us a guided tour of our yacht, the flotilla organizer took us out into the bay in order to familiarize ourselves with the reversing and steerage of the yacht. He told us that the sail on the first day was the longest, at about eight hours, but it was worth it in order to get to the massive unspoiled Hisaranou Gulf. He then bade us goodbye and dived off the boat and swam back to shore.

We chugged towards the mouth of the bay, the sun beating down, the stereo playing chill-out music. There wasn't much wind, but then it began to gust and so, like the complete novices that we were (read 'complete idiots'), we hoisted the full genoa and then every inch of mainsail and turned the engine off. As we left behind the tranquil waters of the bay and headed towards the channel between the Turkish mainland and the island of Kos, we were hit by the full force of the high wind that gusts strongly down the channel and forms a giant natural wind-tunnel!

The wind hit us broadside and knocked us over – almost totally over – and we totally panicked, as you would, because we had absolutely no control. I tried to steer the boat into the wind, but the pressure on the full sails was incredible, and no matter how hard I fought, I wasn't going to beat the wind. We now know that we should have let the wind take us about, but we were terrified that it would turn us over.

After five awful minutes, Kay was horrifically seasick and we were still fighting the wind and the massive list of the yacht. I sometimes think how lucky we were that one of us didn't end up overboard because we were battered at a ridiculous angle for ages.

I instinctively told Kay to let the rope for the genoa go completely, and she undid it from the winch and it began flapping wildly and noisily – but it was a different matter getting the massive mainsail down. It is a fact that you can't drop a mainsail while it is full of wind; the pressure is too great. What you need to do – I now know – is bang the engine back on and rev it up and turn into the wind, so you are head on to it. There is then little or no direct pressure on the sail and you can drop it. Alternatively, you can let the boom out until the sail is head-on into the wind for the same effect.

At the time, we knew nothing of this. We had our theory certificates, but no real practical knowledge – what made us think that we could sail a proper big yacht?! Eventually, it dawned on us that we should use the motor to head into wind and after what must have been half an hour, we had the mainsail down and had somehow managed to get the genoa rope back and get the foresail under control and refurled.

Our problem now was that we were way behind schedule, the sea was rough and the wind still strong – and Kay was totally ill. We decided that we would have to motor the rest of the way, so that was eight hours into a choppy sea, hitting every wave head on.

I have to say that after that baptism of fire, we had a fantastic week's sailing and visited several stunning Turkish bays and harbours, which were completely inaccessible by road and so wonderfully isolated, with just one or maybe two tavernas, which allowed you to park at their moorings if you spent the evening in their hostelry.

We have sailed a lot since and have taken the kids on flotilla holidays around the Ionian Sea and recently around Skiathos and Skopolos, where they filmed *Mamma Mia*. One day, I want to go back to Turkey and sail that same route – without the terror and feeling of total helplessness, of course – because the coastline we explored and spent time in was stunningly beautiful.

We had another near-death experience on Kay's brother Stephen's yacht, *Calista*, off the Bay of Lyons, when we were hit by the

Tramontagne wind that sweeps down France. Stephen had asked us if we would crew for him and his wife Kath on the yacht's maiden voyage from Marseilles to Palma, Majorca via Barcelona, and it was an offer we couldn't refuse.

Their son, Michael, joined us in Marseilles, where the yacht was undergoing sea-trials. We sailed at midday and for eleven hours there wasn't a breath of wind as we motored at a steady seven knots through the Mediterranean. Stephen plotted our position and advised that we were approaching the Gulf of Lyons; Kath said that she'd been reading about the incredibly strong wind that came out of nowhere and blew down through the Gulf. She said that the warning signs were cigar-shaped clouds, but we didn't take a lot of notice because the sailing had been so calm and the weather beautiful.

As the sun began to set, Kath pointed to the distant sky and asked, 'Would you say that those clouds were cigar-shaped?' None of us thought they were.

At about eleven o'clock, Stephen organized 'watches'. Michael and I took the first four hours and everyone else went down below to bed. We continued to motor along surrounded by the placid Mediterranean, illuminated by an incredibly bright, almost full moon that shone in a cloudless, star-filled sky.

Then we felt a breath of wind, and we decided to put up half the genoa and a third of the mainsail. We got them up and trimmed quickly, then knocked the engine off and we were sailing. The wind increased a notch and we hoisted a bit more sail. It continued to increase – and now we had nearly all the sail out and we were proper sailing, real fast, ten, eleven knots: exhilarating.

Then the force of the wind doubled in seconds, then trebled – and we were in trouble. I asked Michael to get Stephen, who by some miracle was fast asleep on his bunk. Stephen came up and assessed the situation, got everyone on deck and switched on the motor. Kath said, 'I told you those clouds were cigar-shaped,' as we struggled to furl the genoa and slowly, very slowly got it in.

By now, the wind was incredibly strong. We had to get most of the mainsail in, so Stephen revved the engine and fought to bring us into the wind. He ordered Michael up to the mast to pull the mainsail down as I eased the sheet, but Kath wouldn't have that!

'No, Michael's not going up there, he's too young to die. Dave, you go!'

Oh right, thanks, I've done all my living, have I?!

I clambered forward and strapped my safety harness onto the mast and tried hard to pull the sail down, but I couldn't get the final reef (needed to secure the sail) onto the hook. Stephen had to come and help – meaning someone else had to take the wheel. Kay, looking a peculiar shade of green, heroically dragged herself off the floor and took control, while Stephen joined me and together we got the last reef on.

As we got back to the cockpit, there was a strange, loud 'bang', which turned out to be the gearbox signalling its surrender; so now we had no control over the yacht and the fifteen-foot waves were coming at us like giant battering rams out of the dark.

We rode it out for about an hour, by which time only Stephen and I had avoided the acute seasickness affecting the others, whom we could see lying on the cabin floor below. Kay was half-sitting, half-lying with a bucket, which she hugged for dear life and occasionally vomited into. Then Michael, who had been the last to succumb, panicked and tried to take the bucket off Kay; she saw that his need was greater than hers and relinquished her grip on it. She crawled to a cupboard and retrieved a frying pan. I remember thinking, 'A frying pan? That's not going to work. That is possibly the singularly worst choice of vomit receptacle imaginable; there is a very real risk of splashback there.'

The sea began to get even bigger and rougher and scarier, and we were taking a hell of a battering, so we decided that we must send out a distress call. We decided not to send a 'Mayday', the call reserved for the most serious of maritime emergencies, but we would send a 'Pan Pan', which is the next most serious. I was despatched down to the cabin to do this.

The three sickies were in a bad state as I set the VHF to emergency channel and sent out a 'Pan Pan', quoting the name of the yacht, brief details of our emergency and our position. No answer. I tried again and again, but no one answered. (We later found out that the antenna had not been connected! The VHF had worked during sea trials because it was tested in the port of Marseilles and transmitted adequately over that limited distance, but it didn't work on the open sea.) So that was it: we were on our own.

We'd been battered for seven hours or so by the time the sun came up. I stupidly assumed that things would be better in the light of day, but I was completely wrong – now I could actually see the size of the waves coming at us!

At about seven o'clock, we spotted a trawler and set off an emergency flare, which they saw and set a course for us, bless 'em. They were circling us about twenty minutes later and we tried to communicate in basic Spanish; I spun the useless wheel to demonstrate that we had no control and shouted in my best Spanish: *'El f**kto!'* I dropped my jeans to show them the colour of my underpants and they sailed off! *Bastardos!*

We were totally gutted by this apparent callousness and I suggested that we try to sail. We put up a bit of the genoa, but it didn't help much … and then we saw the coastguard heading our way. The trawler had obviously been in touch with them and given our position, so not *bastardos* after all. They towed us into the lovely harbour of Roses, north of Barcelona – and just to add insult to injury, our slowly turning propeller snagged a mooring line as we were manoeuvred into a berth!

Kay and I got onto the shore and kissed the ground, vowing never ever to set foot on a yacht again. But despite this, of course, we do still sail and both took part in the Cowes 'Round the Island' race onboard the charity yacht *Prostate UK*.

As we turned with the wind behind us at the Needles, our spinnaker fell off … but that's another story for another day.

Buddy Holly and the Dragon Tattoo

A BRILLIANT BONUS of being a successful stand-up comedian is that you get asked to perform at venues all around the world. I've worked in Singapore, Hong Kong, Dubai, Abu Dhabi, Spain, Germany, Portugal and Ireland ... and inevitably funny stuff happens on every trip. Two trips stand out above the others, though, for different reasons, and they were to Dubai and Hong Kong.

I had been booked to do the Dubai gigs many months previous to the date of travel, which fate contrived to be the week prior to the invasion of Iraq. I don't know how well you know your geography, but Dubai is pretty much next door to Iraq, and understandably this preyed heavily on the minds of entertainers scheduled to make the trip out there in the troubled times. Many acts, mainly American it has to be said, pulled out of travelling, fearing attack from the Iraqi forces, but us Brits are made of sterner stuff. (In any case, we were getting well paid and gold is incredibly cheap out there.)

At Manchester Airport, Kay and I (I always take her with me. It saves kissing her goodbye © Antiques Joke Show 1977) bumped into a bloke I'd met on the club circuit at one time, who was a pretty fair vocalist. He told me that he was going out to perform at the Dubai Country Club in a 'Rock and Roll Legends' type of show. He was Eddie Cochrane; Elvis, Buddy Holly and Roy Orbison were also in the production. He invited us out to see the show if I had time in my schedule, and we chatted about the Iraqi conflict and the performers who were bottling flying out there.

Later, as we arrived at the gate, I was aware of a good deal of noise, agitation and raised voices. Then Elvis came over with a look of disbelief on his face. Eddie asked him what was the matter and he said that Buddy

Holly wouldn't get on the plane! He said his wife didn't want him to go as she was worried sick about him being so close to the war and he wasn't keen on flying anyway (who could blame him?). We followed Elvis back to the heated discussion, where Roy Orbison and the rest of the band were pleading with Buddy to get on the plane, how could they do the show without him?

I was the only one on Buddy's side. 'Leave Buddy alone!' I shouted. 'If Buddy doesn't want to get on the plane, he doesn't want to get on the plane' – because I'm thinking, seriously, the last thing I want on a nine-hour flight to Dubai is Buddy Holly sitting next to me. Buddy didn't fly.

When we arrived at Dubai Airport, it took hours to get through security; it was chaos. There were soldiers with machine guns barking orders at everyone and there must have been over a thousand people in the arrivals hall. We eventually got to passport control and the woman on duty took Kay's passport, studied it, compared the photo and stamped her through.

Then she took mine, studied it, compared the photo, looked puzzled, held the photo up to my face (it is a bad photo), studied it a bit more – and then summoned a big machine-gun-toting military policeman over. She said something to him and he took the passport, studied it some more, and then held up the photo beside me again, just at the moment when the noise and clamour of the arrivals hall seemed to stop, as it sometimes does. Kay timed her moment perfectly and said to the guard in a loud voice, made even louder by the sudden lull, 'I know, he looks like a terrorist, doesn't he?'

I gave her a 'Thanks for that' look as I felt two thousand eyes turn in my direction … but then it was over, the noise resumed and all seemed well – until the guard found the plastic bag full of Coffee-mate in Kay's bag! Well, you can't get it abroad.

I've been lucky enough to play Hong Kong twice and on the first occasion, we flew into the old infamous airport, which the planes had to approach through the skyscrapers, flying at ridiculous angles and with breathtaking proximity. I remember that I was very apprehensive because I knew of the airport's notoriety. The flight went beautifully, and then the seatbelt light came on and the pilot spoke over the intercom.

'Hello,' he said. 'This is your pilot Paul Redmond speaking, we have started our approach into Hong Kong Airport.' I thought, 'He sounds like a confident sort of chap. Probably ex-RAF; squadron leader, I wouldn't be surprised. I expect he's had years of experience in flying this route.'

That made me relax a little bit, but that only lasted for about a second as he continued, 'I'm pleased to say that first officer Andy Peters has volunteered to land the aircraft today,' and I blurted out loud, 'Andy Peters? Shouldn't he be in a broom cupboard somewhere?'

And then I had another thought! Exactly what does 'volunteered' mean?! Was there some sort of argument going on up there? Something like …

Pilot A: I'm not landing it. I landed it last time.

Pilot B: Well, don't look at me, I've flown it all the way here.

Andy Peters: I'll have a go.

Pilots: Will you? Oh, nice one, Andy.

As it turned out, it was a beautiful landing – but guys: think about your choice of words!

The gigs in Hong Kong are at the Punchline Comedy Club, which is based in the Viceroy restaurant, situated right on the harbour front near the famous 'Star' ferry terminal. It's a brilliant Indian restaurant in a stunning location. When you stand onstage, you can see the breathtaking skyline of Hong Kong through the big windows and you think, 'How great is this? Just because I can make people laugh, I get to come to this fantastic city and witness all these fabulous sights!'

There are three comedians on each bill and if you are ever in Hong Kong, I urge you to seek it out. The entrance fee includes an amazing Indian buffet set out on the terrace, which overlooks the manic and exciting Kowloon Harbour and has the skyline as the backdrop. After the buffet, the gig starts inside the restaurant, which is set out with chairs theatre-style, and it's a great show.

I love Hong Kong city: it's one of my favourite places ever. I love the colour, the vibrancy, the noise and the hustle and bustle. I love the fact that it is a stunningly beautiful and very modern city, yet at street level it's still very Chinese, with markets and shops echoing with the shouts of the traders, coloured neon lights flashing on and off all around, and the constant clanging of the old-fashioned trams as they clatter past. In England, we have that saying that you wait for a bus for ages and then three come at once. In Hong Kong, you don't wait hardly a minute and yet still three come at once, painted in garish colours with bells clanging constantly.

And don't forget that Hong Kong is an island that provides many other opportunities for the traveller and tourist. Visit the beaches and the famous Stanley Market; get a tramcar to the top of Victoria Mount and sip a cocktail at skyscraper level whilst drinking in the breathtaking skyline from above!

Hong Kong is famous for its tattoo parlours, which have always been sought out by visitors, most notably the sailors of the Allied fleets. On my first visit, one of the other comedians on the bill, who I knew quite well, decided he wanted a dragon tattoo on his back to complement his already staggering range of body art. I went with him to have a look at examples of the type of tattoo available, and was stunned by the staggeringly huge choice.

I decided to do a bit of sightseeing while he was being tattooed, and so I left him to it and said I'd return in a couple of hours. Whilst out and about, and after a couple of ice-cold Chinese beers, I had this little idea in my head which made me laugh out loud, which is always a certain sign that the idea is brilliantly funny (which I still think it was). In retrospect, I should have definitely thought longer and harder about the reaction that it might provoke – but I didn't, I just did it.

I walked back into the tattoo parlour – suppressing a manic little giggle – and sought out my pal, who was still sitting patiently in the chair while the tattooist worked on his back. I walked straight up to observe the artist's craft from behind and feigned a startled, stunned and shocked expression. Then I shouted in a loud voice, 'No!! He said *"dragon"*, not *"wagon"*!'

That is funny, right? I thought everyone would agree that this was a top joke. I didn't anticipate that my pal would jump up and try to look over his shoulder (which is ridiculous; you can't see your own back. As my daughter once said quite profoundly, when she was just a toddler, 'Daddy, no matter how hard you try, you can never see your chin.' So your back is way out of sight, right?).

Anyway, his instinctive, shocked, in my opinion overreaction caused the tattooist's pen (do they call it a pen?) to zzzzzzzzzzzzzzzzzzz up my mate's back, leaving a trail of dots in its wake. And my mate still can't laugh about it, even though the tattooist bloke managed to incorporate the extra line into a very fancy-looking dragon's tail, I must say.

The second time I played Hong Kong was a couple of weeks before Christmas. The city was lit up like an enormous Christmas tree and Christmas carols blared out of every shop and bar; it was magical.

That is, until I came down with a terrible dose of flu. Real proper flu, I'm talking. Sore throat, runny eyes, banging headache, sky-high temperature, shivers and aches flu. I had four gigs to do and I basically got out of my sweaty wet bed, staggered to the gig, did the show and went back to bed, every single night. It totally ruined my trip because I was confined to bed the whole time.

One night, I must have been delirious because I decided that as I was still suffering after mountains of paracetamol, bottles of cough medicine, Nurofen, throat linctus etc., what I really must try is the traditional medical treatment. After all, I undoubtedly had Hong Kong flu, so what better place to find a natural holistic remedy? I got up at 2 a.m., dressed and made my way down to the other city that never sleeps in search of an ancient Chinese apothecary.

I actually remembered seeing one down a side street in Kowloon on my last visit (possibly a hallucination), so I decided to catch the Star ferry over there – and this, I repeat, is now at 2.30 in the morning. I wandered the back streets of Kowloon for ages … until suddenly it was there! The window was full of weird jars full of dried plants and powders and a few that might have contained insects or tiny lizards or possibly sticks.

I entered the little shop and there he was behind the counter, the archetypal inscrutable Chinese man, complete with wispy beard and pigtail. He looked about 123 years old, give or take. I approached him and then, for some unknown reason, I started speaking to him in English with a slight Chinese accent and broken phrasing, missing out occasional words that I edited out as unnecessary. This isn't as dodgy as it first sounds. I genuinely, in my own head, automatically did this, assuming it would help him understand.

'Hewo,' I said. ('Hewo', for God's sake!) He bowed. Brilliant, I thought. I pointed down my throat and said, 'Soah, soah' (translation: sore), and he nodded. I felt my forehead and said, 'Ho' (translation: hot); he nodded again. I gripped myself with both arms and said, 'Shibber, shibber' – no, really, I did; I thought that 'shibber' was the perfect Chinese translation of 'shiver'. He looked at me sagely as I questioned, 'You ha somthey fo me?' (You have something for me?)

He smiled and ducked down behind the counter, then reappeared, placed a bottle gently before me, and spoke for the first time in almost perfect English! 'This very good medicine.' (Thi beri gu medsin.) I stared at the bottle and said, 'I can get Night Nurse at home, mate.'

He honestly gave me Night Nurse. I said, 'Haven't you got any magical roots or ragwort or horny goat weed or jojoba? Anything? Ginkgo biloba? What about butter?! I know, I'll have butter for my temperature and some vinegar, please; I don't know if you are aware, my wise old friend, that vinegar is nature's cure-all. Oh, and while you're at it, dig us out some knitbone ...' Then I fainted.

Lost in Translation

IT CAN'T JUST be me who goes into half-arsed auto-translation mode, can it? My mates think it's hilarious when I 'speak' Italian or Thai or Indian in those respective restaurants. I order and look up to find them staring at me with stupid grins.

'I'm doing it again, aren't I?'

'You always do it, mate.'

I did it the other week with someone who stuttered. I stuttered back a bit! I wish I didn't do it, because it probably sounds quite patronizing when I write it down, but I honestly don't mean it to be; I just want to be nice and friendly.

I'll tell you something else that's mad; I do it with regional accents as well! I did a couple of gigs in Cork a few years ago; another beautiful part of the world. I've been back on holiday several times since and the south-west and west coast of Ireland are breathtakingly beautiful. If you've never been, please go and take a trip around the Ring of Kerry and the Dingle Peninsula and take time to visit Kenmare and Killarney and Kildare and most other places beginning with 'K'.

I had one of the best nights of my life in a small bar in Knocknagree (another 'K', see?), where a small door from the bar led to a world of years gone by as you passed through it into a dance hall. Johnny O'Leary, the great fiddle player, appeared onstage and said, 'Good evening' to a couple of hundred people, then continued, 'Here we go, then,' and he started playing and didn't stop until midnight. We danced reels and polkas and goodness knows what else under the enthusiastic instruction of the local folk.

Prior to that, on our first morning in Ireland, we went shopping in the small town of Newstreet, where we were staying. The others wanted a coffee, but I said I'd go off for a bit of a wander to see if I could find a shop that sold corkscrews, as we'd forgotten to pack one. I soon discovered a small ironmongers; well, ironmongers and bar, obviously. (Nearly every other shop has a small bar and that, for me, is the hallmark of a civilized society.)

The little Irish fella, dressed in traditional ironmonger's brown overalls, smiled a greeting as I approached him. I smiled back and said without thought or hesitation, 'Would you be having a corkscrew at all?' My brain screamed at me, 'What?! Why are you talking like that?' Why on earth didn't I say, 'Do you have a corkscrew please?' or 'Do you sell corkscrews?'

I maintained my inane, glazed-smile look as the little man said, 'Sure I have,' and wandered off to fetch one. He brought me one and said, 'That will be two euros, please.' I gave him the money and managed a near-normal, 'Thank you so much.' Then he said, 'Would you fancy a glass of stout?' and I looked at my watch, discovered it was almost ten o'clock in the morning, thought this was brilliant and said so: 'To be sure, that would be brilliant.' (!)

He led me to the bar, which was next to the hosepipes and gardening kit. I sat at a table and drank my pint of Guinness, thinking, 'What a wonderful world.' Halfway through my pint, the others walked past and saw me sitting in the ironmonger's window, and I smiled and held up my corkscrew. Result.

I decided that I actually needed to learn a language rather than speak in English with a foreign accent, and so, during my frequent trips to Spain, I took the opportunity to polish up my linguistic expertise. It was not without its hiccups.

I was doing a gig in La Manga when a Spanish waiter told me that '*I cagado en su leche*' is a traditional Spanish greeting, so I tried it out a couple of times – and discovered that it was also a surprisingly good way of seeing the sights at the local accident and emergency department. This spurred me on to learn some Spanish properly, in order to avoid another broken nose, but do you know what? I am so not a natural. I'll give you an e.g. (Is it e.g or i.e? I always get confused. Call it e.g.)

I was in Benidorm recently with seven mates on a jolly. I like Benidorm a lot; I know that it gets a bad press sometimes and there are people who look down their noses at it, but it has so much to offer. The beaches are brilliant – some of the best in Europe – the old town is fab, and its interesting streets and alleys reveal a multitude of small bars and traditional tapas restaurants, some with an unbelievable number of dishes, plus the resort boasts entertainment to suit everybody.

We were in the old town on the way to a show at Benidorm Palace (check it out) and we'd just finished a delicious paella, so I said as much to the waiter: '*La comida es delicioso*' ('The meal was delicious' – well, near enough). My mates were impressed and so was the waiter. Later, I asked for the bill, aiming to impress again – and this is where I made a schoolboy error.

Question for you discernable travellers: what is Spanish for 'the bill'? Correct, '*La cuenta*'. Question two: what is Spanish for 'cheese'? Yes, five points (*cinco punto*) to the fit lass in seat 36C, it is '*queso*'. Now, on paper, they look like completely different words, but now say them phonetically – altogether, everybody on the plane get into the holiday mood – 'Kwenta' and 'Kweso' – and again … (For those more fluid in Spanish than I am, I know it should be 'Kehso', but to a beginner it looks like 'Kweso', okay?)

So I shouted confidently to the waiter, '*La queso, por favor*,' and he looked at me questioningly: '*La queso?*' he said, and I said, '*Sí.*' Then he said something I didn't quite catch, but I think he meant, 'For everyone?' and I said, '*Sí*,' and to illustrate my point (and show off a bit more) I counted out my companions! '*Una, dos, tres, cuatro, cinco, seis, siete, ocho … para ocho.*'

He went, he came back and, honestly, you have never ever seen so much cheese in all your life, all of which he deposited on our table. Of course, I'm a total idiot, so I think that this is a freebie. You know at the end of a meal when they give you stuff for being good customers? I said to the lads, 'Look at this! You don't get this in England. You just get a bit of fruit or some sweets or a rubbish apple liqueur.' And then we get stuck in and about half an hour later, we had just about managed to see off the cheese mountain.

Then one of my mates, Steve, says, 'Come on, Dave, we'd better get a wriggle on, the show starts in fifteen minutes,' so I look for our waiter ('Where can he have got to?') and then he appears and I beckon him over. He approaches and I say, '*La queso*,' and he just gives me a weird look, shrugs and disappears. Two minutes later, he's coming back and Steve says, 'He's bringing more cheese, Dave,' and there he is, wheeling Sainsbury's cheese counter towards us on a trolley. I shouted, 'Noooo!' (in Spanish, obviously).

As a postscript, I am sad to report that Steve is now addicted to cheese – and I mean proper addicted. He has to wear those Kraft cheese slices like nicotine patches. He had a bad period when he snorted Parmesan, but he's on the mend now, thank goodness.

Speaking of drugs (well, you know) …

Just Say No

I DON'T THINK that it's a secret that the use of drugs is commonplace in the wonderful world we call 'show', but I've never been tempted. Possibly it's because of my upbringing, certainly it's because I've seen the effect of drugs first hand, and basically it's because I've never fancied it. I've never smoked a cigarette, not one, not even had a drag, and I take no real credit for that because smoking wasn't a big deal amongst my peers growing up, and so there was no pressure to conform; and in any case, even if I had been tempted, I knew how my parents would react, and I didn't want them to be disappointed in me.

Working on the comedy circuit over the years, I have been offered all sorts of substances and witnessed the effect they have had on my fellow performers. I once saw a comedian on the late show at the Comedy Store storm the audience for the first ten minutes, then lose them completely for the second ten. She came offstage totally confused, 'I don't know what happened. I was going great. I had them, then they'd gone.' I told her that indeed she had done a great ten minutes – but then she'd done the same ten minutes again! Seriously. You have to remember that sometimes you could do five shows on a Saturday night in London, dashing from one venue to another; obviously some performers need a little help keeping 'up'.

Kay is even more naive than I am about the drug scene, bless her. She very rarely accompanied me to shows in those early days when I was travelling extensively, chasing gigs all over the place while she did extra shifts or on-call at the hospital, but there was one occasion when she had come with me, and which we still talk about.

We were in the green room, chatting with three other comics with show time approaching, when the comic who was compèring rushed in late and went straight into the toilet. He reappeared shortly afterwards and asked if anyone had a knife or razor blade. I said, 'No, sorry,' and while the others searched about their person, Kay started looking in her handbag. I whispered through a fixed smile, 'Leave it.' She gave me a look and carried on searching, as one by one the others came up empty-handed. Kay then smiled and offered the object of her search to the comedian. 'I've got some scissors!' she said.

I said, all smiley, 'Please put them away.'

'Why?' she asked, a little confused.

'I'll tell you later.'

Then someone found a knife and the guy ducked back into the loo and came out five minutes later rubbing his nose, and announced, 'There's a line in there if anyone wants it.'

Kay said to me, 'Isn't that nice?' and I said, 'What?' and she said, 'That you comedians write lines for each other.' I looked at her, thinking, 'She's got to be joking, right?' but no, she was all smiles and I thought, 'Yeah, right, it's like a tradition. We write lines for each other and then we leave them in the toilet!' I thought, 'I bet mine's got something to do with cocaine and scissors.'

I once did a gig in Lisbon, another beautiful city, and on the morning after the show, which was a Saturday, Kay and I strolled through the main square and down a pedestrianized road that leads down to the sea. There was a street market and the place was buzzing.

As I looked in shop windows and studied the stalls, I became aware of Kay shouting at a grubby little man, ' "No," I've said! How many times?'

I went over as the man sloped off and asked her, 'What's going on?'

She replied, 'That horrible man has been pestering me all the way down the street. He keeps trying to sell me a block of chocolate and it's not even in a wrapper! Have you seen the colour of his hands? Who would be stupid enough to buy chocolate off him? You wouldn't know what it is.'

Indeed you wouldn't – but I tell you this: you've gotta love her for that, haven't you?

Overnight Success

WITH THE SUCCESS of *Phoenix Nights* and my elevation to minor 'stardom' – gauged by people shouting 'Jerry the Berry!' at me in the street and asking me where the black bin bags were in ASDA – I decided I'd better get myself a fancy London agent and my first choice was Comedy Store Management.

I'd always had a good relationship with the office and the legend that is Don Ward. I met with Charlotte and Don and outlined my plans and they agreed to manage and represent me. Charlotte organized my first ever tour – 'The Overnight Success Tour' – and booked it into theatres of varying sizes around the country. I was apprehensive about the size of the tour and theatres, but Charlotte and Don, as always, were incredibly enthusiastic in their encouragement and support. The tour more or less sold out and I had the best time.

Justin Moorhouse was my special guest on tour. He was a tad overweight and had an unhealthy lifestyle, so he decided that he would take the opportunity while travelling with me to become a vegetarian. I was impressed, and applauded and encouraged this initiative when he announced it in the car on the way to the first tour show in Cambridge.

I'd said that I'd drive to the first couple of gigs, and borrowed my wife's Peugeot 305 as my car wasn't a comfortable ride over long distances. And so it was that we turned onto the A1(M) on a bright sunny March day, an hour into our adventure.

Then Justin saw a Burger King.

'Can we just pop into here? I'm starving,' he said.

I looked at him in disbelief and replied, 'Two words: unhealthy lifestyle. Oh, and one more – vegetarian?'

He smiled weakly and said that he just wanted one last Whopper, just one, last one ever, so I pulled into the services and parked outside the burger place. He emerged minutes later with the biggest double, treble Whopper cheese-type burger whatever-they-call-them and got back into the car.

'I cannot tell you how disappointed I am in you,' I said.

He didn't reply; he couldn't as he'd just taken a massive bite of the giganta-burger. I pulled away and joined the slip road back onto the motorway, giving him a further disapproving look as he took another huge mouthful. He looked back at me, eyes wide now, and said something like 'Mbwwermuborri!'

I shook my head and said, 'You're a man of straw, you are,' at which he became even more agitated, staring just over my shoulder and repeating loudly, 'Mbwwermuborri!'

That's when the lorry hit us. I saw it at the last minute and braced myself as it side-swiped the rear wing and door, while Justin was knocked off his seat. He was instantly concerned about the bright red blood he was covered in. 'I'm bleeding, I'm bleeding!' he yelled.

'No, you're not,' I said. 'That's ketchup.'

I asked him why he didn't warn me and he insisted that he'd been trying to communicate 'through the power of eye'. The lorry driver dismounted his cab and limped towards us, repeating in a monotone, 'Not my fault, not my fault,' and to be fair it wasn't. I braced myself to call Kay at work and told her that one hour into the tour, I'd written off her car and it was mostly Justin's fault for wanting a burger … she took it as a joke and said, 'Yeah, right,' and then hung up.

In retrospect, we were lucky to escape alive because it was a proper massive truck and the car was really bent. We had to get a taxi to Cambridge and the show went really well, with Justin improvising his whole thirty-minute set around the accident and the 'Not my fault' driver. I worked with Justin recently at a charity comedy night for a Special Care Baby Unit and he was brilliant – why he isn't a massive comedy star I don't know, but hopefully his time will come. He is also, by the way, a committed vegetarian now; so top man all round.

One of the highlights of my new career was the nomination of 'The

Overnight Success Tour' for the prestigious *Manchester Evening News* Theatre Awards, in two categories. One was for 'Best Comedy Show' and the other was for 'Performance of the Year', which was voted for by the readers and which included shows from every genre of entertainment: Opera, Dance, Theatre, Music, etc. I was up against Peter Kay's all-conquering 'Mum Wants a Bungalow Tour' in both categories, so I wasn't holding my breath. Peter won Best Comedy Show and Sally Lindsay collected the award for him by reading out the acceptance speech that he'd texted in.

The *Manchester Evening News* Theatre Awards dinner at the Midland Hotel is possibly the best awards show on the planet; I have been privileged to host them in the past. The production of the event is always top class and themed; we walked into a 'Winter Wonderland' through a blizzard of snow the other year. The atmosphere is brilliant; warm and friendly, as you might expect. Bob Hoskins attended one year and said, 'Forget the BAFTAs, this is the bollocks,' and it is. The food is always stunning, the company great: we sat with Jason Manford, Jimmy Cricket, Badly Drawn Boy, the mad teacher from *Corrie* and the Bad Dingle from *Emmerdale* last year and had a right laugh from when the wine starts to flow at 12 noon, through the awards which end at 5-ish, and then onto the evening party.

And so it was that I was a smiling happy drunk by the time the last award was announced. The 'Performance of the Year' is the one to win because, as I mentioned, it crosses all genres and is voted for by the readers. Anyway, the point is that I wasn't listening when they announced the winner, but noticed quite quickly that everyone was applauding and looking at me with weird smiley faces, and then Kay screamed, 'You've won it!' and I staggered onstage and, for the first time in my life, was lost for words, such was the shock and surprise. I was in the car going home when a text on my mobile snapped me out of my trance. It simply said, 'What's he won that for?' which I think must have been sent in error.

I am lucky enough to have quite a few awards on my shelf at home, but the 'Performance of the Year' takes pride of place. It meant that at last I'd made it as a comedian and I'd done it the hard way. I'd done it my way. I'd not compromised; I'd not taken bad advice from a multitude of people who said that I needed to be more outspoken and edgier and provocative to succeed. You are what you are and I am what I am; I can only write and perform material that I think is funny, that makes me laugh.

I realized early days that of course I am not unique and that if I see, hear, think, imagine or invent something that makes me laugh inwardly, then it will probably make the majority of ordinary people laugh as well. My job – and a comedian's skill, I think – is to take these ideas and exaggerate them to wring every ounce of humour out of them, and in doing so, to trigger off other ideas that often take you by surprise and steer you off at a tangent or help develop the same theme further. A good comedian must possess a high level of creativity and, most importantly, lateral thinking, in order to harvest the highest yield of comedy material from a given idea and then deliver the pay-offs with that crucial element of shock and surprise and … timing.

Charlotte did a deal with Universal to film 'The Overnight Success Tour' show at the wonderful City Varieties Theatre, Leeds and to distribute the DVD of the tour. Universal wanted me wearing a white jacket on the DVD cover to 'connect' me with Jerry from *Phoenix Nights*, and also to have small banners saying 'Co-writer and co-star of *Phoenix Nights*', but there were objections from some quarters so I happily reverted to my trademark black PVC jacket and the banners were relegated to the back cover. The DVD sold well in any case and got me a Gold Disc, which hangs in my kitchen.

Round about the same time, I was approached to release Jerry's songs on CD, which sounded like a great idea and I'd have loved to have done, but as I didn't own the rights, it wasn't possible – although they are available on a CD called *The Best of Peter Kay So Far*.

I wrote a new show, 'Living The Dream', which I toured a couple of years later and which Universal again filmed, this time at Oldham Coliseum, which is a special place for me as it holds many great memories of my nights there with Eamonn and Jimmy and the WOW shows in the early years. The show wasn't quite as good as the first one in my opinion, but I was still very pleased with it.

I did an 'Audience With' tour a couple of years later, which I really enjoyed. The audience filled in cards with questions, and while the fantastic Steve Royle, who has been my special guest on all tours, did his set before the interval, I sorted the questions out into some sort of order. I knew that there would always be the same recurring questions, and so I had prepared answers and routines for these, but about half of the questions were particular to that night's audience. Q: 'If you could have a super power, which one would you choose?' A: 'Russia. It's got all that gas and oil for a start.'

As I say, it was great for me because it made me address topics I normally wouldn't have considered, and in doing so generated new ideas and routines, which I later incorporated into my recent 'Best Medicine Tour'. I consider this to be my best show to date and I toured it in well over a hundred theatres nationwide over eighteen months. It received great reviews from critics and audiences alike and the DVD was filmed at Mansfield Palace Theatre in front of a brilliantly enthusiastic audience.

I'm slowly putting together my next tour show and fifth national tour, 'Words Don't Come Easy', for Spring 2011. The core of the show has sprung from an incredibly popular segment of my 'Best Medicine Tour', in which I deconstructed song lyrics. I have amassed a couple of dozen more and will use them to highlight the situations in life where indeed words don't come easy, from parents' rubbish sex-education talks, to adolescent chatting-up techniques, hospital 'speak', newspaper features and 'readers' poems' and many, many others. It should be good and will be coming to a theatre near you! I'd be pathetically grateful if you would come along and have a laugh with me.

Bear with Me

EVERY DAY, I receive requests to help charities either by sending autographed DVDs, books and photos, or by attending events, either as a guest or a performer, in order to raise the profile of the charity and/or raise funds. I still find it strange that the simple fact of me agreeing to participate in these events can make such a difference, but the fact is that it does – such is the power of 'celebrity' (hate that word) – and so I consider it to be a great and satisfying, if surprising, aspect to my job.

I think the job I did in the NHS for all those years was far more important, but nobody ever popped their head into the lab after an arduous, sleepless twenty-hour shift and said, 'Dave, bloody well done last night.' Now, people come up to me in the street and pubs, shops and restaurants to tell me how much they enjoy my work, and I get touching messages from people who say that watching *Phoenix Nights* or my stand-up DVDs has helped them through a particularly tough time in their lives – so I find it difficult to reconcile the two careers. I mean, it's all very flattering and yes, everybody needs a pat on the back now and then, but you have to keep it in perspective, don't you?

My problem is that it's so difficult prioritizing and actioning so many requests, all of which are very worthy causes. While I do always send off signed memorabilia, I can't attend the majority of the events that I'm invited to. I have a waiting list of around a hundred invitations, and requests to perform for charity, with more arriving daily, so it's basically down to a question of logistics based on my forthcoming commitments, combined with how much a particular cause touches me and how it fits in with my personal adopted charities.

A couple of years ago, when the last of our lovely pets passed away, we made the decision not to replace them for the time being because I was now travelling and touring extensively and it was becoming increasingly difficult to find people to look after the animals while we were away. I decided that I would get more involved with animal charities at grass roots level and channel my energies into helping them in this way. I became patron of Pet Rehome, which takes unwanted pets and finds foster homes for them until such time as a suitable permanent home can be found. This is far less traumatic for the pets than being placed in a destitute animals' centre and living for months or years in a cold unwelcoming cage, especially when you consider that a fair number of these pets will have come from loving homes where the owner can no longer take care of them due to illness or old age.

I also support Paws for Kids, which is a unique charity I think and one which I am committed to raising the profile of. It helps children from families where domestic violence is prevalent, who are often deeply affected by witnessing violence to their parent, siblings or pets, whether or not they are themselves victims of an assault. In families where there is domestic violence, pets are often threatened, injured or killed by a violent person as a means of keeping power and control over his partner and her children. *Paws for Kids' 'Safe Haven'* project provides a unique and specialized support service to the victims, their children *and* their pets; helping all involved, physically and emotionally, both in the short and long term. *'Safe Haven'* provides families who have experienced violence first hand with an opportunity to become part of a meaningful, nurturing programme, which aids the development of emotional and relationship skills.

I've also been privileged to open the new Haematology Unit at the Christie Hospital and the new 'skateboard' park and playground at Rainbow House, as well as perform in shows to support Macmillan Nurses, Shelter, Bolton Hospice, The Wonderbus, Special Care Baby Units, The Suzy Lamplugh Trust and many more.

However, I decided a couple of years ago that, rather than send off a donation here and there, it would be far more effective if I donated all the money from selected tour shows to certain charities. Last year, Pet Rehome, Paws for Kids and Animals Asia were my chosen charities.

I mentioned that if a certain cause touches me, I will try my hardest to get involved and help. Such was the case with Animals Asia China Bears Rescue. In China, Vietnam and neighbouring countries, bear bile is used in traditional medicine to treat a variety of conditions, ranging from fever to haemorrhoids. I know, it's ludicrous; even more so when you consider that there are over fifty homeopathic and synthetic alternatives.

Because of this nonsensical 'medicine' of the dark ages, the bears are kept in appalling conditions in horrific torture chambers that they call 'farms'. These beautiful, majestic, stoic animals are kept in tiny cages for up to twenty-five years and milked of their bile. That's *twenty-five years* – can you even begin to imagine the interminable pain and suffering? The method of extraction is achieved by either clamping the bears in a metal corset, through which a steel canula is embedded in their liver to drain the bile, or by randomly sticking needles into the liver in a hit-and-miss, pot-luck attempt at trying to hit the gall bladder! 'Barbaric' doesn't begin to cover it. The cages they are kept in are so small and constrictive that the bear cannot ever stand, move or turn – and again, that's for up to twenty-five years. And of those who were trapped in the wild, many will have at least one paw missing due to traumatic injury in the trap.

So I sent the money from a show to Animals Asia, and they replied and asked if I would host their roadshow in Manchester and the following year in Liverpool, which I said I would. There I spoke with Jill Robinson MBE, the inspirational founder of the charity, and she told me that the money I had sent was sufficient to free two bears from their lives of torture. I was dumbstruck. When I help a charity, what normally happens is that I get a letter thanking me and telling me where the money that I've helped to raise has been sent, so maybe a new incubator for special care or specialized equipment for physically challenged kids, and so on. That is obviously very pleasing and gratifying – but this was something else. I had actually freed two bears from their suffering!

The way this works is that the charity has to buy the bear 'farmer's' licence and take his bears away. Although in China it is still legal to farm bears, I understand that no new licences are being issued, so you effectively reduce the number of farms by one every time you do this.

Jill asked if I'd consider allowing the charity to name the two freed bears 'Spikey' and 'Kay'. Of course I agreed to this. Then they asked if Kay and I would like to fly out to Vietnam, to choose 'our' bears from the eighty that were pending release in an area south of Hanoi and to visit the brand new sanctuary, which was approaching completion. They also suggested a visit to their established sanctuary, which was home to over 200 rescued bears in China, after the visit to Vietnam. I looked in my diary and found a week in November free and we booked our tickets straight away.

It was a whistlestop visit with seven flights in six days. Manchester to Singapore – Singapore Airlines. Singapore to Hanoi – Singapore Airlines. Two days in Hanoi, then Hanoi to Guangzhou (98-point score in Scrabble!) – China Southern Airlines. Guangzhou to Chengdu – China Southern Airlines. (Bear with me, there is a point.) Three days in Chengdu, then Chengdu to Beijing – Air China. Beijing to London Heathrow – Air China. Then the last leg – almost home now, been travelling twenty-two hours – Heathrow to Manchester – British Airways – f***ing cancelled!

The visit was incredible. Three words: emotional roller coaster. There were highs, but also many lows. I knew there would be, but it was still too upsetting at times. Nothing can prepare you for the sight of the bears in their tiny cages. Their sad, desperate, tortured eyes pleading with you. The self-mutilation, endless pacing and mental illness that the continued pain and suffering has caused.

In Vietnam, the practice is now illegal, but many farms still exist under the guise of tourist cafés and restaurants – 'The Black Bear Café' etc. – where customers can have a drink and look at the 'lovely' bears. This is, of course, a front, and in a dramatic twist of fate we stumbled upon the reality of what actually happens when we returned unannounced to one such café. A coachload of Korean tourists were just leaving, having chosen a bear for bile extraction. We discovered the bear unconscious and we found bile on an 'operating' table, together with horrible long needles that had been stabbed into the bear's gall bladder. We filmed the evidence and the panic of the farm owners. We have since submitted it to the Vietnamese government, who have said that it is not sufficient evidence to shut down the 'café'!

On the plus side, we visited the new sanctuary in Vietnam, which is situated in a beautiful spot inside a national park and will provide a wonderful retirement home for the bears.

The established sanctuary in China, meanwhile, is nothing short of stunning. On 200 acres, it has ten bear houses and enclosures and is home to over 200 happy bears, some of whom spent the first ten to twenty-five years of their lives in the horrible 'crush' cages, which are particular to China – and yet these bears have somehow forgiven us for their awful suffering and you can actually feed one or two by hand through the bars of their luxury compounds!

One heartbreaking day, the vets brought a beautiful big bear called Fuzzy into the hospital for her two-year routine health check. I helped clip her paws and took blood from her jugular vein for a full laboratory screen. During the physical examination, we found a mass in her abdomen. The laparotomy revealed a huge liver tumour, which had spread to the lymph nodes. Fuzzy never went back to her enclosure; another victim to the liver cancer that is a common legacy of the years of trauma that the liver suffers during the bile extraction by needle, canula or fissure.

My abiding memory, however, will be a happy one. Seeing the bears free at last, feeding, playing, climbing their platforms, splashing in their pools, foraging for their hidden food and play-fighting – many of them with limbs missing, a result of the terrible snare traps that captured them in the wild. There are thousands of them still suffering and I'm dedicated to help this wonderful charity carry on until all of them are free.

Education is key, I think. You can't go blundering into these countries and lecture them on animal welfare and the rights and wrongs and plain ridiculousness of their traditional medicine because it is exactly that: hundreds of years of tradition. Both sanctuaries have education centres which detail the history of bear farming, with many diagrams and photographs to illustrate the practice, exhibits on show including the cages and the metal corsets, and presentations of the many alternative treatments available. They finish with a tour of the sanctuary, where the happy bears roam in acres of space, foraging for the food that the Chinese staff have hidden early in the morning. Thankfully, I think the message is getting across. Please check out their website animalsasia.org to see at first hand the fantastic work they do.

Schools These Days

A S WELL AS undertaking charity work, I also often get invited into schools to present prizes or give motivational talks or career advice. I am continually amazed at how much the schools and their teaching methods have radically changed since I was hit with a chair leg for defacing a 'Lost Property' notice (which incidentally I did not do – it was Chris Whitehouse).

I've seen this at first hand on more than one occasion recently, and although there have been many, many changes, I'm not convinced that they have all been for the good. It might be an age thing, but I am convinced that somewhere along the way, during the abolition of 'streaming' children and the implementation of liberal teaching methods, PC initiatives, health-and-safety considerations, league tables and scrapping of competitive sport etc., etc., etc., the actual education of our children has suffered and kids aren't as bright at the same stages of development as they used to be ... and an incredibly high number are really thick.

I present to you, mi'lud, evidence to support this.

1. A friend of mine is head of department in humanities in a big comprehensive school near Manchester. He's a good bloke and a great teacher. The other Christmas, he had an idea to organize a 'Form Fortunes' quiz for his class, combining all the aspects of the classic family TV game show with the coursework they'd studied on the Industrial Revolution – a sort of fun revision period. He asked me if I would go in and be 'Les Dennis', and I said of course I would. This is what happened.

The class was very excited and had sorted themselves out into teams of five, as on the TV show. I stood behind a desk placed in front of the blackboard, upon which was chalked the outline for the game and each question's top answers. I called the first two contestants up to the desk, and they shook hands and stood on either side facing each other. I asked if they understood the rules and they said they did and everyone started cheering. I said that the only difference was that we didn't have the electric gadgetry of the TV show and so if they knew the answer, they should bang the desk. They nodded and off we went. This was the first question – I kid you not.

Me: In the Industrial Revolution, a series of canals was excavated in order to facilitate water transport of coal from the pits and cotton from the docks to the hundreds of mills in our region. One of these canals was the Leeds–Liverpool canal, which joined together two British cities. Which cities? (*Honestly.*)

I stood back anticipating a swift response – nothing! I mean nothing, apart from a cacophony of noise and shouting and frustrated banging of the foreheads by our protagonists. The shouting escalated until one of the contestants smashed his hand down hard.

Me: Yes?
Him: Bangladesh.

(*I stand looking at him in disbelief as he turns with questioning eyes to his teammates, one of whom shouts out.*)

Teammate: No! Bang the desk, bang the desk – you dick.

2. I opened a garden centre and was having the guided tour when I was stopped by a few teenagers stood by a sundial. The tallest, spottiest one, who had his black tracksuit bottoms tucked into brown shoes (when was that ever a good look?) and a Burberry baseball cap perched on his head at a jaunty angle, said, 'Hey mister, what's this, then?'

I thought, 'He's got to be fourteen, fifteen – how can he not know?' I said, 'It's a sundial.'

'What does it do?' he asked.

I said, 'Well, you see that there's a circular dial, and it's calibrated all the way round? Well, they're minutes and the Roman numerals are hours, right? And this angular metal central arm here will cast a shadow dependent upon where the sun is in the sky, and if you look where the shadow is on the calibrated dial, it will tell you the time.'

And he studied it for a moment, then looked back at me with raised eyebrows and said, 'I dunno, what will they think of next?'

I have another good friend who teaches in primary school. It's all he's ever wanted to do and on the whole he loves it. He asked me to come in and present some awards and to have a look round. I was happy to do so and after I presented the award, he let me sit in a class of six-year-olds as they had a lesson of natural history, during which he played a DVD of some of the world's biggest animals. The children sat cross-legged on the floor in front of the television: beautiful, innocent, naive, wide-eyed with excitement.

In retrospect, my friend should have had misgivings as soon as the new DVD he'd withdrawn from the library started with the credit, 'Filmed in Xiudeng Zoo, Szechuan, China,' because they aren't renowned for their animal-rights record over there, are they? Rather than sitting at the back of the class with me, he should have positioned himself a lot nearer the 'pause' button – as subsequent events served to underline.

First, there was a huge spider; massive, it was, and hairy and horrible. I'm not a spider fan. Have you ever relaxed soaking in the bath and convinced yourself that a big, big spider is watching you from behind the overflow? If you look closely, you can see its beady eyes.

It was news to me that there are 3,000 spiders for every person on the planet and I don't want mine; so if anyone out there does, they can have them. I've had an aversion to spiders since I was nine and my sister pulled all the legs off one and gave it me to eat as a raisin.

Then this snake appeared. As I say, the DVD was called *The World's Biggest Animals* and this snake was, well, definitely one of the world's biggest animals, I reckon. It was enormous both in length and girth, and the kids squirmed and shuddered as it slithered around – and then it was feeding time. You are way ahead of me, aren't you?

Yes, a keeper in the zoo came to the enclosure and tossed a little puppy in with the snake. A little, fluffy, cuddly puppy – and all the children are saying, 'Aww, little puppy, nice puppy, nice puppy,' and the snake is also thinking something similar as it approaches the puppy. My friend is now running like Steve Austin in slow motion towards the DVD player, he mouths a slow-motion, 'No-o-o—o!' but it's too late as the snake opens its enormous jaws and ... GULP! Swallows the puppy in one, and it's suddenly like a cartoon because this snake is lying there with this puppy-shaped lump about a third of the way down.

And the class goes very, very quiet. There's a shocked silence for about five seconds, and then a little girl on the front row, a pretty girl with blonde hair tied in bunches with red ribbon, says very slowly and deliberately, 'F**k – me!'

My friend does love his job, but he is constantly frustrated by the interminable health-and-safety directives. Every week we hear of some new, ridiculous rule. Kids can't play conkers, have snowball fights or compete in sack races – just in case they get hurt.

Of course, teachers no longer want to take kids on school trips because they fear parents will sue if there's an accident. On BBC News, a teacher said that on school trips, on average, every year, one or two children die. 'One or two'? I hope he wasn't a Maths teacher – one or two? How stringent was that Department of Education survey? Q. 'How many kids died last year?' A. 'Well, one definitely died; the other one we might have mislaid. Having said that, it was in March and it's September now, so what if we put 1.5?'

We used to have school trips at the end of term just prior to the summer holidays. A fleet of coaches would arrive at the school gates and it was a very exciting, yet often disappointing day, because my form went on some totally rubbish school trips; destinations that were the last place on earth you'd rather be. I don't mean Basra (nothing like the brochures) or a Swiss Euthanasia Clinic or Midsomer or 'The Land of Leather' (shit rides); I mean a total letdown. We'd gather in the hall and the headmaster would announce the destinations to a mixture of cheers and jeers. When I was in 4a, this is what happened:

Headmaster: 4c – Blackpool Pleasure Beach. (*Deafening cheers.*) 4b – Chester Zoo. (*Mixed.*) 4a – Cumberland Pencil Museum. (*Total silence – disbelief.*)

A pencil museum?! That's not fair! Why do the thickies in 4c get Blackpool Pleasure Beach? We worked hard to get into the 'A' stream and what's the reward? All you ever wanted to know about graphite! (The first graphite ever discovered was found in the Seathwaite Valley on the side of Seathwaite Fell in Borrowdale in 1500.) I'd rather go to Madame Tussaud's after a fire.

Dead Man Weds

ALTHOUGH I ENJOYED crafting my stand-up tours and gigs, I missed the sitcom writing process when *Phoenix Nights* came to an end. I still had drawers full of ideas and characters and it wasn't long before I was inspired to put pen to paper again.

As I may have mentioned, I have always had an interest in local newspaper stories and the headlines that accompany them, which was prompted when I saw a sign outside a newsagents on my way home from the hospital one night.

The sign said 'Dead Man Weds'. I slammed the brakes on, parked very badly, and got myself a copy of the *Bolton Evening News*. There indeed was the front-page headline: 'Dead Man Weds'. You've got to laugh, haven't you? No sign of inverted commas around the 'dead', so I'm thinking, 'Well, this is Bolton, maybe he was dead. Maybe a dead man did get married.'

I imagined the scene at the reception over a pub in Farnworth:

Wedding guest: Your Billy's not saying much.
Bride: He's dead.
Wedding guest: Is he?
Bride: Yeah, but we'd paid the deposit on the buffet and we'd lose that if we cancelled, so . . .

Of course, what had really happened was that a man had had a heart attack and was, for a few seconds, technically dead, until paramedics shocked him and got it going again and he was now sufficiently recovered to get married.

But regardless of the technicalities, I was hooked. I started collecting weird and wonderful stories and headlines and on my 'Best Medicine' tour I always took the local paper onstage to highlight their regional stories. You may have read my book which comprises a large collection of these, accompanied by my 'hilarious' commentary (publisher speak). It's called *He Took My Kidney, Then Broke My Heart* and did really well. I've had emails from people around the world saying how much they enjoyed the book, which is immensely satisfying.

The upshot of my interest and research was that I soon realized that an obvious setting for a sitcom would be a small rural newspaper office, and so I set about writing what was to become *Dead Man Weds*. I had an idea that every week a big story would happen in the area and that somehow, every week, the newspaper staff would contrive to miss it, reporting instead on some local non-event. I drafted in a new editor, recently forced out of a big newspaper under mysterious circumstances, and followed his attempts to get the *Fogburrow Advertiser and News* back on track as a serious organ.

I sent the script to Nicola Shindler at RED productions because I'd loved everything they'd done (*Our Friends in the North*, *Clocking Off* and *Queer as Folk*, to name but three) and Nicola is such a respected figure in the industry; a reputation that is well deserved. Nicola liked it and asked if she could pitch it to television commissioners and I, of course, was thrilled for her to do so. After quite a long wait and a couple of small rewrites, ITV commissioned the series.

I was over the moon and flattered that they wanted me to play the main role of Gordon Garden, the new editor. I chose 'Gordon' because it was my father's name. I initially wanted to call him Gordon Gordon because I had a back story that he'd been found in a phone box as a baby with a label that simply said 'Gordon'. Hospital staff didn't know if this referred to his Christian name or surname, so played it safe. I can't remember why I changed it now, but I have a vague memory of another sitcom character surfacing at the time with a similar style of name.

The great thing about Nicola and RED is that they include the writer in all stages of the production process, and so I met prospective producers and directors and had a say in the choice. We asked Sarah Smith to produce and Mark Elliot to direct. Sarah had a great pedigree, having produced the first series of *The League of Gentlemen*, which had been a massive hit. Sarah also co-directed and script-edited, and although we had a couple of heated discussions, she was immensely helpful and the script became a lot tighter.

Casting was quite exciting because I had a wish list assigned to each of the main characters – and in every case my first-choice actor accepted. I really wanted Michael Brandon, 'Dempsey' from *Dempsey and Makepiece*, to play the boss of GeneUS, the dodgy American company based in a weird-looking industrial plant on the surrounding moors, and we sent the script to him while he was on holiday in the Caribbean. He got back in touch quickly and said he wanted to do it; as did Johnny Vegas, the fantastic Keith Barron and the brilliant Nicola Stephenson, who I'd once – as a television extra playing a taxi driver – driven away from a screen wedding that she (the bride) had done a runner from.

We auditioned for the 'Also starring' roles. I really wanted Janice Connolly (Holy Mary from *Phoenix Nights*) to be Carol the office clerk, and she did an amazing audition so she was in. Iain McKee was superb as Duane Guffog, the aspiring thespian. The only part we struggled to cast was Gerry Stringer, the old-school journalist in the office. Gerry was apt to get flustered under pressure and was a bit of a fusspot, and we just couldn't find anybody who nailed it – until Alan Rothwell turned up and he totally 'got it'; not surprising, really, because he is one of this country's finest actors in my opinion.

I was asked to suggest filming locations – and of course I pushed for anywhere within fifteen minutes of my house! Although I was lucky with the newspaper offices, which were built in an old mill near the canal in Withnall, the other locations were situated near Castleton in the Peak District, which is an area of outstanding beauty, so quite a result nonetheless.

I'm very pleased with *Dead Man Weds* and count the production and filming of it amongst the happiest times of my life. I think I tried too hard to cram too much into each half-hour, but I've watched it again recently and there are loads of gags hidden away that viewers never got to discover because ITV never repeated it, which was strange because they must have thought quite highly of it; enough to pitch it against the first series of *Desperate Housewives*. They were disappointed with the viewing figures, which can't have been surprising considering the million-pound hype that accompanied *Desperate Housewives*.

But you know what? It's a cracking little show. The ensemble cast bring the small town of Fogburrow to life *and* I got to have a sword fight with 'Dempsey' which was interrupted by a giant turkey – and not many people can say that.

The critics liked it too and it got really good reviews across the board, which makes ITV's decision not to commission a second series even more surprising. I'm in the process of buying the rights back from ITV because I get so many enquiries from the general public asking where they can see it again or buy it on DVD – so watch this space.

Tom-Tom

AFTER MY DAD died, I found Mum a flat in a sheltered accommodation unit, near where I live in Chorley, so I could visit regularly and run her around, as she'd never learned to drive. It was a very nice flat and had the bonus of being in the same development in which her old friends, Mildred and Gordon, lived. Mildred had been my mum's bridesmaid, so they went way back.

At first, everything was good, but I could tell that Mum was getting increasingly bored. She soon grew fed up with a life that consisted of getting up and going down to the Spar for a paper and something for dinner, and then after dinner going down to the Spar to choose something for tea. There were occasional events organized in the social centre, but although she enjoyed some of these, it was clear that she didn't like being on her own for the first time in fifty years or so. Not surprising, really.

Then she met Tom – and after a whirlwind romance she was moving into his house. ('As a lodger, David! Separate rooms, purely a business arrangement.') I was surprised, obviously, but pleased for my mum, who had been transformed overnight and once again had a spring in her step and a twinkle in her eye.

Tom is absolutely nothing like my dad. He's a six-foot-plus, handsome, old-school, ex-guardsman and ex-police officer. He doesn't have much of an interest in the arts or television or reading; he likes to potter and have a go at DIY and drive his motor-home or caravan to explore the Lakes and Cumbria, and sometimes further afield. He is a good man and a strong man and is a great companion for my mum, who in return is a great companion for him.

They were together a couple of years before getting married quietly at Preston registry office in 2005. Kay and I, my brother Pete and his girlfriend Sue were invited at the last minute. It was a lovely day and they look the perfect happy couple in the wedding photos.

Getting It Write

AFTER THE RELATIVE success of *Dead Man Weds*, I got stuck into the writing of another idea I'd had knocking about in my head for years. Based on the premise 'write about what you know', I wanted to write a comedy drama about a small group of painters and decorators. My dad was a painter and decorator, Kay's dad was, her brother is and one of my best mates, Paul, is, so I certainly wasn't short of material.

My dad used to come home and tell us stories about the house he was decorating and the behaviour and antics of the family who lived there. In conversations with the in-laws and Paul, more and more stories came to light, and I became aware of the potential of a disparate group of lads opening different front doors every week to discover and become part of the stories that lied therein. The result was *Magnolia*.

I based my main character on my friend Paul, who is a brilliant bloke with a sharp wit and a heart of gold inside a rough exterior (he won't mind me saying that). He's a six-foot-two skinhead who is often mistaken for my minder when we go out for a drink. People approach him and say, 'Can I speak to Dave?' and depending on his mood he'll say, 'Okay' or 'No' or 'No, f**k off'.

He is incredibly quick with a witty remark or put-down. His small business has been hit hard by the recession and he said the other day after a particularly bad week, 'What a bloody awful week. Just when you think you've hit rock bottom, you find there's a f***ing trapdoor.'

In *Magnolia*, Paul sets up a small company and recruits old mates and lads that he has recently met in prison on the painting and decorating course. On the whole, these are lads who, for a variety of reasons, would normally find it very difficult to find employment elsewhere. He gives them a second chance – but only time will tell if that trust will be repaid.

Nicola Shindler liked the script and pitched it to the BBC, where Cheryl Taylor commissioned it for the new BBC *Comedy Playhouse*. This was a massive thrill because it meant that now I'd written shows for Channel 4, ITV and BBC1. *Comedy Playhouse* showcased six different shows, all of which had the potential to be made into a series, and they seemed very keen on *Magnolia*.

Ralph Ineson was great as Paul, while Chris Coghill, Will Ash and Chris Bisson were totally spot on in their performances as his assorted recruits. Dawn Steele played Paul's wife, and although I'll admit that initially I wasn't keen on the casting, she proved me totally wrong and her on-screen relationship with Ralph was totally believable. The wonderful Shobna Gulati played the barmaid in the local pub, who had to deal with the smarmy Gregg (Mark Benton) trying to chat her up every time he visited. Shobna is one of my absolute favourite actresses and has a brilliant gift for comedy; her timing of the withering put-downs was impeccable. We cast my big mate Steve Royle as a builder, Tom Bowler, and I played a loser known locally as Chernobyl, who wore a shell suit and rode a BMX (as they do). I was desperate for Paul to give me a job, but as I was a walking disaster with the reverse Midas touch – everything I touched turned to shit – Paul steered clear of me (at first!).

Jim Doyle directed and was very gracious in letting me sit in with him on many occasions and offer my opinion on scene set-ups and performance. The end product, if I'm honest, in my opinion wasn't as good as it might have been. It looked good on screen, the critics liked it and agreed that out of the six, it was the one with most potential for a series, but I was slightly disappointed with the edit. I thought it too often slightly missed the mark in both comedy and drama, which in turn affected the pace and 'real' feel of the piece.

Initially, all signs from the BBC were good, so much so that we were fairly confident that it would get a series commission, but, at the eleventh hour, as so often happens, they went cold on it and it never happened. Another huge disappointment for me because it did have great potential and all the actors in it without exception deserved for it to continue.

The thing about being a writer, though, is that there is always another idea just around the corner, ready to light the blue touch paper inside your head and start the gags and comedy set-ups flowing. In recent years, I've had three writing commissions and I've loved creating these new worlds and characters once again.

My first was a comedy drama about a Sunday football team, which was obviously inspired by my love of the world of Sunday football and the players who inhabit it. I was incredibly lucky to get the great Shane Meadows on board early days through Mark Herbert at WARP films, and we assembled a cast and improvised a few scenes around the script a while back. You can see the scenes on YouTube and they're pretty good, I think. In my opinion it's absolutely the best thing I've ever written.

I was also asked by a production company to write a synopsis concerning a group of lads who buy a vineyard in France and go out to try and make a go of it. The piece was called *Sour Grapes*.

The third script commission, meanwhile, was for a script I wrote with a new friend, Terry Milligan. Titled *Bringing in the Sheep*, it concerns Frank, who has gone to live in a hut village in the Himalayas to find the peace and tranquillity for which he yearns. Of course, when he gets up there, it's a nightmare! It's kicking off every day amongst the many weird and wonderful hut-dwellers. It's a sparkling, slightly odd script – a sort of *Father Ted* meets *League of Gentlemen*, but I know that it's very funny. However, the feedback we've had so far is that it's too 'high concept', which is a vague and oft-used term in commissioning, but maybe the 'high' relates to the Himalayas.

Another television producer asked if we could maybe set it up Mount Snowden, missing the point completely! It really does make you wonder how they get these jobs. I explained that if he went up Mount Snowden and found his life a living hill (I mean hell), he could simply walk down or get the train, and that the whole point of him living in the Himalayas was that he was stuck there, he'd burnt his bridges and had to stay there for the foreseeable (hopefully a minimum of three series) future. The script is still doing the rounds and I still have hopes for it.

Currently, I'm writing a comedy drama with original music called *Best of Times*. It's about a young woman (Sumo) who has leukaemia, but is in remission, and who is searching, with the aid of her friends and community, for a suitable bone marrow donor. It's all hands to the pump as her friends leave no stone unturned in their search for Sumo's missing mother and late father's twin brother. They organize donor drives, and her closest friend and soon-to-be boyfriend, Paps, who works in telesales, tries phoning every person in the directory with her uncle's name – pity he's called Tom Jones, but hey, it's only a matter of time. There is a massive twist at the end and it's coming together very well. I've had a few pieces of music written for it already, courtesy of my good friends Sean and Harry.

They do say write about what you know, and this project combines knowledge gained from my work in haematology, my kid brother's long, courageous battle with lymphoma (more on that later) and my ex-wife's work in organ donation. I want to highlight the need for more donors of both organs and bone marrow/stem cells and to highlight through the vivacious Sumo a fact that we noticed in the hospital labs, which was that the patients had a much better prognosis if they were upbeat and positive in their approach to their battle with their disease. Patients who could still laugh and who had a bright disposition and outlook always did so much better than those who became introspective and self-pitying.

Lastly, I want to highlight that there have been tremendous advances in the treatment of the malignant blood diseases and that where once, not too long ago, there was no hope, there is now, thankfully, much hope.

TV Tales

IN 2005, I was fortunate enough to be asked to be a team captain on a new quiz show called *8 Out of 10 Cats*, which was based on the results of national surveys such as 'What is Birmingham's favourite vegetable?' (It's not the oven chip or Jasper Carrott, as you might expect, but the onion.) Having become a familiar face to TV viewers, and with my stand-up background thrown in for good measure, the producers very flatteringly thought I'd be a good fit with the show. Jimmy Carr was lined up to host and Sean Lock was to be the other team captain, and as they are two of my favourite comedians, I jumped at the chance.

The programme, of course, went on to become a great success and was a fantastic experience. I did four series and met some great people from all walks of the entertainment world, including one of my all-time comedy heroes, Joan Rivers, who was on my team twice. Joan Rivers sat next to me! I brought in my battered copy of her autobiography *Enter Talking* and sheepishly, during a gap in filming, asked if she would sign it, which she did and added a lovely message.

It was a great show to do for many reasons, not least the excellent team at Zeppotron/Endemol, including Ruth Phillips, Richard Osman and the script associates, especially Dom and Aiden, who were always encouraging and supportive. I left 'by mutual consent' as they say after series four – because I wasn't enjoying it any more and it showed. I'd had a lot of stress in my personal life, which I'll outline later, but that should never creep into your work and I was poor in series four.

I never really 'enjoyed' the show as such anyway, in all honesty, as I found it incredibly stressful. It sort of took over my life because I'd be constantly looking at newspapers and television for topical news stories that might come up in the big opening round. I'm not a quick-thinking comic; well, I am in the pub amongst my mates, I'm incredibly quick on the funny line and a skewed take on events, but up against other, sharper comics, I'm a second or two too slow, and that's a long time in comedy. To compensate, I'd over-prepare, writing lots of gags about whatever the week's big news stories were, even though I knew there were only five questions and if two big stories broke on the day of the show, I'd be stuffed. I am so in envy of quick-witted comics, who appear to be funny on the spot or view a subject from left-field, and Sean Lock is a master at this.

I also have a problem in general with gags that are based on personal attacks on people in the public eye and because of the nature of the quiz, there was plenty of opportunity to do this. I find that not only are the 'celebs', politicians, royal family etc. easy targets, but also they can't answer back. We can't believe everything we read or hear in the news, so why have a pop at people who can't defend themselves?

The main criticism I received from the producers was that I was too generous and should fight to get my material in, rather than letting other guests dominate, but I was always of the opinion that we were making an entertainment show and so everyone should get their best lines in. I didn't like the growing competitive element of the show, where even your own teammates interrupted you to get their lines in first. I found that incredibly rude and ungracious; we're all in this to do well and entertain, and yes, of course there needs to be an edge, but that needn't exclude basic generosity.

I suppose you might say that I highlight these aspects because they weren't my strong suit and I struggled. Having said that, I wouldn't have missed it for the world.

A short while later, out of the blue, I landed another TV opportunity which was much more my sort of thing. To my complete surprise, I was offered the job of hosting the new, revamped series of *Bullseye*.

I turned it down at first. I thought it could turn out to be a bit of a poisoned chalice because for generations of fans of the show out there, there could be only one man who could host the show and that was Jim Bowen. After discussions with the television people and the quiz creator, however, it became clear that for one reason or another Jim wouldn't be hosting the new series, and so I thought, 'Well, sod it! It might as well be me then.'

It was filmed at Yorkshire TV and I had a wonderful time doing it, thanks to the brilliant crew and production team. It was literally laugh-a-minute over there, and working with the darts legend that is Tony Green was the icing on the cake.

It was quite a surreal experience at first: hosting a show that you've been a fan of for so many years. A show that was a Sunday teatime institution throughout the country. Before every show, Tony and I would stand backstage before the audience came in and record 'Bully's Prize Board', how mad was that? I used to pinch myself when Tony shouted, 'In ONE!' and I would read from the list of typical *Bullseye* prizes, 'Make finding lost treasure an absolute pleasure with this Viking metal detector!' 'In TWO!' 'If you're going to stew it, you're gonna need this cruet.' (Kay wrote that one.) A cruet set in a twenty-first-century game show!

The production lads wrote most of the prize descriptions in this style and slipped the odd saucy one in. I remember one prize was a yellow inflatable jet-ski (how brilliant is that?). My line was, 'It's the only thing yellow I want in my pool.' The naughtiest one was for a Brevill grill, which was, 'If browning your meat is your idea of a treat, you'll love this grill!'

My good mate Steve Royle came over and did the studio warm-up for me, which was brilliant. He also helped me with some of the interview questions required for the contestants and their 'interesting' experiences, 'unusual' hobbies and 'funny' stories.

Actually, we did have some bizarre stories – and I pass on here the most bizarre of the lot. Two girls were on the show and they had a funny story about something that had happened while they were getting ready to go out for a night on the town. One of the girls told me that they had a sort of ritual where her friend came round to her house and they had a drink of wine and had a bath together! Rum enough there, but there was so much more to the story.

She told me that one night her friend had weed in the bath water for a laugh (?!), so guess what she'd done? I said that I couldn't imagine and she said, 'I did a poo!'

Total silence in the studio, she carried on undeterred, '... and it floated towards her.' They are both laughing hysterically now and, as Jimmy Cricket would say, there's more. She said, 'So I scooped it up and rubbed it on her breasts.'

Okay, now that is one of the most offensive, disgusting stories I have ever heard – but even more shocking was that they thought it was (a) hilarious (b) acceptable behaviour and (c) okay to recount to millions of viewers on television!

Another favourite concerned a bloke who was a bus inspector. I said that I was surprised that there was still a need for inspectors because all buses seemed to operate a pay-the-driver-on-boarding system and he replied, 'I know! They're the buggers we're after.' I often wonder how that was received in the bus depot the day after the show went out!

We recorded forty shows and they went well, I think. I got good reviews and *The Times* reviewer wrote a very flattering piece and said I was the natural successor to Jim Bowen, which is an immense compliment. Weird thing is that they are constantly re-running them on Challenge TV, together with my *Chain Letters* shows of fourteen years ago!

Typical *Bullseye* question on 'Spelling': 'Henry V defeated the French at the battle of Agincourt, the battle of Agincourt. Can you spell "Henry"?'

The Spice of Life

IN ONE MEMORABLE week in November 2005, I achieved two incredible ambitions. The first was appearing on the Royal Variety Performance in front of HRH Queen Elizabeth and Prince Philip, and the second guesting on *Parkinson*.

The Royal Variety was staged in Cardiff in 2005 and was an amazing experience for someone who, only five years before, had been working in the NHS. I couldn't sleep the night before the show, so nervous was I, and at breakfast on the day of the performance I had to keep pinching myself after spotting yet another famous face in the dining room.

Our breakfast took ages coming and Kay, who is incredibly impatient, kept glaring at the entrance to the kitchens behind me every time the doors opened.

Some time later, Cliff Richard passed us on his way out. As he passed, he turned and looked quizzically at Kay, who had a strange look on her face. I asked her what was wrong and she said quietly, 'Did he look?' and I said, 'Yes. Why?' and she told me that she hadn't realized for ages that Cliff was sitting at a table right in front of the kitchen entrance. He'd probably thought she'd been staring at him aggressively for the last twenty minutes!

We were taken to St David's Hall, the venue, at around 9 a.m., issued with passes and directed to my dressing room. On the way down the corridor, a double door opened just as we approached it and there was Cliff coming through. You should have seen his face when Kay passed him.

I had to go to make-up and Kay came with me. As I sat in the chair, the bloke next to me said hello and I looked in the mirror and saw it was

Cliff. Just then, Kay appeared in the background. He saw her and I swear jumped in his seat. Was this mad woman stalking him?!

Once the show got under way, there was a technical hitch just before I was due on. I was standing in the wings when they sent for Cliff to fill in and he arrived with acoustic guitar, which he tuned in the wings, oblivious to all around him. It was pretty cramped in the wings and he accidentally leaned on Kay, then turned to apologize, saw 'that woman' again and went 'Argh!' before going onstage!

Before that, it had been an exhausting day of sitting around for hours doing nothing, then rehearsing and then doing a technical run-through, which did provide a moment of great comedy. Shirley Bassey was headlining (obviously in Cardiff) and as she sang her final number, all the other acts wandered on to surround her. She took a bow and exited, her music kept playing as we took our bows, and she dashed under the stage and onto the lift, which would bring her up for a dramatic reappearance through the stage trapdoor. It all worked well up to this point – when the lift suddenly stuck and only Shirley's head and shoulders appeared! She's belting out 'I Am What I Am' or something similar through our legs. Very funny.

Showtime arrived and I was on about third from the end, before Bryn Terfel and Shirley Bassey, two massive Welsh megastars. The show had dragged on through technical difficulties; I got on at around eleven o'clock, so I'd been there for fourteen hours and was dead on my feet and a total bag of nerves. Worse, the audience were all tired and bored and really just wanted Bryn and Shirley on, then they could go home.

Michael Parkinson was supposed to go on and give me a big build-up, but there wasn't time. He introduced me offstage and I heard a low groan from the audience before I walked on to only a smattering of applause (very rude, I remember thinking). There wasn't a Royal Box and the Queen and Prince Philip were seated on a raised plinth in the stalls, right in the performers' eyeline. I was now bricking it – and then I swear that the Queen looked at her watch. I think it was a Casio because her face lit up blue and she looked like a giant second-class stamp.

The combination of tiredness and nerves resulted in me completely forgetting my set and I did ten minutes of new, brand new material about my grandma wanting one of those baths with a door in them. New untried material on the Royal Variety Show! Still, it went okay. I got away with it, as they say.

The week afterwards, I achieved my main lifelong ambition: to walk down those stairs on *Parkinson*. As Michael had co-hosted the Royal Variety, we started by chatting about that and I got laughs from recounting my experiences. The interview went brilliantly well, I couldn't have asked for better, and then came the unexpected bonus of staying onstage while the other guests were interviewed and interacting with them.

'Them' being Rachel Weisz, Katie Melua and Paul McCartney! Kay had already played another blinder, mistaking Rachel Weisz for a production runner during rehearsals and asking her if she could show her where the ladies' toilet was. While onstage in between recording breaks, we all chatted about music and I spoke with Paul McCartney, an absolute hero of mine, about our common interests of animal welfare and vegetarianism.

One of the absolute highlights of my career.

My Brother Pete

I'VE LEFT THIS chapter till the end because I knew it would be the most difficult to write. I've mentioned Pete in places along the way, but his story and the way it impacted on my life deserves further explanation.

I had just turned eight when Pete was born and because of the big age difference, I didn't play a huge role in his formative years and didn't have the same sibling relationship with him as I did with Joy, who was only three years younger than me. I left primary school while he was still a toddler and when I left grammar school, aged sixteen, he was only eight. At weekends and after school, I played out with my friends and so, unless I had to babysit him, we saw little of one another, except at family meal times and holidays.

It's no surprise, then, that I remember little of his early years until he got quite a bit older and started secondary school, by which time I was eighteen. I do remember witnessing him split his head open on the edge of the coffee table when he tripped and fell in the lounge. It was a nasty cut and I thought, 'No amount of butter is going to heal that wound.'

Pete was always a happy-go-lucky kid and into everything. He was spoiled a bit because he was the youngest, but it didn't really have any effect on him. He did okay at school, but not brilliantly because he was 'easily distracted', as they say, and 'easily led'.

After a couple of false starts, Pete got a job in the laboratories of a bleach works just outside Bolton and started studying for his ONC. He met Bev when he was nineteen/twenty and they got engaged quite soon afterwards. They got married at the Victoria Hall in Bolton and had the reception in a basement Italian restaurant. There was a thunderstorm and I remember the restaurant leaking water and getting a little flooded. It was perhaps a sign of things to come.

Pete became sick shortly afterwards and when we look at the wedding photos, we always say, 'Why on earth didn't we notice that there was something wrong with him?' He looked happy in the photos and sported his big beaming grin, but it was obvious that he'd lost a load of weight and was looking really gaunt.

He was admitted to Bolton Royal Infirmary for tests while I was working at the General Hospital in Haematology. The blood tests showed a degree of anaemia, but nothing much else. It was what is known as the 'Anaemia of Chronic Disorder' (ACD), which is secondary to an underlying condition.

They found the underlying condition a few days later on X-ray. It was a tumour growing on and around his heart – 'mediastinal' is the terminology. It was a very unusual presentation, especially in such a young person, and the consensus of opinion was that it could be a benign growth or possibly Hodgkin's Disease, which does present in early adulthood and is a tumour of the lymphatic system.

I remember going round to Mum and Dad's when the results came through and we had a group hug and cry, during which I tried my best to reassure them that even if it was Hodgkin's Disease, the cure rate using specific chemo and radiotherapy was extremely high. We hoped, obviously, that it would be benign, but I had doubts because he was so ill and had lost so much weight.

The biopsy, which was examined in the Histopathology lab at the General Hospital, surprised everybody because it showed a malignant Non-Hodgkin's Lymphoma (NHL), which is extremely unusual in someone of Pete's age and was, at that time, very difficult to treat and cure. I always wondered if it might have been triggered by the concentrated chemicals he was using at work, but I'd better leave that there.

I thought it best that I tell him, so I phoned the ward and told them not to say anything until I'd spoken with him and went straight down to the ward. As I approached his bed, he said in his own cheeky style, 'You drew the short straw, did you?' It seems that the message hadn't got through and a junior doctor had spilled the beans. I tried to be very upbeat about the situation and told him that the prognosis was good and there had been great advances in treatment of NHL. He took it all onboard and was very positive in his approach to whatever the future held in store.

He was transferred to the Christie Hospital near Manchester, which is one of the finest cancer treatment centres in Europe, and which we are so lucky to have on our doorstep. After his assessment, we were given more bad news, which was that as the tumour was on and surrounding his heart, they couldn't risk radiotherapy. The only hope was high-dose chemotherapy to shrink the tumour to a size and position where they could access it.

He started this regime while further tests were undertaken to establish exactly which type of NHL he had. At one visiting time early in the treatment, a doctor told my parents that the results were back and that they wanted to see Pete's wife Bev the following morning, and that someone should accompany her because it wasn't good news. This was devastating, but perhaps unsurprising, because Pete's condition had deteriorated more over the past few days.

My mum and dad went with Bev to see the doctor while I waited by the phone at work and then for the first time during his illness, a small shaft of light shone through the darkness. The doctor was initially going to tell them that Pete's condition was terminal, but overnight supplementary test results had been received, which now gave Pete a slim chance of surviving the gruelling treatment. Any chance was a chance, and so we were uplifted by that information and very upbeat when we visited Pete.

Over the next few weeks, Pete was hammered with chemotherapy, which made him very ill, but was successful in shrinking the tumour enough to get at it with radiotherapy. I visited when I could and his wife Bev was an absolute rock for him, which must have been very difficult for her, especially now that she discovered she was pregnant. This news obviously gave Pete a boost and even more cause to beat this awful disease. My parents, who must have been devastated, were absolutely focused in their support, travelling to the hospital most nights.

It's a terrible admission, but many nights I tried to think of reasons not to go. I was busy at work, it was November and so the journey there and back was in the dark … The hours at the Christie were desperate, seeing my kid brother tortured by the treatment and seeming to fade. Then of course I gave myself a smack round the head and told myself to stop being so incredibly selfish and to try to imagine what Pete was going through each and every hour of the day. That he couldn't take a night off because he was feeling a bit tired and worn down by it all.

I visited him on my own one night about a month into his treatment and he appeared a lot brighter. He seemed to have improved significantly in the couple of days since I'd last seen him; so much so that he said that he fancied a pizza! I said I'd nip out and get one for him, but he said no, he wanted to go out for one and suddenly he looked, in his eyes, a bit like his old self again. The staff said that it would be alright and so we went out in search of a pizza place!

It did seem that he had turned a corner and he got stronger every time I saw him. They allowed him to go home for short periods and on one occasion, with his hair falling out in clumps, he decided to go to his old mate Lol's, who was a hairdresser, to have the lot shaved off. Lol is quite a character and a laugh-a-minute and was weirdly one of my best friends at school, so considerably older than Pete, but they had met through mutual friends on nights out in town and struck up a firm friendship. So Pete turned up at Lol's shop and asked for a haircut, and Lol said that he was really sorry, but he had no availability that day. Pete removed his bob hat to reveal his half-bald, half-tufty look and said, 'If you don't shave this off, I'm going to stand outside your shop and shout, "Look what Lol did to me!"' Lol cut his hair.

Pete had to undergo more radiotherapy and he became ill again with lung abscesses, which had to be drained. I visited him in a side ward in Manchester Royal Infirmary and was shocked at how ill he was. He went through so much pain in those months of treatment it was heartbreaking.

Then he began to come through it, and doctors became more optimistic that he was in remission and that the disease was undetectable and the side effects were calming down. Because he hadn't worked, obviously, for a couple of years now and his immediate prospects were not at all bright, he was given a council house, where he went to live with Bev and his beautiful new daughter Zoe.

But this wasn't good enough for Pete. He didn't want to live off handouts, and so he resolved to do something about it. Firstly he enrolled in the Open University to do a degree in IT. Information Technology was in its early stages at the time and he had recognized the potential of obtaining a qualification in what was to become a major global technology.

He then convinced his bank manager that he should give him a mortgage based on his sickness and invalidity allowance. The bank manager was obviously sceptical about Pete's ability to keep up the repayments over the term of the mortgage and he insisted on obtaining a report from Pete's consultant regarding his prognosis. Thankfully, Pete got the mortgage and bought a house on Halliwell Road in Bolton, which fell within the council's regeneration area. He applied for and got a full grant for the house and set about restoring the property into a beautiful terraced house.

In time, he obtained his degree and started working for a Manchester firm, quickly progressing through the ranks because he was a natural at computer programming and software solutions. Over the next few years, apart from a setback when he needed a new hip after they found that the chemo had destroyed one of his joints, he stayed well, remained in remission, got back to his old mischievous self, had a son, Christian (even though they told him the treatment would make him sterile!), and bought an old Porsche! He became more successful at work and hooked up with his old mates for nights out and partying.

He loved to party. He lived life to the full, as the saying goes (and who can blame him?). He found that he had a good singing voice and karaoke became a bit of a passion; I can hear him crooning 'Mack the Knife' now. He more often than not belted out a couple of his hero David Bowie's tracks, 'Jean Genie' in particular. He became well known on the karaoke circuit and later sang duets with Zoe, who has inherited a brilliant voice.

Then his marriage broke down. Pete and Bev were divorced and the associated costs in terms of maintenance etc., added to his other financial pressures (for he had bought a new house without first selling the one on Halliwell Road, and had consequently got into a lot of debt), broke him financially and for a time psychologically. But, as these things do, slowly his situation improved. He got into a bit of debt again in later years, but I was lucky enough then to be in a position to help.

Pete moved into a new place in time and seemed a lot happier. It was around then, however, that he revealed that he'd not been feeling so well, suffering terrifically high temperatures and night-sweats, which left him feeling weak and exhausted. I insisted he went to the doctors because (I kept to myself) severe night-sweats can be an indicator of something serious occurring at cellular level. He had tests, which all came back normal, thank goodness, and soon after he met Sue, who was his neighbour. He brought her over to our pub in Chorley one night out of the blue and they seemed very much an item already.

Over the months, Pete recaptured his vigour, enthusiasm and lust for life, thanks to this relationship, but he still had episodes of illness with the night-sweats recurring. Pete and Sue were, on the whole, extremely happy together and they shared a passion for cooking, always coming up with incredible recipes using sometimes unusual ingredients. He loved a drink as well; his favourite tipple of cider was 'Cheeky Vimto', to which he quickly introduced Sue.

His doctor sent him for a scan after another bout of illness, but it came back clear, which surprised me in a good way. Meanwhile, he and Sue continued their intense courtship. I think, no, I'm sure that she loved Pete more than anyone else did. She always called him 'Gorgeous', always.

It became obvious that something was wrong with Pete as his periods of illness increased, and they sent him for a second scan. I was driving back from a gig when he phoned me with the results, which shocked me to the core.

'They've found a tumour,' he said and I could hear the fear and despair in his voice. I asked where and he told me that it was in the same place as his NHL tumour, mediastinal presentation. I said that although this was devastating, he shouldn't be too down because even if it had returned, there was a good chance that chemo and radiotherapy could cure it again. Indeed, advances in treatment over the intervening twenty-odd years meant that he should be confident about beating it again. Pete, to his credit, did seem to take heart from the words and told me, 'I've beat it once – I'll do it again.' You quite often see it said, in obituaries, that people lost their battle with cancer. Pete didn't have a battle, he had a full-blown war.

I also tried to give him hope by reminding him of the fact that the tumour hadn't been visible on the scan from earlier in the year, so it must be quite a recent event, and so more susceptible to treatment. That's when he told me that they had reviewed his earlier scan and that the tumour was present and that somebody had missed it. How can somebody deserve so much terrible luck? Still, let's stay positive and get it blasted, eh?

He had a biopsy a couple of days later and phoned me on the way back from another gig to give me more unexpected and devastating news. The tumour wasn't NHL, it was lung cancer, thought to have been caused by the intensive radiotherapy to the area all those years ago! It can happen, but I didn't think it possible after all this time. He said that they might be able to remove it surgically and I thought that that was really encouraging.

He was admitted to Blackpool Hospital for surgery, but when they opened his chest, they found that they couldn't get at the tumour because it surrounded one of the major arteries. This pattern was to be repeated time and time again over the following months: small rays of hope lifting the soul, only to be extinguished suddenly by unexpected, awful twists of fate. How he kept going, how he kept smiling when he must have been screaming inside, continually baffled me and generated within me the most amazing respect, admiration and love for my brother as I accompanied him to interminable appointments for blood tests, X-rays, CAT scans, MRI scans, PET scans, consultations etc. The last PET scan was undertaken because it had been discovered that now he also needed a double heart bypass! How's your lucky rabbit's foot business doing, Pete? Then a heart surgeon agreed to undertake the procedure as the tumour appeared to be inactive.

Now you see a ray of hope? Now you don't. The radiotherapy showed that the cancer had spread into his liver and that it was inoperable and that was that: abandon hope.

He was put on various combination chemotherapy treatments and battled away for months, getting weaker along the way. Sue was there for him every waking minute and most of the other hours of the day and we owe her so much for her care of him. I got over to see him almost every other day over the months and we always, always had a laugh, even during the last months when he was confined to bed. His indefatigable sense of humour was simply astounding. Who else could crack a joke like this at the pinnacle of their illness, when yet another doctor asked him the latest in a long line of stupid questions?

'How do you feel, Pete?' the doctor asked.

Pete slowly opened his eyes and said, 'With my fingers.'

My mum and Tom visited regularly and through her suffering, she always put a brave face on for Pete. She was only doing what you would expect any mother to do under the circumstances, I suppose, but it must have been tearing her apart inside to see her youngest child endure such pain. She was amazing through it all and handled it with dignity and compassion and gained total respect for the way she coped with the terrible events over the years of Pete's illness. She was always there for him, even though she lived quite a distance away. Sometimes she would sleep on the couch to be near him on the nights when she couldn't bear to leave.

Pete rallied now and again and we'd go out for a meal or a drink. I got him a big-screen TV for Christmas and he got a Wii and loved playing on that. He and Sue came to the Hi-Life Dining Awards at the Hilton Hotel in Manchester and we had a great night and Sue fell out (not) with Pete because a woman sat next to them kept chatting him up! He enjoyed it so much that he vowed that he'd be back the next year and David, the Hi-Life boss, said he'd be very welcome, although I think we all thought in our hearts that he wouldn't be there.

Pete and Sue and Christian came to our house in Spain in July. Although Pete was very ill from the flight and travel when he got here, he had a brilliant time after a good rest and watching him enjoy himself made us all enjoy the holiday that bit more.

Inevitably, there were sad moments. I was stood with him one night, watching the sun going down over the mountains, when he said, 'I'll never see this again, Dave' – how sad is that? I often think about that moment, especially when I'm watching a sunset or sitting in the garden in the spring sun. I think that it's so unfair that after all he went through over the years, all the pain and suffering, all those moments of hope that were extinguished, how unfair that he can't see the sun rise or hear the birds sing or have a laugh with his mates or enjoy a glass of wine on a long hot summer night and yet I can. He was my kid brother, he was eight years younger than me. After the moment on the terrace, we went in the house and suddenly he was crying and he turned to me and said, 'I am so scared,' and I had no real answer, no real words of comfort other than 'Don't give up on me now. There's always hope.'

Back at home, autumn came and I was back on tour. Pete arranged to bring some friends to come and see the show with him and Sue, even though he was very ill. He made it, of course, and loved it and we went for a drink afterwards and he bragged about his 'famous' brother. Because that's one thing I haven't mentioned about Pete: he was my biggest fan. He supported me all the way through my career, he sang my praises to anyone who would listen and he loved everything that I did. He never begrudged me my success, he never once compared my life to his and felt that it was unfair that I had done so well and he had got the shitty end of the stick. He never felt sorry for himself or, at least, never showed it. He was brave and honest and true, my brother.

As the year passed, Pete became sicker. The steroids he was taking had bloated his features and the constant morphine he was on had deadened his sharpness, but he was still 'Gorgeous' to Sue.

I went with him to his hospital appointment as usual on 8 November, two days before his forty-eighth birthday. He asked the consultant how long he had left and the consultant said, 'Realistically, a couple of months.' Pete thought for a while and then said, 'Alright, then, I'll have the last two months in 2050!' I still don't know how he did that. And the thing is, he didn't do it for himself, he did it for his family, to defuse the tension and to make us smile.

'Two months' meant that the consultant could definitely give him until Christmas to live. Just till Christmas. Pete said that his daughter Zoe was getting married in June and he needed to be there, but the consultant shook his head and said that he couldn't guarantee that.

I remember the walk out of the consulting room, through the hospital to the car park as if it was yesterday. Pete said something like, 'Not the best news in the world,' and, not for the first time during his illness, I was semi-speechless, managing to mutter a few platitudes, trying to put myself in Pete's position; how do you deal with the fact that at such a young age someone has told you definitively that you will soon be dead?

Pete dealt with it by setting himself 'goals', which included going out on New Year's Eve in Darwen as he always had, getting to the Hi-Life Awards as he'd promised – and walking his beautiful daughter down the aisle at her wedding, which had hastily been brought forward to March, which was the earliest date available. I thought that he might make the first two, but the wedding?

He went out 'early doors' on New Year's Eve, but went back to the flat early, only to get a second wind and go down to the club where his mate was a bouncer. They had a great night on 'cheeky Vimtos' and didn't get in until the small hours.

The Hi-Life Awards were at the end of January and I didn't think he could possibly make it, but as the date approached, he confirmed that he wanted to go, but had nothing to wear as his disease-riddled body had swollen so much. I bought him a dress suit and, on the night, my son Steve drove him over to Manchester and he went to the Hi-Life Awards.

The day after, he was terribly ill and I couldn't get him out of bed for a while, but he said that he wouldn't have missed it. Again, I tried to get myself into his head: how do you cope with the knowledge that you are about to die and yet still push yourself to achieve things? Where does that motivation come from? I find it an astounding and courageous trait.

Cutting a short story short, Pete made it up to Washington, Tyne and Wear for Zoe's wedding to Karl. Zoe had been courting Karl for ages and then she was taken in by Karl's wonderful family, who take every credit for helping form the lovely girl she's turned out to be.

Although Pete was confined to a wheelchair by now, Sue drove him up the night before to the hotel he'd booked. The hospice he'd been attending in Blackburn had said that they could arrange for him to stay in a hospice in the North-East, and we all encouraged him to accept the offer, but he wouldn't. It was the only time that we argued over the two years because I felt strongly that he should get up there early and rest before the big day, and he got angry and said no, he wanted it be 'normal' and he wanted to do it his way. He made it clear that if it was the last thing he was going to do in his life, he was going to do it right.

And he did – and there we were on a beautiful March day, stood in the church awaiting the arrival of the bride. When Zoe made her entrance, looking absolutely stunning, Pete rose from his wheelchair, his chest swelling with pride – and he walked his daughter down the aisle. It is a moment that all of us who loved him will never forget.

My brother Peter died in hospital on 25 March 2008 in his mother's arms. I was privileged to be there, along with Sue, Zoe, Karl, Christian and Tom. He looked at me intensely minutes before he died, and held his hands up. I took one and said, 'It's alright, Pete, I'm here.'

I think about Pete all the time. I have a few photos of him in happier times around the place, one sitting on the promenade railings at Blackpool, another on a beach somewhere and one taken with me at Zoe's wedding. On all of them, he has this great big smile and sometimes, when I look at them, I can't bear it that he's gone forever.

I don't believe in God and heaven and hell, but if, by the odd chance, I'm wrong, I hope that Pete's in that great betting shop queue in the sky, behind my dad and grandad.

I organized the funeral. Sue told me that the only thing he really wanted was a horse-drawn carriage to carry him to the church, so I arranged this for him. As the beautiful black-and-gold carriage was pulled by two big black horses sporting black feather plumes up Chorley Old Road where we all grew up, the traffic stopped and people paused to watch. Many bowed their heads as a mark of respect, and I thought, yes, he would have loved this.

Life Goes On

ZOE, WHO HAD been a bit of a tearaway in her youth, has blossomed into a beautiful, thoughtful and caring young lady. Her husband Karl is a diamond, as are his close family, who took Zoe in and treated her like one of their own. To them, on behalf of us all, thank you. Zoe is pursuing a nursing career now and is excelling in doing so.

Christian had a rough time during the last couple of years of Pete's illness. He was only fourteen when the cancer came back and he had to deal with his father's illness along with the rest of us. I think in an odd sort of way he felt neglected during this period; an important period for him with his schooling and his journey into adulthood. He rebelled and has had a confused couple of years, living first with his girlfriend's family and more recently in college accommodation. He has got his act together and is doing a public services course, hoping to get into the police or paramedics, though I have a feeling that he might pursue computing like his dad. Christian is very much like Pete, impulsive and headstrong, but he has grown into a great lad who is caring and generous. A son that his dad would have been proud of.

I've said before that my kids are well and happy. They are my greatest achievements in life, even though, as I've also said, I take little credit for the great people they've become. The best thing that's come out of the comedy successes I've had is that I've been able to help them get on the property ladder and I will always be there for them, no matter what they want or need.

Kay and I are very happy (or she's putting on a bloody good show). She retired from the Blood Transfusion labs and works as my PA now.

We spend a lot of time in Spain and love the way of life out there. I still miss Pete more than I can say, especially when I walk round the pool and stand where we stood a few short years ago, looking at the sun going down over the mountains. I constantly count my blessings and try very hard to enjoy every single day of my life.

The work keeps coming in, and I'm lucky enough to have that sort of brain that keeps surprising me by coming up with new ideas – for stand-up shows, scripts, books and even quiz shows. I'm really looking forward to touring again in 2011 with my 'Words Don't Come Easy' show because I still love stand up and the sound of laughter.

I'm often asked about my hopes and ambitions for the future. I'd like very much to get my Sunday football script made for TV or film, and I'd especially like my *Best of Times* story to get made, as it's inspired by both my and Pete's experiences, and written from the heart. I'd also like to direct a sitcom.

I'm drawn to acting, and would love to tackle a challenging part or two. I haven't had much experience away from *Phoenix Nights*, *Dead Man Weds* and *Magnolia*, but I've really enjoyed some of the other roles I've taken on: playing 'Pemberton', a golf professional convicted of child molestation (she looked sixteen!) in Channel 4's BAFTA-winning prison drama *Buried*; a small part in *Clocking Off*; and playing a priest in Neil Fitzmaurice's new film *Charlie Noades R.I.P.*

But you know what? If none of that happens, that's okay – because I've had more than my share of good fortune and two amazingly disparate careers, both of which I've loved on the whole … and not many people can say that.

My mum turned eighty this year and has again had another heartbreaking year. Her husband Tom was diagnosed with prostate cancer early in 2009, which spread into his bones in January. So this year, as in so many recent years, my mum has spent most of her life in hospital wards and clinics, hospices and scan units. Day upon day she would sit by his bed, holding his hand and comforting him and reminiscing about the short yet wonderfully happy time they'd had together. Tom died on 31 July 2010, a few days after I finished this book. Bless him.

I have gained so much respect for my mum over the last few years. She has not been well herself, and yet has had to be strong first for my dad, then my brother and then Tom. These should have been her twilight years, but have become her nightmare years, yet she just gets on with it. A lesser woman would have been crushed.

I'm sure (I know) she has her moments of despair and desolation, but she continues to bounce back. People say that I'm a lot like her. I wish.

In Loving Memory of

Gordon Bramwell
15 May 1929 – 6 January 2002

Peter Bramwell
10 November 1959 – 25 March 2008

Index